MW01046624

THE HOLY SPIRIT IN THE
SYRIAN BAPTISMAL TRADITION

GORGIAS LITURGICAL STUDIES

4

The Holy Spirit in the
Syrian Baptismal Tradition

SEBASTIAN P. BROCK

GORGIAS PRESS
2008

First Gorgias Press Edition, 2008

Copyright © 2008 by Gorgias Press LLC

All rights reserved under International and Pan-American Copyright Conventions. No part of this publication may be reproduced, stored in a retrieval system or transmitted in any form or by any means, electronic, mechanical, photocopying, recording, scanning or otherwise without the prior written permission of Gorgias Press LLC.

Published in the United States of America by Gorgias Press LLC, New Jersey

ISBN 978-1-59333-844-2

GORGIAS PRESS
180 Centennial Ave., Suite 3, Piscataway, NJ 08854 USA
www.gorgiaspress.com

Library of Congress Cataloging-in-Publication Data
Brock, Sebastian P.
 The Holy Spirit in the Syrian baptismal tradition / Sebastian P. Brock. -- 1st Gorgias press ed.
 p. cm. -- (Gorgias liturgical studies ; 4)
 1. Holy Spirit. 2. Baptism--Syrian Church. I. Title.
 BT121.3.B76 2008
 234'.161--dc22

2008024645

The paper used in this publication meets the minimum requirements of the American National Standards.

Printed in the United States of America

TABLE OF CONTENTS

PREFACE

This study was originally written at the suggestion of the Revd Dr Jacob Vellian, in whose monograph series, The Syrian Churches Series, it was first published in India (as vol. 9, in 1979); it was subsequently reprinted, again in India, as an enlarged second edition in 1998. In the present third edition the bibliographical references to secondary literature have been brought up to date, a number of smaller revisions made, and some indexes provided. In the second edition, two further chapters were added, on the Transition to a post-baptismal anointing (as ch. 10; reprinted from B. D. Spinks (ed.), *The Sacrifice of Praise. Studies ... in Honour of A. H. Couratin* [Bibliotheca "Ephemerides Liturgicae" Subsidia 19; 1981], pp. 215–25), and on the Holy Spirit as feminine (inserted earlier, as ch. 2; reprinted from *Aram* 3 (1991), pp. 249–57). The first of these is also included here, as Appendix 1, but the second has been replaced by another article on the same subject, since the one in *Aram* has recently been reprinted elsewhere, in my *Fire from Heaven, Studies in Syriac Theology and Liturgy* (Variorum Reprints, Aldershot, 2006), ch. VI. Thus the present Appendix 2 is now taken from my chapter in J. Martin Soskice (ed.), *After Eve. Women, Theology and the Christian Tradition* (London, 1990), pp. 73–88. I am most grateful to the editors and publishers of these two pieces for permission to reprint them here, where they appear in a lightly revised and updated form.

When the original book was published very little had been written on the Syriac baptismal tradition, but in subsequent years a considerable number of important studies have appeared, most notably those on the anointings by Gabriele Winkler (in her *Das Armenische Initiationsrituale*, 1982, and elsewhere) and by Baby Varghese (*Les onctions baptismales dans la tradition syrienne*, 1989), as well as more general works by Francis Chirayath, *Taufliturgie des Syro-Malabarischen Ritus* (1981), Thomas Finn (*Early Christian Baptism and the Catechumenate: West and East Syria*, 1992), Joseph Chalassery (*The Holy Spirit and Christian Initiation in the East Syrian Tradition*, 1995), Kilian McDonnell, *The Baptism of Jesus in the Jordan*, 1996), Mathew Kizhakearanjaniyil (*East Syrian Baptismal Theology*, 2001), Emmanuel Kaniyamparampil (*The Spirit of Life. A Study of the Holy Spirit in the Early Syriac Tradition*, 2003), Baby Varghese (*West Syrian Liturgical Theology*, 2004), Bryan Spinks (in the first section of his *Early and Medieval Rituals and Theologies of Baptism*, 2006), and

Mgr Jacques Ishaq (*Le rite du Baptême dans la liturgie chaldéo-assyrienne*, 2007 [in Arabic]).

I am most grateful to Fr. Jacob Vellian for his gracious permission to republish this work with Gorgias Press, to Dr George Kiraz who kindly suggested the idea, and to Dr Katie Stott, of the editorial staff of Gorgias Press, who saw to the task of inserting the many corrections and additions.

Sebastian P. Brock
Oxford

ABBREVIATIONS

BAPTISMAL *ORDINES*

B = Melkite service attributed to *Basil,* quoted from Assemani.

D = Anonymous service in British Library, Add. 14,518 (D corresponds to the siglum used in 'Studies').

JS = Maronite service attributed to *Jacob* of Serugh, quoted from Assemani.

S = Syrian Orthodox service attributed to *Severus.*

SA = Editions of *Severus* in Assemani.

SH = Homs edition of *Severus.*

T = Syrian Orthodox service attributed to *Timothy,* quoted from *Le Muséon* 83 (1970).

U = East Syriac service, quoted from Urmia edition.

For details of the editions, see chapter III. In the text the *ordines* are quoted as *Basil, Jacob, Severus, Timothy* (italicized).

OTHER ABBREVIATIONS

Assemani = J. A. Assemani, *Codex Liturgicus Ecclesiae Universae,* I–III (Rome, 1749/50).

'Baptismal themes' = S. P. Brock, 'Baptismal themes in the writings of Jacob of Serugh,' *OCA* 205 (1978), pp. 325–47.

Brev. Chald. = *Breviarium iuxta Ritum Syrorum Orientalium id est Chaldaeorum,* I–III (Rome, 1938) (reprint of 1886 edition).

'Consecration' = S. P. Brock, 'The consecration of the water in the oldest manuscripts of the Syrian Orthodox baptismal liturgy,' *OCP* 37 (1971), pp. 317–32.

CSCO = Corpus Scriptorum Christianorum Orientalium (Louvain).

Diettrich = G. Diettrich, *Die nestorianische Taufliturgie* (Giessen, 1903)

'Epiklesis' = S. P. Brock, 'The Epiklesis in the Antiochene baptismal *ordines,*' *OCA* 197 (1974), pp. 183–218; reprinted in *Fire from Heaven,* chapter VII.

Fire from Heaven = S. P. Brock, *Fire from Heaven. Studies in Syriac Theology and Liturgy* (Aldershot, 2006).

ET = English translation.

Fenqitho = *Breviarium iuxta Ritum Ecclesiae Antiochenae Syrorum*, I–VII (Mosul, 1886–96).

Murray, *Symbols* = R. Murray, *Symbols of Church and Kingdom: a Study in Early Syriac Tradition* (Cambridge, 1975; revised edn, Piscataway NJ, 2004).

OC = *Oriens Christianus* (Leipzig/Wiesbaden).

OCA = *Orientalia Christiana Analecta* (Rome).

OCP = *Orientalia Christiana Periodica* (Rome).

PG = *Patrologia Graeca*.

PO = *Patrologia Orientalis*.

PS = *Patrologia Syriaca*.

SCS = The Syrian Churches Series (ed. J. Vellian; Kottayam).

Siman, *L'Expérience* = E-P. Siman, *L'Expérience de l'Esprit par l'Église d'après la tradition syrienne d'Antioche* (Paris, 1971).

'Studies' = S. P. Brock, 'Studies in the early history of the Syrian Orthodox baptismal liturgy,' *Journal of Theological Studies* ns 23 (1972), pp. 16–64.

METHOD OF CITATION

Most writers are quoted either by section number (§), or page number (p.) with an indication of the editor: this will suffice to enable those who wish to locate details of publications in C. Moss' *Catalogue of Syriac Printed Books and Related Literature in the British Museum* (London, 1962) or I. Ortiz de Urbina's *Patrologia Syriaca* (Rome, 1965; second edition), and, for the period 1960–1990, my *Syriac Studies. A Classified Bibliography, 1960–1990* (Kaslik, 1996), and for 1991–1995, 1996–2000, and 2001–2005, the continuations of this in *Parole de l'Orient* 23 (1998), 29 (2004), and 33 (2008) respectively. Cp also chapter III, on sources.

For writers edited in the CSCO I quote the page number of the text volume only, since these numbers are given in the margins of the translation volumes.

Ephrem is quoted from Beck's edition in CSCO, where available, (by hymn number, stanza, and (if necessary) line).

Jacob of Serugh's Homilies are quoted from Bedjan's edition, I–V (Paris/Leipzig, 1905–1910; reprinted Piscataway NJ, 2006); the reprint has an extra vol. VI, which includes the Homilies by Jacob included at the end of Bedjan, *S. Martyrii qui et Sahdona quae supersunt* (Paris/Leipzig, 1902), which are cited as Bedjan S.

I have avoided over literal translations, and at times, where the context requires it, my renderings are somewhat interpretative.

A simplified form of transcription is employed, and for typographical reasons *he* and *het* are represented by *h*, *semkat* and *sade* by *s*, *tet* and *tau* by *t*.

1 INTRODUCTION

(1) SCOPE AND AIMS

Syriac Christianity is unique in that it represents a genuinely Semitic form of the Gospel which itself was preached originally in Aramaic. Although the New Testament itself reached Syriac by way of Greek, the thought forms, imagery, and religious vocabulary of the earliest Syriac writers—above all Aphrahat, Ephrem and the liturgical poets—are very largely Semitic and owe little or nothing to the influence of Greek culture. As such, Syriac Christianity can genuinely claim to be an indigenous Asian representative of Christianity, and not a European export. This is not, of course, to deny the very great influence which the Greek-speaking church subsequently had on all the Syriac churches, in particular over the period c. AD 400–700;[1] but what is important here is that this Greek element—now thoroughly assimilated as part of the general liturgical and literary heritage of the Syriac churches—is a secondary one.

This double heritage, Semitic and Greek, where the two elements are sometimes kept separate, sometimes fused, lends to Syriac tradition a peculiar richness, the effects of which may be seen in almost all spheres of the life of the Christian community. It is a heritage, moreover, which is common to all four churches which employ, or have in the past employed, Syriac as their liturgical language, the Syrian Orthodox, the Maronite, the Melkite,[2] and the Church of the East.

The extraordinarily rich theology of the Holy Spirit that is characteristic of the Syrian Orthodox tradition has already received fine presentation by Father Emmanuel-Pataq Siman in his *L'Expérience de l'Esprit par l'Église d'après la tradition syrienne d'Antioche* (1971). The present book is both more, and at the same time much less, ambitious in its aims: more ambitious, in

---

[1] As a matter fact this Greek element was itself largely the product of the bilingual Greek-Aramaic/Syriac culture of Syria-Palestine: in liturgy and hymnography, as well as in art and architecture, Syria-Palestine appears to have been one of the most creative areas of the late antique world.

[2] Syriac was used (often, since the 11th century, alongside Arabic) in Melkite liturgical texts up to the 16th century.

that I have tried to present Syriac tradition in its entirety, rather than just one branch of it; less so, in that I have confined myself to an exploration of the various roles of the Holy Spirit in one particular sphere, namely that of Baptism.

Taking as a starting point the baptismal services themselves of the several Syriac churches, my aim has been to try to bring out the distinctive features of this Syriac tradition, drawing particularly on the earlier and less Hellenized writers as a source from which to illustrate and comment on the liturgical texts. Although I have attempted to present the Syriac tradition as a whole, attention has of course throughout been paid to individual ecclesiastical and historical developments.

Inevitably, in a field such as this where the workers are few, any attempt at synthesis must at the same time involve extensive preliminary research on the primary sources: this has meant that a certain amount of documentation is necessary in order to validate my presentation of the material; nevertheless, for the sake of the general reader, technical discussions have been kept to a minimum. It is to be hoped that, in trying to cater to a limited extent for the interests of the scholar as well as those of the general reader, the result is not simply a failure to please either.

In broad terms it seems likely that the present baptismal texts of the Syriac churches reached approximately their present form in the sixth and seventh centuries—a period of great liturgical creativity all over the Christian world. Needless to say, these texts contain elements of varying antiquity, and the process of accretion, resulting from shifts of interest over the course of time, has led to a certain amount of duplication and inconsistency; sometimes it is possible and valuable to sort out the early from the late, sometimes not. In any case it would be wrong to assume that later additions always represent a deterioration; rather, they can often be seen either as logical developments (such as the post-baptismal, anointing, unknown in Syriac tradition before the fifth century), or as enrichments, illuminating yet further facets of the many-sided sacrament of Baptism.

It is the period up to c. 400 which represents Syriac Christianity in its most purely Semitic phase, while the subsequent three centuries or so constitute a period of hellenization. The Arab conquests in turn heralded the advent of a rather different outlook in the Syriac churches: this was a time of consolidation, rather than of creativity. This new situation is reflected, from our point of view, in the development of the liturgical commentary, a thoroughly prosaic successor to the poetic exuberances of an Ephrem, Narsai or Jacob. Thus for the most part it is from the earlier writers, rather than the commentators, that I have preferred to illustrate the liturgical texts, since these seem to me to be theologically more interesting and to show a greater profundity in their understanding of the many dimensions of the baptismal mystery.

There are two particular matters preliminary to a study of the baptismal texts themselves which require our attention briefly in the Introduction. The first is the biblical foundations of the vocabulary associated with the working of the Spirit in Syriac tradition: as might be expected, it turns out that a high proportion of this vocabulary finds its origins in the Syriac Bible. The second point is concerned with the understanding of time, and the distinction, recognized by anthropologists as operative in the religious thinking of practically all cultures, between sacred and profane time, seeing that this is something fundamental to a proper understanding of Syriac liturgical tradition.

(2)   THE HOLY SPIRIT IN THE SYRIAC BIBLE

Although 'Spirit of Holiness' is a term that occurs occasionally in the Old Testament (Ps. 51:12: Isaiah 63:10–11), alongside the very common 'Spirit of the Lord,' it will come as a surprise to many that *ruha d-qudsha*, 'Spirit of Holiness' is quite a frequent term in some Jewish texts, in particular the Palestinian tradition of the Aramaic translations of the Old Testament, or Targumim. Whereas Targum Onkelos, the official Babylonian targum, normally employs the term 'Spirit of Prophecy' (a phrase known to some early Syriac writers too), the earlier Palestinian Targum texts prefer 'Spirit of Holiness.' Thus, for example, at Numbers 27:18, Joshua is described as 'a man on whom there dwells the Spirit of Holiness from before the Lord.'

The word for 'spirit' or 'wind' happens to be feminine in the Semitic languages, and this of course has had certain consequences for the use of the term *ruha* when applied to the Holy Spirit.[3] Early Syriac writers consistently construe *ruha d-qudsha* as a feminine, and it is clear from a few oft-quoted texts that the Holy Spirit was actually regarded as mother in some circles. This understanding is first found in a quotation preserved by Origen and Jerome from the almost wholly lost Gospel according to the Hebrews:[4]

> (Christ speaks) Even so did my mother, the Holy Spirit, take me by one
> of my hairs and carry me away on the great mountain of Tabor.

---

[3] The Holy Spirit of course also inherits much imagery from the feminine figure of Wisdom, popular in post-exilic Judaism.

[4] E. Hennecke and W. Schneelmelcher, *New Testament Apocrypha* (London, 1963), I, p. 164.

In Syriac writers it is rare to find the Holy Spirit described specifically as a 'mother,' but there is one well known passage where this is the case: Aphrahat, in his *Demonstration* 18.10. 'On virginity and marital continence (*Qaddishuta*),' denies that Gen. 2:24 ('a man shall leave his father and mother...') refers to ordinary parents:

> Who is it who leaves father and mother to take a wife? The meaning is as follows: as long as a man has not taken a wife, he loves and reveres God his Father and the Holy Spirit his Mother, and he has no other love. But when a man takes a wife, then he leaves his (true) Father and his Mother.

The same interpretation is found in Greek in the Macarian homilies.[5]

We can see how later generations came to object to this description of the Holy Spirit if we look at one of the beautiful invocations to the Spirit in the *Acts of Thomas*. In §27 Judas Thomas stands by the font and anoints the heads of King Gundaphor and his brother, and his prayer includes, in the Greek (but not the Syriac), the words 'Come, compassionate Mother...' Although Syriac was the original language of the *Acts of Thomas*, the surviving texts in this language have undergone a little expurgation, and the phrase 'compassionate Mother' has been dropped as unsuitable, and so survives only in the Greek translation which has received less attention from later editors.

As we shall discover below, the verb *rahhef*, 'to hover,' is frequently used of the action of the Holy Spirit, derived from Gen. 1:2 and Deut. 32:11. That this is essentially a feminine action in the eyes of Syriac writers can be clearly seen from two comparatively late writers who compare the Holy Spirit to a mother. Sahdona,[6] writing about 600, speaks of the man 'who has been held worthy of the hovering of the all-holy Spirit, who, like a mother, hovers over us as she gives sanctification, and through her hovering over us, we are made worthy of sonship.' Nearly three centuries later

---

[5] See Murray. *Symbols*, p. 318 (and in general on this subject, pp. 142–50, 312–20). In the *Didascalia* (§9; ed. Lagarde, p. 36) the deacons are said to represent Christ, but the deaconesses the Holy Spirit; cp also chapter IV, note 34. See further, Appendix 2.

[6] Ed. de Halleux, I, p. 32. For *rahhef*, see further my *Fire from Heaven. Studies in Syriac Theology and Liturgy* (Aldershot, 2006), ch. XIV.

Moshe bar Kepha[7] describes in a homily how the Holy Spirit 'hovered over John the Baptist and brought him up like a compassionate mother.'

Although we shall find many pointers to the feminine character of the Holy Spirit in the baptismal texts, the actual title 'mother' does not, to my knowledge, occur, and the nearest we come to it is in a baptismal *qolo*[8] beginning 'stretch out your wings, o holy church, and receive the perfect sheep to whom the Holy Spirit has *given birth* in the baptismal water…'

For the majority of writers, however, it would be unwise to stress their consciousness of the femininity of the Spirit. Moreover it should be remembered that *Logos*, the Word, was also rendered by a feminine Syriac word, *melta*, and in the Old Syriac version of St John's Gospel it is still construed as a feminine (in the Peshitta however, and in later Syriac writers generally, *melta*, 'Word,' is always treated as a masculine). It is in fact quite likely that the existence in second- and third-century Mesopotamia of a number of pagan triads consisting of father, mother and son (e.g. at Palmyra, Hatra), may have acted as a deterrent against the development of this sort of imagery in ecclesiastical circles.

From the late fourth, and especially fifth, century onwards, under Greek influence, *ruha*, '(Holy) Spirit,' came to be construed as a masculine. In the biblical translations the process has begun in the Peshitta New Testament (though in many places a feminine verb is left), to be completed in a consistent way in the Harklean (and probably already in the Philoxenian) version. In non-biblical texts we find examples of the feminine lingering on into the early centuries of the Islamic period, surviving especially in liturgical texts. For some reason the feminine adjective *qaddishta*, however, tends to be avoided, while a feminine verb after *ruha d-qudsha* is much more likely to survive. On occasions one finds *ruha* construed as both feminine and masculine in the same sentence, and in poets like Jacob of Serugh it seems to be considerations of versification that mainly govern the choice.

Actually it is Jacob of Serugh, together with a number of Syrian Orthodox contemporaries, who preserves one of the rare instances of a piece of fundamental exegesis which does seem to be governed by considerations of the gender of *ruha*. In a homily on the Annunciation he stresses on several occasions that the 'Spirit' and 'Power' of Gabriel's greeting in Luke 1:35 ('The Holy Spirit shall come upon you and the Power of the Most High

---

[7] Ed. Nurse, *American Journal of Semitic Languages and Literature* 26 (1909/10), p. 95.

[8] SH, p. 43.

shall overshadow you') are not synonymous, as is commonly assumed to be
the case. The Spirit, according to Jacob, came first and his role was to
cleanse, while the Power was the Word?[9]

> It was necessary for the Holy Spirit to come before the Only-Begotten;
> for it was the Spirit, and then the Power, that dwelt in the pure Virgin.

A little below the 'Power' is again defined:[10]

> The Power of the Most High, that is the child from on high...
> he is Christ, the Power of the Father, as is written.

The same concept is found in both Severus and Philoxenus,[11] as well as in
other Syrian Orthodox writers, and still features in the *Fenqitho*.[12] In origin
the exegesis would appear to go back to the difficulties that were felt to
arise in the verse if the Spirit is regarded as feminine; this can be seen from
a remark to be found in the Coptic Gospel of Philip, a work of the second
century with Syrian affinities:

> Some have said that Mary conceived of the Holy Spirit. They are wrong,
> and they do not realize what they are saying, for when did a woman ever
> conceive of a woman? (§17).

In the biblical texts, and especially in the Old Testament, 'Spirit' is
used very often in the sense of an impersonal force, but for the most part
the Fathers do not take into account the difference between the impersonal
and personal uses of the term 'spirit' in the bible, and Theodore of Mopsuestia was exceptional in this respect, in that he denied that the Old Testament showed any knowledge of a distinct person or hypostasis of the
Spirit;[13] Theodore's historically-minded view, taken over by some East
Syriac writers, to some extent anticipates that of modern scholarship. The
other Fathers, however, looked at the matter differently: what the writers of
the Old Testament books themselves understood by the term 'spirit' was
only of secondary importance to them, since in their view the Church is
able to interpret what these writers say in the light of revelation of the Holy
Spirit in the New Testament; thus they feel justified in reading back this

---

[9] Ed. Bedjan, S, p. 631 (cp pp. 642, 682, 733).

[10] Ed. Bedjan, S, p. 632.

[11] E.g. Severus, *Philalethes* (ed. Hespel), p. 132; Philoxenus, *De Trinitate et Incar-
nations* (ed. Vaschalde) p. 95; *Letter to the Monks of Senun* (ed. de Halleux), p. 60.

[12] E.g. *Fenqitho* IV, p. 872a.

[13] *Comm. on Haggai*, PG 66, col. 486.

newly-gained knowledge into the Old Testament. This deeper understanding is on a completely different plane from the purely historical understanding, and should not be confused with it.

Because of this outlook it will be important to look at the activities of the Spirit in the Old, as well as in the New, Testament, since the biblical evidence is formative in many areas of phraseology and imagery. In the following pages the Peshitta is used throughout, and the Hebrew and Greek are only mentioned when these differ in any notable way.

In the Old Testament the verbs most commonly found where 'spirit' is the subject are as follows

(1) 'reside upon': Num. 11:26; 2 Kings 2:15; 2 Chr. 15:1, 20:14; Isaiah 11:2 ('rest and reside upon'; the Hebrew and Greek only have one verb).

(2) 'be upon': Num. 24:2; Judges 11:29; 1 Sam. 19:20, 23.

(3) 'put on': Judges 6:34 (Greek 'empower'); 1 Chr. 12:19; 2 Chr. 24:20.

(4) 'take': 1 Kings 18:12; 2 Kings 2:16 (Greek 'find'); Ezra 3:12, 8:3, 11:1 and 24.

(5) 'lead': Ps. 143:10; Isaiah 63:14.

(6) 'hover' (*rahhef*): Gen. 1:2.

Although it only occurs once in connection with the Spirit in both Hebrew and Syriac, the verb *rahhef*, 'hover' is perhaps the most important word of all, for it has become, together with *aggen* ('overshadow,' taken from the New Testament), a technical term for the action of the Holy Spirit in Syriac writers. The verb is actually quite common in the Peshitta Old Testament (in contrast to the Hebrew), and it translates the Hebrew 'have pity or compassion on' in several places (e.g. Isaiah 27:11, 30:18; Jer. 13:14). The noun *ruhhafa* is also used a number of times, always translating Hebrew words for 'mercy, pity' (e.g., Prov. 3:22; Isaiah 63:9). In one passage, Zech. 12:10, it is specifically associated with 'Spirit': 'spirit of *ruhhafa* and mercy.'

Looking next at passages where 'spirit' is the object of a verb, the most important words are the following:

(1) 'give': Num. 11:29; Isaiah 42:1; Ezek, 11:19.

(2) 'fill with': Exod. 28:3, 31:3, 35:31.

(3) 'pour out': Isaiah 44:3; Joel 2:28; Zech. 12:10.

(4) 'send': Ps. 104:30; Isaiah 48;16.

(5) 'partake of': Ps. 51:11.

In the New Testament, the Old Testament phraseology of Isaiah 11:2 ('rest upon') is picked up in 1 Peter 4:14, but apart from this there are a number of new verbs used of the Spirit's activity: the Spirit 'comes'[14] (Luke 1:35; Acts 1:8, 19:16), 'is upon' (Luke 2:25; cp Gen 41:38 'is in'), 'descends' (Matt. 3:16, Mark 1:10; Luke 3:22, John 1:32); 'breathes' (John 3:8), 'dwells in' (Rom. 8:9,11; 2 Tim. 1:14), and above all 'overshadows' (*aggen*). This last term, which is hard to translate exactly, has evidently become a technical term for the Spirit's activity from an early date in the Syriac-speaking church, for it is used to render a number of different Greek verbs: thus it translates *episkiazo* 'overshadow,' in the Annunciation message of Luke 1:35, and the same verb again at Acts 5:15; it translates *epipipto*, 'fall upon,' twice used of the Spirit in Acts 10:44 and 11:15. With subjects other than 'Spirit' *aggen* renders *skenoo* and derivatives in John 1:14 (where the Word is subject), Acts 2:26, and 2 Cor. 12:9 (where the 'power of Christ' is subject).

The term *aggen* in fact has its background in the Peshitta Old Testament and the Targumim,[15] but never in the context of the 'spirit.' In the narrative of the Sinai theophany God tells Moses 'I will cause my hand to overshadow (*aggen*) you until I have passed by' (Exod. 33:22). The Hebrew verb which *aggen* translates here is *skk*, 'hedge in, protect'; in the light of the etymologically related word *gnona*, 'bridal chamber,' it is interesting that the Syriac translators have evidently associated the Hebrew verb *sakak* with *sukkah*, 'canopy, tabernacle, or booth,' used in the Jewish wedding ceremony (compare also the Peshitta at Job 1:10, 3:23).

Elsewhere *aggen* always translates Hebrew verbs meaning 'protect' (e.g. 2 Kings 19:34; Isaiah 31:5; cp also Wisdom 5:16). In the Old Testament texts the 'Lord' is always subject of the verb, and it is only in writings of the intertestamental period that we find a shift in usage: in Wisdom 19:8 the Lord's 'hand' is subject (developed from passages such as Exod 33:22, and Ps. 138:8, 'cause your hand to overshadow me, Lord'); in Ben Sira 23:18d the subject is 'shade,' while in IV Ezra 7:122 it is 'the glory of the Most High' which will 'overshadow those who have lived in chastity.'

Seeing that *aggen*, 'overshadow' has become a technical term in Syriac, it is very possible that the non-biblical Greek word *epiphoitao*, itself fre-

---

[14] In the Hebrew Old Testament the Spirit '*comes* on me' in Ezek. 3:24, but the Peshitta translates by 'enters in.'

[15] E.g. Targum Exodus 12:13 'I will overshadow (protect) you with my Memra.' The verb is understood as being etymologically related to Hebrew *magen* 'shield.' For further details on the usage of *aggen*, see my *Fire from Heaven*, chapters X–XIII.

quently used of the Spirit's activity in liturgical and patristic Greek texts, is in fact a rendering of *aggen* which originated in a bilingual, Syriac-Greek, speaking area. Certainly the converse is found, for *epiphoitao* occurs in the epiclesis of the Greek Anaphora of St James, and in the Syriac eucharistic epicleses modelled on this anaphora this verb is rendered either by *aggen* or *rahhef* (or derivative nouns).

There is one important New Testament passage, however, where *aggen* is not used; this is in the Transfiguration narrative, where the Greek *episkiazo* is rendered by *atel*, 'give shadow,' in Matt. 17:5 = Mark 9:7 = Luke 9:34.

Turning to transitive verbs where the Spirit is subject, we find 'seize' (Acts 8:39), 'teach' (Luke 12:12; John 14:26), 'comfort' (Acts 9:31 where the Peshitta uses a noun rather than a verb), 'search out' (1 Cor. 2:10), 'give life to' (2 Cor. 3:6), 'announce, make known' (John 16:13f with different verbs in the Old Syriac and Peshitta; Heb. 9:8), 'testify' (Acts 20:23; Heb. 10:15) and 'lead' (John 16:13; cp Mark 4:1: Luke 4:1). Only the last of these has its basis in the Old Testament.

Where the Spirit is the object of a verb, however, the Old Testament provides the model for 'give' (Luke 11:13 etc.) 'send' (John 14:26; Gal. 4:6), and 'pour out' (Acts 2:17–18; Tit. 3:5). New verbs are 'receive' (John 20:22), 'quench' (I Thess. 5:19) and 'grieve' (Eph. 4:30).

Finally two negative point should be made: the verb *shken*, 'reside,' is only used of birds in the Syriac New Testament (Matt. 16:32 Old Syriac; Mark 4:32 Peshitta). In view of the importance of this verb—and especially the noun *Shekina*[16]—in Jewish literature, this is not without interest. Secondly, it should be noted that the Johannine name for the Spirit, *parakletos*, is simply transliterated in the Syriac Gospels; in earlier Syriac writers the term is not at all common (perhaps due to the fact that Mani had appropriated it to himself).

The Syriac Bible serves as the source for most of the phraseology employed by the later liturgical texts in connection with the activities of the Spirit. Besides *rahhef* and *aggen*, three other verbs with biblical antecedents would seem to be particularly characteristic of Syriac tradition: come, rest and reside on. One group of verbs, however, stands out as having no obvious biblical origin: in early Syriac tradition the Holy Spirit 'mixes' or 'min-

---

[16] In some (late?) East Syriac liturgical texts the corresponding form *shkinta* is quite often found. The verb is occasionally used in epicleses, eg. U, p. 68 (oil).

gles'[17] in with the baptismal water, the bread and the wine, and the baptized themselves. To quote but a single example, according to Ephrem Christ came to baptism 'in order to mix (*da-nmazzeg*) the invisible Spirit in with the visible water.'[18]

(3) SACRED TIME AND ORDINARY TIME[19]

Right at the outset it will be helpful to consider the understanding of the nature of time which underlies all our texts. It is widely recognized that most religions know of two quite different kinds of time: besides ordinary, historical, time, there exists a second dimension of time, best referred to as 'sacred' or 'liturgical' time. Ordinary time, the succession of moments in history, requires no special explanation. Sacred time, however, is not concerned at all with the sequence of events in ordinary time (indeed it can reverse them); rather the concern of sacred time lies in the salvific content and meaning of an event or events that take place either in primordial time, 'in the beginning,' or (and this is particularly characteristic of Judaism and Christianity) at a point or points in historical time. These salvific events continue to be effective throughout history, and can be 'recaptured' at any point in historical time, since they are eternally present in sacred time. In Judaism sacred time is recaptured pre-eminently in the Passover ritual, while in Christianity the entry into sacred time takes place primarily in the eucharistic liturgy. Each Sunday becomes, in sacred time, the day of the Resurrection:[20]

> On this day the Son, the Firstborn, is risen from the grave, giving joy and gladness at his resurrection to those above and those below...

The feast and the salvific event it celebrates likewise run together in sacred time, even though far separated in historical time. Thus the first of Ephrem's hymns on the Nativity begins:

---

[17] *mazzeg, hlat* (e.g. U, p. 67 (oil). The only possible biblical source seems to be Isaiah 19:14. Syriac writers also frequently speak of the baptized being 'mingled' in the flock (e.g. *Acts of Thomas* §156: 'mingle them in your sheep' and often in the *ordines* themselves), for which compare Gen. 30:40. The verbs are also used of the union of the divine and human natures of Christ (as *sunkerannumi* in some early Greek writers), though later on this language fell into disrepute.

[18] *Sermo de Domino Nostro* §55.

[19] Cp also my 'The poet as theologian,' *Sobornost* VII 4 (1977), pp. 243–50.

[20] *Fenqitho* VI, p. 407a (Lilyo, Third Sunday after Pentecost).

This day my Lord has given joy to kings, priests and prophets,
for on it their words have received fulfilment and have all become fact;
for a Virgin today has given birth to Emmanuel in Bethlehem,
the word that Isaiah uttered has today become reality.

(H. Nativ. I. 1–2)

Likewise in Greek the early sixth-century poet Romanos begins his famous Nativity *kontakion* with the words 'The Virgin today gives birth to him who is beyond all being.' Such phraseology is commonplace in all Syriac liturgical texts, and one further example, for Epiphany, must suffice:

On this night the Holy Spirit has hovered like a dove, and the springs have surged with water. (*Fenqitho* III, 273; Lilyo)

This 'entry' into sacred time is effected by the Holy Spirit. At the epiclesis in the eucharistic liturgy the bread and wine effectively 'become' the body and blood of Christ, and at the consecration of the baptismal font the water 'becomes' the Jordan water into which Christ stepped at his own baptism; it also 'becomes' the water which flowed from his side at the crucifixion (John 19:34). In both the Eucharist and in Baptism a salvific event (or series of events) in the life of Christ is represented, by means of the conjunction of sacred time—the eternal now—with that moment in historical time at which the liturgical action takes place; the conjunction of the two times is brought about by the power of the Holy Spirit.

Sacred time thus represents an objective reality, but one of which the Christian's experience is essentially subjective.

As we shall see, Christian baptism is associated with various events in the course of the Incarnation, in particular Christ's own baptism, the piercing of his side on the cross, and his death, burial and resurrection. Although each of these events is separate from the others in historical time, in sacred time they are identical, each possessing the salvific effect of the Incarnation as a whole. The dramatic possibilities of this interplay between the two times is constantly exploited by the liturgical poets.

Christian baptism is linked with sacred time in a further way as well, for at his baptism the Christian is understood to be entering already, in sacred time, the kingdom of God; he is now capable of anticipating, as it were, the life or the resurrection.[21] The Old Syriac translation of Luke 20:35–6 seems to be making this point:

---

[21] For the anticipation of the angelic life by ascetics and saints in this world, see my 'Early Syrian Asceticism,' *Numen* 20 (1973), pp. 1–19.

Those who have become worthy to receive that world (i.e. the kingdom) and that resurrection from the dead, do not marry, nor can they die, for they have been made equal with the angels, and being sons of the resurrection they are like the sons of God.

The tension between what is 'already' in sacred time and what is 'not yet' in historical time is here very obvious, but the important point to realise is that the 'gift of the Spirit' which the Christian receives at baptism provides him or her with the *potential* for continually entering the Kingdom, for making the 'not yet' into the 'already,' since it is the Holy Spirit who once again effects this conjunction of the two times. The Eucharist, which formalizes the bringing together of sacred and historical time, effected by the Holy Spirit, also provides the Christian with a model: by co-operating with the Holy Spirit who dwells within him, by not 'constraining' the Spirit, the Holy Spirit will effect his own entry into sacred time; the Kingdom of heaven is thus 'within you.'

Seen in this light, the Christian life is a continual striving to make sacred and historical time effectively one. Only by allowing the Holy Spirit to operate can this be brought about.

2 THE SYMBOLS OF THE SPIRIT

In the early Christian writers three symbols of the Holy Spirit stand out: fire, dove and the oil. Of these by far the most prominent and important in Syriac tradition is that of fire.

(1) THE HOLY SPIRIT AS FIRE

In the 73rd of his *Hymns on Faith* Ephrem provides, as an illustration of the Trinity, the example of the sun: the sun corresponds to the Father, the light to the Son, and the heat to the Spirit (*H. Fid.* 73.1). The analogy is particularly helpful, in Ephrem's eyes, for the way it helps to explain the penetration of the Holy Spirit into the created world:

> The might of the Spirit's heat resides
> in everything, with everything, yet it is wholly with the One
> and is not cut off from the Radiance,
> being mixed in it, nor from the Sun,
> being mingled with it. (*H. Fid.* 74.3–4)

The Holy Spirit as fire above all consecrates;

> In fire is the symbol of the Spirit,
> it is a type of the Holy Spirit
> who is mixed in the baptismal water
> so that it may be for absolution,
> and in the bread,
> that it may be an offering. (*H. Fid.* 40.10)

The consecrating fire of the Holy Spirit has its origins in the Old Testament, where, besides such passages as Isaiah 6, the descent of fire on a sacrifice is seen as the sign of its acceptance (e.g. 2 Chr. 7:1). This was a concept that was much extended in post-biblical Judaism and in early Christianity. In the Targum to the Song of Songs 5:1 God is represented as saying that, as a sign of his acceptance of Solomon's sacrifice in the Temple (2 Chr. 7:1), 'I sent fire from heaven and so I consumed the whole offerings and the sacred sacrifice.' Theodotion, the Jewish Greek translator of the

Old Testament, rendered Gen. 4:4 with the words 'and God *burnt up* Abel's offering,' thus providing an explanation of how Abel knew that his sacrifice had been accepted. Aphrahat, in his *Demonstration* 4 on Prayer, lists the Old Testament instances of the descent of fire to assure his correspondent that 'when Abel and Cain offered up their offerings both together, living fire, which was doing service before God, came down and licked up Abel's pure sacrifice, but did not touch Cain's because it was impure (*Dem.* 4.2).

The Holy Spirit as 'fire' thus has two aspects: the fire is a sign of acceptance of a sacrifice, and at the same time it also consecrates it. In the case of the coming of the Holy Spirit on to the baptismal oil and water the former aspect is of course not applicable, but at the Eucharist both aspects are very much present.

The consecrating role of the fire can be seen very well in the Syriac *Acts of John*; the Apostle prays over the baptismal oil and 'immediately flaming fire was there over the oil, without the oil itself burning.'[1] Fire *over* the baptismal water was seen by Constantine, according to Jacob of Serugh's poem on his baptism.[2] More frequently, however, the water itself is described as going up in flames; this goes back to an ancient tradition that the Jordan went up in flames at Christ's own baptism.[3] In the case of Christ's own baptism it is of course Christ himself who effects this, not the Holy Spirit (though Jacob speaks of 'the Spirit of Christ' going ahead and heating the water); in Christian baptism, however, it is the Holy Spirit who sets aflame the water. Thus in the long list of exorcisms common to the Maronite service and the Syrian Orthodox one attributed to Timothy we find: '...the Father rejoices, the Son exults, the Spirit hovers; the baptismal water is set aflame with fire and the Spirit...'

At the Eucharist the descent of the Holy Spirit as fire at the epiclesis similarly consecrates the bread and wine; as a poem by Balai, on the consecration of a church at Qenneshrin, puts it: 'the priest stands, he kindles fire (i.e. by uttering the epiclesis), he takes bread, but gives forth the Body, he receives wine, but distributes the Blood.'[4]

---

[1] Ed.Wright, p. 42, cp p. 58.

[2] Ed. Frothingham, p. 235–6 = Bedjan VI, p. 318.

[3] See especially C. M. Edsman, *Le baptême de feu* (Uppsala, 1940), pp. 182–90. In the Rabbula Gospels of AD 586 one of the marginal illustrations depicts this. For the imagery of fire, see further my *Fire from Heaven*, chapter V.

[4] Ed. Overbeck, p. 252.

The 'fire' of the Holy Spirit is also imparted to the baptized in the Eucharist, thus effecting a continuing process of sanctification in them. Ephrem's tenth *Hymn on Faith* is worth quoting at length in this context:

> In your Bread there is hidden the Spirit who is not consumed,
> in your Wine there dwells the Fire that is not drunk:
> the Spirit is in your Bread, the Fire in your Wine,
> a manifest wonder, which our lips have received.
>
> When the Lord came down to earth to mortal men
> he created them again in a new creation, like angels,
> mingling Fire and Spirit within them,
> so that in a hidden manner they might be of Fire and Spirit.
>
> The Seraph could not touch the fire's coal with his fingers,
> but just brought it close to Isaiah's mouth;
> the Seraph did not hold it, Isaiah did not consume it,
> but us our Lord has allowed to do both.
>
> To the angels who are spiritual Abraham brought
> food for the body, and they ate. The new miracle
> is that our mighty Lord has given to bodily man
> Fire and Spirit to eat and drink.
>
> Fire descended in wrath and consumed sinners,
> the Fire of mercy descended and dwelt in the bread.
> Instead of that fire which consumed mankind,
> you have consumed Fire in the Bread and you come to life.
>
> Fire descended and consumed Elijah's sacrifices,
> the Fire of mercies has become a living sacrifice for us:
> Fire consumed the oblation,
> and we, Lord, have consumed your Fire in your oblation.
>
> (*H. Fid.* 10.8–13)

Fire, like water, is an ambiguous symbol—it can also be destructive. But in the case of the Holy Spirit as fire, what is destroyed is only what is impure or evil:

> Your Bread slays the Greedy one who had made us his food,
> your Cup destroys Death who had swallowed us up.
> We have eaten you, O Lord, we have drunken you—
> not that we would consume you up, but through you we shall be saved.
>
> (*H. Fid.* 10.18)

Or

> When Moses signed and anointed

the sons of the Levite Aaron,
fire consumed their bodies,
fire preserved their clothes.
Blessed are you, my brothers,
for the fire of mercy has come down,
utterly devouring your sins,
purifying and sanctifying your bodies. (*H. Epiph.* 3.10)

Narsai adapts the same idea to the font:[5]

As though in a furnace the priest recasts bodies in the baptismal water;
    and as in a fire he consumes the weeds of mortality
...by the heat of the Spirit he purges away the rust of body and soul.

We are not far here from the eschatological imagery of the 'river of fire.'[6]

In many passages the concept of the Holy Spirit as fire is tied up with the image of the pearl, much beloved by Syriac writers. According to ancient mythology, when lightning strikes the mussel in the sea, the mussel opens as a direct result of this conjunction of disparate elements, fire and water.[7] In his famous set of five poems on the Pearl,[8] Ephrem meditates on the many analogies with the Incarnation that the pearl offers: Christ the Pearl is born through the coming of the Fire of the Holy Spirit upon Mary the mussel. From an early date the consecrated eucharistic elements also came to acquire the technical name of 'pearls.' 'Christ gave us pearls, his Body and holy Blood,' says Ephrem in his *memra* on the Sinful Woman.[9] Here again it is the descent of the 'Fire' at the epiclesis which has given rise to the terminology. As Jacob of Serugh puts in his *Homily on Ezekiel's Chariot*, in the context of the cherubs' 'coals of fire':[10]

It is not the priest who is authorized to sacrifice the Only-Begotten
or to raise up that sacrifice for sinners to the Father's presence:
rather, the Holy Spirit goes forth from the Father
and descends, overshadows and resides in the bread,
making it the Body, and making it treasured pearls
to adorn the souls that are betrothed by him.

---

[5] Ed. Mingana, I, p. 343.
[6] On which see Edsman, *op. cit.*, pp. 57–63.
[7] Cp Edsman, *op. cit.*, pp. 190–9.
[8] H. Fid. 81–5.
[9] *Sermones* II. iv. 9–10.
[10] Ed. Bedjan, IV, p. 597.

As a final example to illustrate the activities of the 'Fire of the Spirit' we may quote a fine passage of Sahdona, where he compares prayer to a sacrifice:[11]

> The beginning of our prayer should be watchful and alert, and with suffering of heart we should let streams of tears pour down our cheeks. The whole of our service should be completed according to the will of God, so that it may be without spot and acceptable to him. Then the Lord will be pleased with us and take pleasure in our offering; smelling the sweet scent of the pure whole-offering of our heart he will send the fire of his Spirit and consume our sacrificial offerings, raising up to to our mind with them in the flame to heaven, and we shall see the Lord, our delight, without perishing, as the stillness of his revelation falls upon us and the hidden things of his knowledge are depicted in us. The spiritual joy settles in our heart, together with hidden mysteries which cannot readily be described in words for the simple. In this way we should make our bodies a living, holy and acceptable sacrifice that is pleasing to God in our rational service.

(2)   THE HOLY SPIRIT AS A DOVE

At Christ's baptism the Holy Spirit descended in the *likeness* of a dove, and on the basis of this episode the dove has, from at least the fifth century on, been a regular symbol of the Holy Spirit in Christian art.[12] In the sixth century, however, both Severus and Philoxenus objected to the use of this symbolism in the fashion for making 'eucharistic doves'; their objection did not stem (as has sometimes been supposed) from iconoclast tendencies, but from the pagan associations of the dove in the pre-Christian cult centred at Mabbugh.[13] It is perhaps because of such pagan connotations that 'dove' symbolism is not so prominent in Syriac writers as it is in those of other Christian traditions.

There is, however, one early text where the image of the dove is prominent, the 24th of the Odes of Solomon, which opens:

---

[11] Ed. de Halleux, III, p. 7.

[12] Among Syriac illuminated manuscripts, see for example the illustration of Pentecost in the Rabbula Gospels of AD 586 (J. Leroy, *Les manuscrits syriaques à peintures* (Paris, 1964), II, plate 34; cp plate 73–4, Annunciation in Vat. syr. 559).

In the (late) Targum to the Song of Songs, the turtle-dove of 2:12 becomes the 'Holy Spirit of salvation.'

[13] Cp my 'Iconoclasm and the Monophysites,' in *Iconoclasm* (ed. A. Bryer and J. Herrin; Birmingham, 1977), p. 54.

The dove flew over the head of our Lord Christ
for he was her head;
she sang above him
and her voice was heard...

The scene of this very obscure poem is certainly Christ's baptism, but it is not clear whether the dove is used as a symbol of the Holy Spirit, or whether the author did not yet know the Gospel accounts and was simply using the bird as a recognition motif.[14]

It is possible that the vocabulary of 'flying,' very frequently found in connection with the activities of the Spirit, derives from the imagery of the Holy Spirit as a dove, but then it could just as well have had its origin in the use of the verb *rahhef* 'hover' in Gen. 1:2, or the phrase 'wings of the Spirit/wind' in Ps 104:3, both passages frequently alluded to by Syriac writers. (The Gospel accounts of Christ's baptism do not use 'fly,' only 'come down').

Passages such as the following,[15] where the Holy Spirit is described straight-forwardly as a dove, seem to be exceptional:

Come, my brethren, let us go and see that Tree planted by the streams of water, whose leaves never fall. In its summit the heavenly Eagle makes its nest, in its branches, the Dove, the Holy Spirit; its roots pour forth the water of baptism, into which sinners go down to be baptized, and come up pure.

On the whole Syriac writers prefer to use 'dove' imagery in quite a different context, and derived from another biblical passage, Song of Songs 6:8: it is Mary who is the dove, and she bears the heavenly Eagle[16] the 'Ancient of Days' (Dan 7:9), as in the following beautiful stanza:[17]

A young dove, she carried
the Eagle, the Ancient of days,
singing praise as she carried him

---

[14] So S. Gero, 'The Spirit as a dove at the baptism of Jesus,' *Novum Testamentum* 18 (1976), pp. 17–35.

[15] *Fenqitho* III, pp. 259b-60a (Lilyo on Epiphany); cp also chapter IV note 34.

[16] Here of course the Son, in contrast to the extract just cited. Christ as an 'eagle' is quite common in Syriac writers, e.g. Ephrem, *H. Eccl.* 1.3.4; *Sermones* II. iv. 58; *H. Nativ.* 4.3; Cyrillona (ed. Bickell), p. 573; Jacob of Serugh (ed. Bedjan) 11, p. 615 S, p. 767; *Fenqitho* II, p. 102b etc.

[17] Ed. Lamy II, col. 543 (Hymns on Mary), translation in my *Bride of Light. Hymns on Mary from the Syriac Churches* (Moran Etho 6; Kottayam, 1994), pp. 44–5.

in her lovely songs:

'O my Son most rich, in a tiny nest
you have chosen to grow; melodious harp,
you are silent like a child, please let me sing to you
with the lyre whose chords stir the Cherubim;
pray let me speak to you.'

Later poets, such as Jacob of Serugh,[18] take up this imagery of Mary as the dove, and develop it in many different ways.

There would seem, then, to be a tendency in most Syriac writers to move away from seeing the dove as a symbol of the Holy Spirit, and to transfer the imagery to Mary. This can already be observed in Ephrem's typological treatment of the dove at Christ's baptism, which he sees as prefigured by Noah's dove (Gen. 8:9–11), the bearer of the olive leaf:

The ark marked out by its course the sign of its preserver,
the cross of its steersman, and the wood of its sailor
who has come to fashion for us a church in the water of baptism:
with the three-fold name he rescues those who in her live;
in the place of the dove, the Spirit ministers her anointing
and the mystery of her salvation. Praises to her Saviour.

(H. Fid. 49.4)

Although Noah's dove here serves as a type of the Holy Spirit in Christian baptism, Ephrem also implies an element of contrast; in another poem he shifts away from this altogether, and prefers to see Noah's dove as 'related to Mary'[19] instead!

The dove gave comfort to Noah in the flood, and related to the dove is
    Mary (John 12:3–5):
instead of a leaf, she depicted symbolically the death of the Son by
    means of fine oil;
in the alabaster vase that she poured over him, she emptied out on him
    a treasury of types:
at that moment the symbols of oil found their home in Christ, and oil,

---

[18] E.g. ed. Bedjan, S, p. 742 (Mary the dove visits Elizabeth the eagle); p. 767 (mankind is the dove, Christ the eagle); *apud* Overbeck, p. 396 (the Church is the dove). Gregory of Nyssa in his commentary to Song of Songs 6:8 describes the Holy Spirit at Christ's baptism as 'the Mother of the chosen dove (ie. the Church).'

[19] Ephrem here as elsewhere fuses two Mary's together (for this feature see Murray, *Symbols*, pp. 146–8, 329–35.)

that treasurer of symbols, handed over the symbols to the Lord of symbols.
Creation conceived the symbols of him, but Mary conceived his actual
limbs.

(H. Virg. 6.7)

In that Noah's dove brings an olive branch, it is also understood as conveying olive oil ; as one of the Epiphany hymns ascribed to Ephrem puts it,
more directly:

> The olive leaf arrived
> carrying the symbol of anointing;
> those in the ark rejoiced at its coming
> for it brought the message of salvation.
> You (*sc.* the baptized) too rejoiced at the coming
> of this holy oil;
> your bodies laden with guilt were joyful,
> for it brought the same message of salvation.

(H. Epiph. 3.8)

This brings us to our next point.

(3)   THE HOLY SPIRIT AND OLIVE OIL/MYRON.

Olive oil is very closely associated with the Holy Spirit in Syriac literature,
but this is because oil was understood as the ideal 'conductor' for the power
of the Spirit, rather than as an actual symbol of the Spirit.[20] As Ephrem puts
it:

> This oil is the dear friend of the Holy Spirit, it serves him, following him
> like a disciple. (*H. Virg.* 7.6.1–2)

---

[20] Note, however, the anonymous East Syriac commentator (ed. Connolly), II,
p. 104: 'The horn of oil represents the Holy Spirit'; and Isho'yahb I (ed. Chabot, in
Synodicon Orientale), p. 186–445: 'the holy oil of anointing symbolizes the garment of
sonship and of incorruption, and is the promise of the anointing that comes from
the Holy Spirit,' Timothy II, *On the Sacraments* III.9 (Vat. syr. 150). Likewise Daniel
of Tella comments on Ps. 23:5 ('my head with oil'): 'by the 'head' he means the
mind which receives the gifts of the Holy Spirit at baptism: with the baptismal
anointing there enters into the soul the divine draught which makes it drunk' (for
this theme, see chapter VIII); and on Ps. 45:8 he comments: 'the 'oil' is the Holy
Spirit who came down upon our Lord in (*sic*) the Jordan' (Harvard syr. 75, f. 76,
109).

Thanks to the play on words available in Syriac, the olive oil (*meshha*) is much more commonly understood as a symbol of Christ (*mshiha* 'the anointed') in our texts;[21] as Ephrem puts it later on in the same poem:

From whatever angle I look at the oil, Christ looks out at me from it.

(*H. Virg.* 7.14.6)

There is, however, another important biblical passage which associates the Spirit with oil and anointing, Isaiah 61:1. The Septuagint version, which is quoted in Luke 4:18 (cp Acts 10:38), reads 'The Spirit of the Lord is upon me, wherefore he has anointed me'; here the Spirit is the subject of the verb 'anointed,' but this is not the case in either the original Hebrew or in the Peshitta Old Testament, which have 'wherefore the *Lord* has anointed me.'

In the later baptismal commentaries it is stated that 'the holy Mar Severus says in one of his writings that the myron typifies the Holy Spirit.'[22] The source for this statement is Severus' letter to John the soldier or 'Roman,'[23] where he speaks of 'perfecting' Arians who are received into the orthodox church and says that they are 'imprinted with myron' and that 'we thus indicate that the Holy Spirit, whose type this imprint is, is the perfecter of the gift that is given by baptism.' Characteristically the Syriac commentators prefer to see the myron as symbolizing Christ, rather than the Holy Spirit.

---

[21] Christ is also the olive, the source of oil: cp Murray, *Symbols*, pp. 322–4.

[22] E.g. Moshe bar Kepha, *On Myron* § 13.

[23] See my 'Severos' Letter to John the Soldier,' in G. Wiessner (ed.), *Erkenntnisse und Meinungen II* (GOFS 17, 1978), pp. 53–75, esp. p. 73. For myron, see below, ch. V (2) (c).

3 THE SOURCES

(1) THE SERVICES AND THEIR STRUCTURE

(a) The Services

The Syriac baptismal services fall into four groups, the East Syriac, the Syrian Orthodox/Catholic, the Maronite, and the Melkite.

(i) The East Syriac (Assyrian and Chaldean)

The East Syriac baptismal service is attributed to the catholicos Isho'yahb III (649–59), who was the author of extensive reforms in many areas of the liturgy. No edition of the oldest available manuscripts is available, and there is a certain amount of variation over details between the different printed texts; in particular certain westernizing modifications have been made in Chaldean editions. In the present book I have used the 1890 edition, printed by the Archbishop of Canterbury's mission at Urmia (modern Rezaiyeh) in *Liturgia sanctorum apostolorum Adaei et Maris*. The text, with Latin translation, will also be found in volume 1 of J. A. Assemani's *Codex Liturgicus* (1725). Among modern editions printed in the Middle East, the Chaldean edition of 1907, and the Assyrian edition (by E. Y. Kelaita) of 1926, both printed at Mosul, may be singled out for mention.

To accompany the Urmia edition, an English translation was made, published in 1893 (*The Liturgy of the Holy Apostles Adai and Mari*, pp. 63–82). G. P. Badger had already made an earlier translation in his *The Nestorians and their Rituals* (London, 1852), pp. 195–214. An English translation of Kelaita's edition (1928) was made by K. A. Paul and G. Mooken, and published in 1967 (*The Liturgy of the Holy Apostles Adai and Mari, together with the Liturgies of Mar Theodorus and Mar Nestorius and the Order of Baptism*, Trichur, Kerala).

A German translation, based on the Urmia edition but making use of a number of manuscripts as well, was made by G. Diettrich, *Die nestorianische Taufliturgie* (Giessen, 1903). Another, using the 1928 edition, is published by J. Madey and G. Vavanikunnel in *Taufe, Firmung und Busse in den Kirchen der Ostsyrischen Ritenkreises* (Einsiedeln, 1971), pp. 22–63 (an appendix, pp. 65–70, lists the differences between this and the Chaldean service).

The East Syriac service certainly underwent some development in the middle ages, and many manuscripts attribute the service to Elias (III; 1176–90) or (less frequently) Yahballaha (III; 1281–1317), as well as Isho'yahb. All surviving manuscripts are later than these reforms, and so the early commentaries, in particular the one attributed to George of Arbela [see below (2) (d)], are of great importance since they describe a more primitive structure.

(ii) Syrian Orthodox/Catholic

1. The standard baptismal service in use is normally attributed to *Severus* although some manuscripts give Jacob of Edessa, Paul of Tella, or even Barhebraeus as the name of the compiler. Comparison of later manuscripts and printed editions with the earliest surviving manuscripts (of the 8th–10th century) indicates that there exists a certain fluidity in the content and (to a lesser extent) the structure of the service, and the position of several prayers and formulae connected with the anointings is unstable. More will be said of this below.

The service was first printed in Europe in 1572, with a Latin translation by Guy Lefevre de la Boderie, at the famous Antwerp printing house of Christopher Plantin. For European readers unfamiliar with Syriac script the text was also given at the bottom of each page in Hebrew characters. This particular text was reprinted (= SA II), together with that of a number of other manuscripts of the Severus service, in volumes I–III of Assemani's magnificent collection of liturgical texts, the *Codex Liturgicus;* each text, however, is inconveniently spread over the three volumes, and so reference to this work is very awkward (see the table below). The Latin translations which accompanied these texts were reprinted in H. Denzinger, *Ritus Orientalium* (Würzburg, 1863), volume 1.

A modern Syrian Orthodox edition was made by the late patriarch, Mar Ignatius Ephrem Barsaum, and published at Homs in 1950; this gives separate services for boys and girls, but there is very little difference otherwise between them. This edition, which has the title *Ktobo da'modo qadisho,* served as a basis for a new edition, with a facing English translation published in 1974 by Mar Athanasius Yeshue Samuel (*The Sacrament of Holy Baptism according to the ancient rite of the Syrian Orthodox Church of Antioch.*)

An earlier, Syrian Catholic, edition had been published at Charfet (Lebanon) in 1922, by the Syrian Catholic Patriarch, Mar Ignatius Ephrem Rahmani; this was translated into French by Mgr G. Khouri-Sarkis and published in *L'Orient Syrien* 1 (1956). This edition contains a few westernizing modifications. There are also several Syro-Malankar editions (Kottayam, no date; Pampakuda, 1900, 1936 and 1950); an analysis of this form of the service is given by E, R. Hambye, 'Le baptême dans les églises syriennes de l'Inde,' *L'Orient Syrien* 1 (1956). pp. 255–66.

An English translation of the service as found in India was made by J. Hough in *The History of Christianity in India from the Commencement of the Christian Era* (1845), pp. 645–50. A detailed study of the early manuscripts of the service attributed to Severus will be found in my 'Studies in the early history of the Syrian Orthodox baptismal liturgy,' *Journal of Theological Studies* n. s. 23 (1972), pp. 16–64; the section of this article dealing with the anointings is reprinted in J. Vellian (ed.), *Studies on Syrian Baptismal Rites* (Syrian Churches Series 6; Kottayam, 1973), pp, 100–18. An English translation of the prayer of consecration of the water, based on the oldest manuscripts, was made by me in 'The consecration of the water in the oldest manuscripts of the Syrian Orthodox Baptismal Liturgy' *Orientalia Christiana Periodica* 37 (1971), pp. 317–32.

2. There exist two short services, for use in cases of need, one attributed to Severus, the other to Philoxenus. The former is printed in Assemani's *Codex Liturgicus* II, pp. 300–306, and in the Homs edition of 1950; the latter in *Codex Liturgicus* II, pp. 307–8. A further short service, not available in print, is attributed to Iohannan bar Shushan (died 1072). Latin translations of the short services attributed to Severus and Philoxenus will be found in Denzinger, pp. 316–18.

3. Another full service, attributed to Timothy of Alexandria, also exists, but it is no longer used, and is known only from two old manuscripts. This has been edited by me, (together with a translation and commentary) in 'A new Syriac baptismal *ordo* attributed to Timothy of Alexandria, *Le Muséon* 83 (1970), pp. 367–431. The translation alone is reprinted in J. Vellian (ed.), *Studies on Syrian Baptismal Rites* (1913), pp. 72–84. This service provides a link between the main Syrian Orthodox service attributed to Severus and the Maronite one.

4. A single manuscript in the British Library, Add. 14518 of the 9th or 10th century, contains a baptismal service that has connections, not only with the two other Syrian Orthodox services, attributed to Severus and Timothy, but also with the Maronite service attributed to Jacob of Serugh. Unfortunately the title is lost, and the final part of the service, containing the baptism and (presumably) a post-baptismal anointing, is lost. An analysis of the structure of this anonymous service is given in my article 'A remarkable Syriac baptismal *ordo* (BM Add. 14518),' *Parole de l'Orient* 2 (1971), pp. 365–78. The edition and translation are published in *Parole de l'Orient* 8 (1977/8), pp. 311–46.

(iii) Maronite

The service employed by the Maronites is attributed to Jacob of Serugh, and was printed, with a Latin translation, in *Codex Liturgicus* II, pp. 309–50, III, pp. 184–7. Of the editions printed in Lebanon the most important is that published at Bkerke in 1942, entitled *Ktobo d-tekse l-teshmeshto d-roẓe qadishe*. A photographic edition of three important manuscripts, together with French translation and study, is available in A. Mouhanna, *Les rites de l'initiation dans l'Église maronite* (OCA 212; 1980). Only the oldest manuscripts, which do not go back earlier than the 15th century, are free from Latinizing influences (especially in the baptismal formula, where the traditional Syrian passive, 'N is baptized,' has frequently been altered to the western 'I baptize N'). In certain other respects, however, the Maronite service retains some extremely archaic elements.

Some variant prayers etc, taken from other manuscripts, can be found in Latin translation in Denzinger, I, pp. 334–50 (cp also P. Dib, 'L'initiation chrétienne dans le rite maronite ,' *Revue de l'Orient Chrétien* II, 5 (1910), pp. 73–84).

There is also a short Maronite service, attributed to Basil. The Syriac text is not available in print, but a Latin translation is included in Denzinger, I, pp. 358–9.

(iv) Melkite

Today the Melkite Church, both Orthodox and Uniate, follows the Constantinopolitan rite and employs Arabic as its main liturgical language. Prior to the Byzantine reconquest of Syria in the late 10th century, however, the Melkite church fully belonged to the native Antiochene liturgical tradition, and their liturgical texts of this period were mainly written in Syriac. In the present book it is only with the original *Antiochene* baptismal texts of the Melkite Church that we are concerned.

The full service is attributed to Basil, and is to be found, with Latin translation, in Volume III of *Codex Liturgicus*, pp. 199–237. There is also a short service, preserved in a single manuscript which is of particular interest, since it is the only surviving Syriac liturgical text which preserves the original Antiochene pattern of having *only* a pre-baptismal anointing (on this, see further below). This text was edited by me (with an English translation) in 'A short Melkite baptismal service in Syriac,' *Parole de l'Orient* 3 (1972), pp. 119–30.

(b) The structure of the services

For our purposes only a few guiding lines need be given here, paying special attention to those features which are particularly associated with the activity of the Holy Spirit, namely the use of oil; for the various epicleses, see chapter V(1)(a).

It goes without saying that over the course of time all the services have altered in various ways from their original form. Many of them, for example, have been profoundly influenced by the structure of the eucharistic liturgy; this applies in particular to the Maronite and East Syriac services, but it is also very noticeable in several old texts of the Syrian Orthodox services attributed to Severus and Timothy.[1]

As in other liturgical matters the East Syriac tradition stands apart from the three West Syriac ones, although, as we shall see, the same basic structure is present. Moreover, right at the end of the service there are surprisingly some word for word correspondences with the Melkite service, which do not appear to have been noticed before.[2]

Of the West Syriac traditions *Severus* and *Basil* stand closest together, and their prayers of consecration of the water basically represent two more or less independent translations of the Greek text still found in the Byzantine rite.[3] Links between these and the Maronite *Jacob of Serugh* are provided by *Timothy* and the anonymous text of Add. 14518. Between these various services a number of prayers are to be found in common (often in differing places in the services).

The two main constituent elements of all the oriental baptismal rites are oil/myron and water. Although the Antiochene tradition is characterized by the proliferation of anointings (a subject we shall shortly have to deal with), one thing is quite clear: anointing with oil and baptism are inseparably linked, and the attempt of many European writers to associate the gift of the Spirit with the one *or* the other is misguided, and the subject should not be discussed in the light of western developments in the baptismal liturgy, with the separation in time between baptism and confirmation/chrismation. As Philoxenus of Mabbug says, 'we receive the Holy

---

[1] See 'Studies,' pp. 40–4, 61–3, and *Parole de l'Orient* 2 (1971), pp. 365–78.

[2] Thus U, p. 73 (at the 'crowning') corresponds to B III, p. 231; even more clearly, one of the closing prayers in U (p. 74, 'The new children worship you…) is found in expanded form in B III, pp. 229–30.

[3] The texts are set out in 'Studies,' pp. 44–59.

Spirit through the oil *and* the water.'[4] Needless to say, passages can be found, both in the liturgical texts and in commentators on the service, which, taken by themselves, look as if they associated the gift of the Holy Spirit with the one, rather than the other; but looking at the tradition as a whole, it is quite clear that this is not a question of either/or: the one without the other would be totally unthinkable. The oil and the water balance each other just as much as do the Institution Narrative and the Epiclesis in the eucharistic liturgy: to give all the emphasis to the one at the expense of the other is an approach that all good liturgical scholars today would abhor.

A little must inevitably be said about the complicated problem of the anointings in the Syrian tradition. All the full services which come down to us contain anointings both before and after the baptism proper, although in some texts of the East Syriac rite the priest simply lays his hands on and signs the newly-baptized with the sign of the cross, without use of oil (so the Urmia edition).[5] In the various services there is a considerable interaction between the prayers and formulae used in connection with the various anointings, but the one thing that is fairly stable is their position within the service, and so this will provide a useful framework for our discussion.

Position I: accompanying the inscription of the candidates (sometimes just a consignation without use of oil). This belongs to the catechumenal rites, originally separate in time from baptism; it is not of much further relevance to us here.

Position II: after the completion of the catechumenal rites, but preceding the consecration of the water.

Position III: following the consecration of the water, but before the baptism proper.

Position IV: following the baptism, and preceding the Communion. The terminology used of the priest's action in connection with these different anointings is fairly stable (although the Melkite and Maronite traditions tend to use one term for all positions), so that the following pattern obtained is fairly certain:

Position I: 'seal' (*htam*)
Position II: 'sign' or 'mark' (*rsham*)

---

[4] Homily on the indwelling of the Holy Spirit, ed. Tanghe, p. 46. Another 6th century writer, John of Tella, states that 'without the holy oil or myron baptism is not complete' (ed. Lamy in *Dissertatio de Syrorum Fide et Disciplina in Re Eucharistica* (Louvain, 1859) pp. 84–5).

[5] For details see Diettrich, pp. 83–8, and below, chapter IV (i) (c).

Position III: 'anoint' *(mshah)*
Position IV: 'imprint' *(tba')*[6]

The anointings in positions I and II normally concern just the fore-head, that in position III the whole body, and that in position IV the organs of sense (for unguents used, see below).

It is now generally recognized that the multiplication of anointings in the Antiochene rite came about as a result of the fusion of several diverging traditions. Thus, the secondary nature, within the Antiochene tradition, of the post-baptismal anointing (position IV) is absolutely certain: it was intro-duced into the area in the fifth century, and probably a number of quite different factors led to its widespread adoption.[7] The situation with the anointings at positions II and III is much less clear.

Before the fifth century the Antiochene rite knew of no post-baptismal anointing at all, as can be seen from descriptions of baptisms in the *Acts of Thomas* and of *John*, as well as from the writings of Aphrahat and Ephrem in the fourth century. Writing in Antioch in the 390s John Chrysostom still does not know of any anointing after baptism (although he speaks of two

---

[6] In the present East Syriac service there is no anointing in position II, but it is clear that the one in position I (called the *rushma*) originally belonged in position II. In the anonymous commentary (ed. Connolly II, pp. 106–9) the consignation in position IV is called *huttama;* to judge by p. 108 line 24, oil was used with it.

[7] Various reasons have been given: thus Ratcliff argued for the influence of the Jerusalem liturgy ('The Old Syrian baptismal tradition and its resettlement under the influence of Jerusalem in the fourth century,' *Studies in Church History* 2 (1965), pp. 19–37, reprinted in ed. J. Vellian *Studies on Syrian Baptismal Rites* (SCS 6); cp 'Stud-ies,' pp. 38–9), while Botte suggested that it came about as a result of the practice of anointing heretics who returned to orthodoxy ('Postbaptismal anointing in the ancient Patriarchate of Antioch' in ed. Vellian, *Studies...*, pp. 63–71 (French original in *Miscellanea Liturgica..G. Lercaro* (Rome, 1967) II)). It is equally possible that the shift towards a cathartic understanding of the *rushma*, resulting from a new empha-sis on baptism as a burial, provided a sufficient reason for the introduction of the post-baptismal anointing associated with the Spirit (cp chapter IV (I)). On this subject see especially G. Winkler, 'The history of the Syriac prebaptismal anointing in the light of the earliest Armenian sources,' in *II Symposium Syriacum* (OCA 205; 1978), pp. 317–24, and 'The original meaning of the pre-baptismal anointing and its implications,' *Worship* 52 (1978), pp. 24–45; B. Varghese, *Les onctions baptismales dans la tradition syrienne* (CSCO 512, Subsidia 82; 1989), and 'Meaning of baptismal anointings according to the West Syriac baptismal texts,' *The Harp* 2:1/2 (1989), pp. 21–30; also Appendix 1, below.

before it), despite the fact that the canon 48 of the Council of Laodicea (380?)[8] had specified that there should be one.

The earliest evidence for a post-baptismal anointing in the Antiochene area comes with the *Apostolic Constitutions* (VII.22.43–4), perhaps dating from the very end of the fourth century; in a Syriac source it is first to be found in the Syriac translation of Theodore of Mopsuestia's catechetical homilies (see (2) (c) below). In the course of the fifth century the new practice must have penetrated deeply into the whole area, since our sources from this time onwards almost all know it; there are, however, important exceptions, especially among Syriac writers: Narsai, active in Edessa and Nisibis, and Jacob of Serugh, active in Osrhoene, neither know of any post-baptismal anointing as late as the fifth, or even early sixth, century. That the original Antiochene pattern lingered on here and there until a very much later date is shown by the survival of the 11th/12th-century short Melkite service where the post-baptismal anointing is absent. The same ancient pattern is also implied very clearly in two related Syriac baptismal commentaries, one attributed to John Chrysostom, the other anonymous.[9]

The problem of the anointings in positions II and III is much more complicated and we cannot go into this matter in detail here. It should be said that there is a great deal of interchange in the prayers and formulae used with these two anointings among the various texts.[10] Furthermore, an anointing in position III is entirely absent in the form of *Severus* employed by the Syrian Orthodox in Iraq and India. This is certainly no recent innovation, since this pattern is already attested in a tenth-century manuscript (British Library Add. 14493), as well as in most of the *Syriac* commentaries on the baptismal service, going back to Pseudo-Dionysius' *Ecclesiastical Hierarchy*, translated into Syriac first by Sergius of Reshaina in the sixth century. It seems likely that this pattern represents the Tagrit, as opposed to the Antioch, rite; whether or not this provides an archaic survival is unclear.

An examination of the earliest sources, in particular the accounts of baptisms in the *Acts of Thomas* and the *Acts of John*, indeed strongly suggests

---

[8] *Nomocanon* (ed. Bedjan), p. 24. See also S. Voicu, 'Textes peu connus concernant l'onction prébaptismale,' *Irénikon* 64 (1991), pp. 268–82. For a claim that a post-baptismal anointing is already attested in Syria in the second century, see Appendix 1, note 1.

[9] See below, (2) (d). The description of Melkite baptism in al-Biruni's *Feasts of the Melkites* (PO 10, pp. 301–2) interestingly enough mentions only a pre-baptismal anointing, of the whole body.

[10] See 'Studies,' pp. 24–40 for S.

that originally there was just a *single* pre-baptismal anointing, and that the name for this was the *rushma*, 'sign' or 'mark': almost certainly only the head was involved. As we shall see in chapter IV, the *rushma* was primarily associated with the mark of ownership and the conferring of sonship and the royal priesthood.

The duplication of the pre-baptismal anointing appears to have been brought about by a number of different, but related, considerations. Contact with other liturgical traditions, where the pre-baptismal anointing was essentially exorcistic and protective, brought about a re-thinking of the meaning of this anointing in the Syrian rite. At the same time, the fact that bathing practice in antiquity made use of oil to anoint the whole body prior to bathing, led to the inclusion of the entire body, and not just the forehead, in the pre-baptismal anointing.[11] Practical considerations, such as the division of labour between priest and deacon (specifically mentioned in some texts) would easily lead to the actual duplication of the pre-baptismal anointing, employing position II for the priest's anointing of the forehead and position III for the deacon's anointing of the rest of the body. No doubt local variations assisted in the process of duplication, as well.

By the end of the fourth century commentators such as John Chrysostom no longer associate the gift of sonship and royal priesthood with either of the pre-baptismal anointings they describe; instead they transfer these to the baptism proper, leaving the two anointings with only the idea of ownership and protection.[12] This situation no doubt eased the transition to the next stage, the introduction of the post-baptismal anointing in position IV,[13] which in effect took over many of the attributes once connected with the original pre-baptismal *rushma*.

In the following chapters, where prayers connected with any of the anointings are quoted from the various baptismal services, the position (I, II, III, or IV) will always be given.

Finally a word needs to be said about the unguent used for the anointings. In the earliest texts we only find mention of *meshho*, '(olive) oil.' At the end of the fourth century John Chrysostom uses the term *myron* for the pre-

---

[11] Cp J. Mateos, 'Théologie de baptême dans le formulaire de Sévère d'Antioche,' *OCA* 197 (1972), pp. 135–61: he considers that the *rushma* denoted primarily a mark of ownership, whereas the *mshihuta* was essentially borrowed from bathing practice.

[12] For the probable reason, see chapter IV (1), and Appendix 1.

[13] The use of fragrant myron for this anointing has its counterpart in the practice in antiquity of using scented unguents after bathing.

baptismal anointing, interchangeably with *elaion* 'oil.'[14] Later usage in West Syriac tradition of course confines the term *myron* to post-baptismal anointing, and it is this *myron* which is specially consecrated on the Thursday of Holy Week,[15] and which became the subject to treatises by John of the Sedre, Jacob of Edessa, George bishop of the Arabs, Moshe bar Kepha, Dionysius bar Salibi, and many others. Commentators of the early Islamic period speak of two constituents of *myron*, olive oil and balsam,[16] but from the thirteenth century onwards the present practice of employing a large number of ingredients was taken from the Coptic church.

Myron is absent from the East Syriac tradition, and their writers stress that olive oil was the only constituent.

Besides being used for anointing the candidates, in all the Syrian rites oil is also poured on the baptismal waters during the course of the long consecration prayer. Some texts simply speak of 'horn of oil' being used at this point (thus the East Syriac and Melkite services; also *Timothy* and some early manuscripts of *Severus*[17]), while others (*Jacob* and the printed editions of *Severus*) specify *myron*. 'Myron' is already spoken of in this context by pseudo-Dionysius in the early sixth (or even late fifth) century, and the term is taken up by the main Syrian Orthodox commentators, such as Jacob of Edessa, Moshe bar Kepha and Dionysius bar Salibi.

One last point in connection with the oil should be mentioned here. The oldest descriptions of baptism that we find in the *Acts of Thomas* and *Acts of John,* and in Narsai, include in the baptismal rite a consecratory prayer said over the oil to be used for anointing. Such a prayer is to be found in the later formularies that come down to us only in the East Syriac, Melkite and Maronite rites.

---

[14] E.g. ed. Wenger, p. 145. This early ambivalence is reflected in the rubrics of some early manuscripts of S in connection with the anointing in position II; cp 'Studies,' p. 29.

[15] Originally by any bishop, but from the 12th or 13th century onwards reserved to the Patriarch. Maunday Thursday as the time for the consecration of the myron was already the norm in the late 6th century: cp John of Ephesus, *Eccl. Hist.* III. 29. Cp Siman, *L'expérience,* pp. 97–8.

[16] E.g. Jacob of Edessa, George, Moshe bar Kepha, who all compare the 'composition' of the myron with that of Christ: cp chapter V (2) (c).

[17] See *Le Muséon* 83 (1970), p. 420. Only in the Melkite *Basil* is the coming of the Holy Spirit to consecrate the water specifically connected with the pouring of the myron (cp 'Epiclesis,' p. 191).

(c) Concordance to baptismal *ordines* in Assemani and Denzinger

Syrian Orthodox Severus: [18]

SA I =   Assemani   II,   pp.   261–300;   III,   pp.   168–74;
             = Denzinger. pp. 302–9.
SA II =   Assemani II, pp. 261–300 (lower text); III, pp. 175–84;
             = Denzinger, pp. 309–16.
SA III =   Assemani I, pp. 219–40; II, pp. 214–26; III, pp. 146–52;
             = Denzinger, pp. 267–79.
SA IV=   Assemani I, pp. 240–58; II, 226–37; III, pp. 152–9;
             = Denzinger, pp. 280–88.
SA V =   Assemani I, pp. 258–76; II, pp. 238–43; III, pp. 159–62;
             = Denzinger, pp. 288–95.
SA VI =   Assemani   II,   pp.   243–61;   III,   pp.   162–8;
             = Denzinger, pp. 295–301.
Short services: Severus: Assemani II, pp. 300–6 = Denzinger, pp. 316–7.
             Philoxenus: Assemani II, pp. 307–8 = Denzinger, p. 318.

Maronite Jacob of Serugh:

   JS = Assemani II, pp. 309–50; III, pp. 184–7; = Denzinger, pp.
334–50.

Melkite Basil:

   B = Assemani III, pp. 199–237: = Denzinger, pp. 318–27.

(2)   THE COMMENTARIES AND OTHER LITERATURE ON BAPTISM

There is a rich literature in Syriac on the subject of baptism, and the aim of
this section is simply to enumerate the more important illustrative sources
upon which I draw in the following chapters. The list is deliberately selec-
tive and is certainly not designed to be complete; for reasons stated in the
introduction it is the earlier literature that I shall mainly be using. Besides
bibliographical information, some brief explanatory notes are appended. A
few influential writings of Greek origin are also included.

---

[18] For the manuscript basis of the texts in Assemani, see J. M. Sauget, 'Le Codex Liturgicus de J-L. Assemani et ses sources manuscrites pour les *ordines* de
l'initiation chrétienne selon la tradition syro-occidentale,' *Gregorianum* 54 (1973),
339–52.

(a) Syriac literature before c.400.

(i) The Odes of Solomon

These beautiful but mysterious poems originate probably in Syria, and would seem to belong to the mid second century AD. They survive almost complete in Syriac; one is now known in Greek and a few are incorporated in Coptic into the Gnostic work *Pistis Sophia*. Whether they were originally written in Greek or Syriac is still unclear.[19] Their allusiveness makes them hard to use, even though many of them are generally agreed to be baptismal in character.

The standard edition, with English translation (not always very satisfactory), is that by J. Charlesworth, *The Odes of Solomon* (Oxford, 1973). There is now a detailed commentary by M. Lattke, *Die Oden Salomos* I–III (Freiburg/Göttingen, 1979–86). Still useful for its references to later Syriac baptismal texts is J. H. Bernard, *The Odes of Solomon* (Texts and Studies VIII.3; Cambridge, 1912).

(ii) The Acts of Thomas

This famous work was written in Syriac and translated into Greek. Since the surviving Syriac manuscripts have been revised in places, the original wording of the text (considered unorthodox by later scribes) has sometimes been preserved only in the Greek translation, which has escaped such doctrinal revision. The work, which may date back to the 3rd century, contains a number of descriptions of baptisms: §§25–7, 49–50, 121, 132–3 and 157–8.[20] In all but §§49 and 132 (where the oil is not mentioned) we have explicitly the characteristic early Antiochene sequence, anointing-baptism. §§ 27, 121 and 157 contain prayers said in connection with the anointing, while 121 and 157 also have prayers said over the oil.

There are editions of the Syriac text by Wright, Bedjan and Lewis;[21] an English translation with commentary was published by A. F. J. Klijn, *The*

---

[19] I incline to the former view, but cp J. A. Emerton in *Journal of Theological Studies* ns 18 (1967), pp. 372–406 and 28 (1977), pp. 512–4.

[20] The section numbers correspond to the pages of Wright's edition of the Syriac text as follows: §§25–7 = pp. 191–4; §§49–50 = pp. 217–9; §121 = p. 291; §§132–3 = pp. 301–2; §§157–8 = pp. 323–4.

[21] W. Wright, *Apocryphal Acts of the Apostles* (London, 1871) (with English translation; from B. L. Add. 14645 of AD 936); P. Bedjan in *Acta Martyrum et Sanctorum* III (Paris, 1892) (mainly from Berlin, Sachau 222 of AD 1881); A. Smith Lewis,

Acts of Thomas (Leiden, 1962); Klijn also made a brief study of the descriptions of baptism, 'Baptism in the Acts of Thomas,' in ed. J. Vellian, *Studies on Sytian baptismal rites* (SSC 6, 1973), pp. 57–62. See now S. E. Myers, *Spirit Epicleses in the Acts of Thomas* (Tübingen, 2007).

(iii) The Acts of John

The Syriac *Acts of John* represent a different work from the Greek *Acts*. They contain two descriptions of baptisms,[22] both of considerable interest; these are studied by Klijn in 'An ancient Syriac baptismal liturgy in the Syriac Acts of John,' *Novum Testamentum* 6 (1963), pp. 216–28. Once again, only a pre-baptismal anointing is known.

(iv) Aphrahat

Although no single *Demonstration* is devoted to baptism, several of them deal incidentally with the subject, in particular nos 6, 7, 11 and 12. I use the edition of Parisot in *Patrologia Syriaca* I–II. There is a complete English translation by K. Valavanolickal, *Aphrahat, Demonstrations* I–II (Moran Etho 23–24; Kottayam, 2005), French by M-J. Pierre in *Sources chrétiennes* 349, 359 (1988–9), and German by P. Bruns (1991–2).

A good study of the subject of baptism in Aphrahat was made by E. J. Duncan, *Baptism in the Demonstrations of Aphraates the Persian Sage* (Washington, 1945). One chapter of this, on the administration of baptism (= pp. 104–32) is reprinted in ed. J. Vellian, *Studies on Syrian Baptismal Rites* (SCS 6, 1973), pp-16–36. Cp also R. Murray, 'The exhortation to candidates for ascetical vows at baptism in the ancient Syriac church,' *New Testament Studies* 21 (1974), pp. 59–80 (on *Dem.* 7).

(v) Ephrem

Ephrem's hymns contain many references to baptism; among the most important hymns for our purpose we may list: *Hymns on Faith* 7, 10, 40, 41, 49, 65, 81–5; *Hymns on Virginity* 1, 4–7 (on oil), 37, 46; *Hymns on the Church* 36, *Hymns on Nativity* 1, 16; *Hymns against Heretics* 22, 56. The Epiphany hymns, all specifically on baptism, are mostly not by Ephrem himself, but they may

---

Acta Mythologica Syriaca (Horae Semiticae 3–4; London. 1904) (from Sinai syr. 30 of 5th/6th century, incomplete). Another archaic prayer over oil for baptism is preserved in the Zuqnin Chronicle; on this see my 'An archaic Syriac prayer over the baptismal oil,' *Studia Patristica* 41 (2006), 3–12.

[22] Text in Wright, I, pp. 42–3, 58.

well be early. Of Ephrem's prose works, the *Sermon on our Lord* and the *Commentary on the Diatessaron* may be singled out.

Throughout I use E. Beck's editions of the hymns in CSCO, giving references by hymn, stanza (and line); the following table gives the volume numbers in the CSCO (the second volume of each pair is the German translation):

Hymn cycle	CSSO vol.	Scriptores Syri
Hymns on Faith	154–5	73–4
against Heresies	169–70	76–7
On Paradise, against Julian	174–5	78–9
on the Nativity, on Epiphany	186–7	82–3
on the Church	198–9	84–5
on Nisibis	218–9, 240–1	92–3, 102–3
on Virginity	223–4	94–5
on Fasting	246–7	106–7
on Unleavened Bread, on the Crucifixion, on the Resurrection	248–9	108–9
On Abraham Qidunaya, on Julian Saba	322–3	140–1
Verse Homilies on Faith	212–3	88–9
Prose Homily on our Lord	270–1	116–7
Verse Homilies I	305–6	130–1
II	311–2	134–5
III	320–1	138–9
IV	334–5	148–9
Nachträge	363–4	159–60

The hymns preserved only in Armenian translation are published by L. Mariès and C. Mercier in *PO* 30 (with Latin translation), and by C. Renoux in *PO* 37 (with French translation).

The Syriac original (incomplete) of the *Commentary on the Diatessaron* was edited by L. Leloir (Dublin, 1963, supplemented by Leuven, 1990), and there is an English translation of the complete work by C. McCarthy (1993), using the Armenian version to fill in those portions still missing in Syriac.

The main collections of English translations available are:

J. B. Morris, *Select Works of St Ephrem the Syrian* (1847). This includes the Hymn on Faith, not available yet in a more recent translation.

S. P. Brock, *The Harp of the Spirit. 18 Hymns of St Ephrem* (2nd edn, 1983).

K. McVey, *Ephrem the Syrian, Hymns* (1989): Hymns on the Nativity, Virginity, and against Julian.

S. P. Brock, *St Ephrem the Syrian, Hymns on Paradise* (1990).

C. McCarthy, *St Ephrem's Commentary on Tatian's Diatessaron* (1993).

E. G. Mathews and J. Amar, *St Ephrem the Syrian. Selected Prose Works* (1994).

S. P. Brock, *Bride of Light. Hymns on Mary from the Syriac Churches* (Moran Etho 6; Kottayam, 1994).[23]

S. P. Brock and G. A. Kiraz, *Ephrem the Syrian. Select Poems* (Provo, 2006).

For translations of individual hymns see my 'A brief guide to the main editions and translations of the works of St Ephrem,' in *Saint Éphrem. Un poète pour notre temps* (Patrimoine Syriaque, Actes du Colloque; Antélias, 2007), pp. 281–307 (an earlier version can also be found in *The Harp* 3:1–2 (1990), pp. 7–29). There is a complete bibliography on Ephrem by K. den Biesen, *Bibliography of St Ephrem* (2002).

There are special studies on baptism in the writings of Ephrem by E. Beck, 'Le baptême chez S. Ephrem,' *L'Orient Syrien* 2 (1956), pp. 111–36, and by G. Saber, *La théologie baptismale de Saint Ephrem* (Kaslik, Lebanon, 1974).[24]

(b) Syriac literature of the fifth and sixth century

(i) Narsai

Narsai has two well-known homilies which give a description of the baptismal ceremonies and their meaning. They were first printed (in reverse order) by A. Mingana in his edition of Narsai's homilies (Mosul, 1905; his nos 22 and 21); these, along with Narsai's other liturgical homilies, were translated into English by R. H. Connolly in *The Liturgical Homilies of Narsai (Texts and studies* VIII. 1,1909).[25] There are French translations by P.

---

[23] This includes the Hymns on Mary, wrongly attributed to Ephrem, which are published T. J. Lamy, *Sancti Ephraern Syri Hymni et Sermones* (Malines, 1886) II.

[24] Cp also L. Mitchell, 'Four Fathers on Baptism' in (ed.) J. Vellian., *Studies on Syrian Baptismal Rites* (SCS 6), pp. 37–56, with pp. 43–7 on the Epiphany hymns. Mitchell also deals with John Chrysostom, Theodore and Narsai.

[25] Narsai also has a homily on Epiphany (ed., with ET, by F. G. McLeod in PO 40.1 (1979), pp. 70–105), but this is concerned with theology more than with liturgy.

Gignoux in *L'Initiation chrétienne* (Paris, 1963), pp. 195–247, and (of no 21 only) by P. Brouwers in *Mélanges de l'Université Saint Joseph* 41 (1965), pp. 177–207, and (of no 22) by A. Guillaumont in *L'Orient Syrien* 1 (1956), pp. 189–207.

Narsai describes only one anointing, the pre-baptismal *rushma*, and he dwells at length on the consecration of the oil used for this. This oil is seen primarily as 'imprinting' the mark of Christ's ownership, and 'giving' the Spirit (Mingana I, p. 367), seen mainly in terms of the power to wage war with Satan. It is remarkable that Narsai has no mention of 'sonship' in his two homilies.

(ii) Jacob of Serugh

Jacob wrote three homilies specifically on baptism, 'on the three baptisms' (of the Law, of John and of Christ), 'on the baptism of Christ,' and an exhortation to baptism (nos 7–9 in vol. I of Bedjan's edition, pp. 153–211), and baptismal themes occur in many of his other homilies; of particular interest is the homily on the baptism of Constantine (ed. Frothingham),[26] and the end of the long recension (ed. Strothmann)[27] of the third poem on Thomas in India.

To Jacob, the twin sources of Christian baptism are Christ's own baptism in the Jordan (which he sees as the betrothal of the Church to Christ) and the piercing of Christ's side on the cross (John 19:34). Though he never gives any description of the baptismal service, it would seem from a number of passing allusions that he knew of no post-baptismal anointing. (In general Jacob shows much greater interest in the water and its symbolism than in the oil). An outline of what Jacob has to say on the subject of baptism will be found in my 'Baptismal themes in the writings of Jacob of Serugh,' in *II Symposium Syriacum* (OCA 205; 1978), pp. 325–47.

(iii) Philoxenus

Of particular interest for our subject is Philoxenus' fine homily on the indwelling of the Holy Spirit, edited (with French translation) by A. Tanghe in *Le Muséon* 73 (1960), pp. 39–71; ET in my *The Syriac Fathers on Prayer and the Spiritual Life* (Kalamazoo, 1987), pp. 106–27. There are of course several

---

[26] An incomplete version of the homily, wrongly ascribed to Ephrem, had earlier been published by Overbeck.

[27] In *Göttinger Orientforschungen*, I. 12 (1976); the short recension was published by Bedjan in vol. III of his edition of Jacob.

references to baptism in his other works, and among these one might single out a passage in his *Three tractates on the Trinity and the Incarnation* (ed. Vaschalde, CSCO 9), pp. 118–24, at the end of which he gives an outline of the rite of baptism (which includes a post-baptismal anointing with myron), as follows:

> …they stand naked on a hair mat, with their tunics off; the exorcism is recited over them in a loud and awe-inspiring voice; they blow on and rebuke the rebel, out of whose power they have been brought. Then each receives on his forehead the mark (*rushma*) of the cross; next looking at what follows, he is anointed with holy oil, is baptized three times in the worshipful names (of the Trinity); when he goes up, he is imprinted with the oil called myron, and is clothed in resplendent white garments; he is then escorted amid lighted candles and psalms (into the church) (p. 124).[28]

(c) Works in or translation from Greek

(i) *Basil of Caesarea (+379)*

Basil's exhortation to baptism (*PG* 31, cols 424–44) is to be found in two different Syriac translations, in British Library Add. 14543 (6th century) and Cambridge Add. 3175 (10th/11th century). Basil is quoted several times by the West Syriac commentators on the baptismal service.

(ii) *Gregory of Nazianzus (+389)*

Gregory's homilies are likewise to be found in two different Syriac versions; the second, made by Paul bishop of Edessa in the early seventh century, was a revision of the earlier translation. The earlier rendering of the homily on baptism (*Oratio* 40, *PG* 36, cols 359–428) is to be found in three manuscripts, the later revision in two.[29]

---

[28] It seems probable that Philoxenus is describing the consignations in positions II, III and IV, rather than, I, III and IV, since the consignation in position I regularly comes *before* the exorcism.

[29] For details see A. van Roey and H. Moors, 'Les discours de saint Grégoire de Nazianze dans la littérature syriaque,' *Orientalia Lovanensia Periodica* 4 (1973), pp. 121–33, and 5 (1974), pp. 79–125. Both versions of Hom. 40 are now edited by J-C. Haelewyck (Corpus Nazianzenum 14; 2001).

(iii) John Chrysostom (+407)

Although John wrote in Greek, he is one of the most important witnesses for the Syrian baptismal rite in Antioch in the last decade of the fourth century. Many of his works, including some baptismal catecheses, were translated into Syriac, but no study of these has yet been made. There are three main collections of his catechetical homilies, that in *Patrologia Graeca* 49, and those published by Papadopoulos-Kerameus (1909) and Wenger (Sources chrétiennes 50; 1985). There is an English translation by P. W. Harkins, *St John Chrysostom, Baptismal Instructions* (1963), and French re-edition of three by A. Piédagnel in Sources chrétiennes 366 (1990). A study of the rite known to John was made by T. Finn, *The Liturgy of Baptism in the Baptismal Instructions of St John Chrysostom* (1967).[30]

John knew of two pre-baptismal anointings, but of no post-baptismal one. For reasons explained elsewhere,[31] John associates the 'descent of the Spirit' upon the candidates with the moment when the priest places his hand on their head during the baptism proper. The pre-baptismal anointings are linked with the idea of the oil as 'dazzling Satan' (Wenger, Cat.II.24), or as preparing athletes for spiritual combat. He uses the terms *elaion* (olive oil) and *myron* interchangeably.

(iv) Theodore of Mopsuestia

Theodore's *Catechetical Homilies* survive only in Syriac translation, edited first by A. Mingana in *Woodbrooke Studies* 6 (1933) with an English translation,[32] and then again by R. Tonneau (with a French translation) in *Studi e Testi* 145 (1949).

Three homilies are devoted to the baptismal ceremonies (nos 12–14 in Tonneau's edition), constituting the second, third and fourth homilies 'on the Mysteries' (the first being devoted to the Lord's Prayer).

---

[30] For John Chrysostom (as well as Theodore, Cyril and Ambrose), see also H. M. Riley, *Christian Initiation: a Comparative Study in the Mystagogical Writings of Cyril of Jerusalem, John Chrysostom, Theodore of Mopsuestia and Ambrose of Milan* (Washington, 1974). Only excerpts from Cyril of Jerusalem's Catechetical Homilies seem to have been translated into Syriac.

[31] See chapter IV (1). The phrase 'gift of the Spirit' occurs in *Cat.* VI. 1 (ET p. 101).

[32] A slightly abbreviated translation of homilies 13–16 is given in E. Yarnold, *The Awe-Inspiring Rites of Initiation* (Slough, 1972), pp. 176–263.

Besides two pre-baptismal anointings, Theodore knows a post-baptismal one as well, although it has been argued that the section on the last is an interpolation.[33] As with John Chrysostom (and for very similar reasons) Theodore sees the 'gift of the Holy Spirit'[34] conferred at baptism proper. His description of the pre-baptismal anointing at position II is remarkable for the absence of any mention of the Holy Spirit (the *rushma* is for him simply a mark of identity, denoting entry into the flock or army of Christ), although his emphasis on *parrhesia* here implies that the catechetical tradition in which he has working once saw the *rushma* as conferring sonship, and hence (by implication) the gift of the Holy Spirit.[35] The pre-baptismal anointing in position III is for Theodore just 'a sign that you will receive the garment of immortality.' As far as the post-baptismal anointing is concerned (if the description goes back to Theodore), we are given the parallelism: Christ's baptism followed by the descent of Spirit: Christian baptism followed by the post-baptismal anointing.

(v) 'Athanasius' (?Athanasius II + 494)

A baptismal address, attributed to Athanasius, to be found in British Library Add. 14727.[36] Although the work (which was known to Dionysius bar Salibi) is certainly not by Athanasius the Great, it is probably of Egyptian origin (though influenced by the Jerusalem catechetical tradition), and may possibly belong to the later patriarch of Alexandria, Athanasius II (488–94). The work is concerned with the contrast between Jewish and Christian purification and anointing, and the author refers only to a post-baptismal anointing with myron.

(vi) Pseudo-Dionysius

The true identity of the author of the famous writings ascribed to Dionysius the Areopagite still eludes modern scholarship, although a date of c.500 seems assured. Chapter 2 of the *Ecclesiastical Hierarchy* contains an outline of the baptismal service (with anointings in positions II and IV, the latter using

---

[33] Cp C. J. A. Lash, 'L'onction post-baptismale de la 14e homélie de Theodore de Mopsueste: une interpolation syriaque?,' in *XXIX Congrès International des Orientalistes Résumés* (Paris, 1973), pp. 43–4.

[34] The phrase is found in ed. Tonneau, p. 416–7 (cp 408–9).

[35] See below, chapter IV (2) (b).

[36] Edition with English translation in my 'A baptismal address attributed to Athanasius,' *OC* 61 (1977) pp. 92–102. The Greek original is lost.

myron) which was to exert considerable influence on all the later West Syriac commentators; one late East Syriac writer, Timothy II [1318–32(?)] also makes considerable use of Ps.Dionysius, but he seems to know the corpus only at second hand, by way of Bar Hebraeus. The Ps.Dionysian writings were translated into Syriac in the early sixth century by Sergius of Reshaina; his work was later to be revised in the late seventh century, by Phokas of Edessa.[37]

It is interesting that some of the Syriac commentators[38] on the corpus here and there adapted or supplemented the text of *Eccl. Hier.* 2 to conform with actual Syrian Orthodox liturgical practice.

(vii) Severus (+ 538)

Severus' work for the most part survives only in Syriac translation. His homilies include six catechetical ones[39] (nos 21, 42, 70, 90, 109, 123) and six on the feast of Epiphany (nos 10, 38, 66, 85, 103, 117).[40] There are also several hymns on baptismal themes,[41] and a letter to John the Soldier (or 'Roman') which is concerned with the myron.[42]

(viii)   Canonical literature

Numerous important references to the rite of baptism are to be found in the canonical literature in Syriac, part of which is of Greek origin. For our present purposes, however, these references are of less importance, and so only the briefest of indications need to be given here.

The *Didascalia*, surviving complete only in Syriac, is an important early document for baptismal practice in the Antiochene area: the description of

---

[37] Cp J. M. Hornus, 'Le corpus dionysien en syriaque,' *Parole de l'Orient* 1 (1970), pp. 69–94, and G. Wiessner, 'Zur Handschriftenüberlieferung der syrischen Fassung des Corpus Dionysiacum,' *Nachrichten der Akademie der Wissenschaften in Göttingen,* Phil.-hist. Kl. 1972, pp. 165–216.

[38] Notably John of Dara.

[39] Cp F. Graffin, 'La catéchèse de Sévère d'Antioche,' *L'Orient Syrien* 5 (1960), pp. 47–54.

[40] There are also five homilies on the 'entry to the baptistery' (nos 40, 69, 88, 106, 121).

[41] Nos 90–101 in *PO* 6.

[42] Edition with English translation in the *Festschrift* for W. Strothmann, ed. G. Wiessner, *Erkenntnisse und Meinungen* II (GOFS 17; 1978), pp. 53–75. Several other letters deal with the question of whether Chalcedonians who renounce the Chalcedonian formula should be anointed or not (notably *Select Letters* V. 6).

the rite in chapter 16[43] knows two pre-baptismal anointings (of the head and of the whole body), but no post-baptismal one. Although the Greek original probably belongs to the third century, the Syriac translation cannot be early (as is sometimes claimed) since it contains features of translation technique which betray a date of at least the sixth century.

The *Testamentum Domini* was translated into Syriac by Jacob of Edessa in the late seventh century, and forms the first two books of the so called Octateuch of Clement of Rome.[44] The standard edition by Rahmani (1899) can now be supplemented by the text in the West Syriac *Synodicon* published by Vööbus from Damascus patr. 8/11.[45] The work makes use of the *Apostolic Tradition*, and the detailed outline of the baptismal rite (II.1–10)[46] shows little real affinity with extant Syriac baptismal texts.

For discussions on baptism in the native Syriac canonical literature, reference may be made especially to C. Kayser, *Die Canones Jacob's von Edessa übersetzt und erläutert* (Leipzig, 1886), and Vööbus' edition of the West Syriac *Synodicon*.[47]

(d) The Later Commentators

(i) *West Syriac Commentators*[48]

The long tradition of interdependent West Syriac commentaries on the baptismal service probably goes back to a short commentary attributed to John Chrysostom, and edited by Rahmani[49] from a manuscript of AD 882, now in the Library of the Cincinnati Historical Society. Closely related to this

---

[43] Ed. Lagarde, pp. 70–1 = ed. Gibson, pp. 134–6 = ed. Vööbus, pp. 172–6 (ET by Connolly, pp. 146–7).

[44] For the complex manuscript tradition, see R. G. Coquin, 'Le Testamentum Domini: problèmes de tradition textuelle,' *Parole de l'Orient* 5 (1974), pp. 165–88.

[45] CSCO 367, 375 = Scr. Syri 161, 163 (1975–6).

[46] Ed. Rahmani, pp. 110–33 = ed, Vööbus, pp. 27–39.

[47] See also his *Syrische Kanonessammhmgen, I. Westsyrische Originalurkimde* IA–B, in CSCO 307, 317.

[48] Cp in general W. de Vries, *Sakramententheologie bei den syrischen Monophysiten* (OCA 125, 1940), ch. IIA–B.

[49] In *I Fasti della Chiesa Patriarcale Antiochena* (Rome, 1920), pp. x-xiii. The work is also known in a Sogdian translation which means that it must have been known in East Syriac circles as well; this has been edited by N. Sims-Williams, *The Christian Sogdian Manuscript C2* (Berlin, 1985), pp. 110–20.

text is an anonymous commentary in British Library Add. 14496.[50] Since these two commentaries do not yet know of a post-baptismal anointing it is likely that they go back to at least the fifth century, if not earlier; of the pre-baptismal anointings, only that in position II is mentioned.

Later expansions of these commentaries, incorporating references to the post-baptismal anointing and (in some cases) material derived from Ps. Dionysius' *Ecclesiastical Hierarchy*, are to be found in Charfet ms 4/1 (attributed to Severus), British Library Add. 14538 (anonymous)[51] and in the commentaries on the baptismal service by George bishop of the Arabs[52] (+724), La'zar bar Sabta[53] (early 9th century), Moshe bar Kepha[54] (+903), Dionysius bar Salibi[55] (+1171) and Bar Hebraeus[56] (+1286). Jacob of Edessa (+708) has left an important outline of the service in a letter to Addai.[57]

There are also a number of tractates on the Myron; of these I have used the ones by the Patriarch John of the Sedre[58] (+648), Jacob of Edessa,[59] George bishop of the Arabs,[60] and Moshe bar Kepha.[61]

---

[50] This is edited, with ET, in *OCP* 46 (1980), pp. 20–61, and reprinted in *Fire from Heaven*, chapter XV.

[51] These are edited in *OCP* 46 (see previous note).

[52] Ed. (with ET) R. H. Connolly and H. W. Codrington, *Two Commentaries on the Jacobite Liturgy* (London, 1913), pp. 11–15 (= 3*–7*); for other manuscripts see 'Studies,' p. 21 note 3.

[53] Vat. syr. 147, ff. 126–30 (I have not seen this work).

[54] English translation by R. A. Aytoun in *The Expositor* VIII. ii (1911), reprinted in ed. J. Vellian, *Studies on Syrian Baptismal Rites* (SCS 6), pp. 1–5; cp 'Studies' p. 21, note 4.

[55] I use Mingana syr. 214, ff. 15b–24b. This has now been edited, with English translation, by B. Varghese (Moran Etho 29; Kottayam, 2006).

[56] In Book VI of his *Candelabra of the Sanctuary*, edited by R. Kohlhaas, *Jakobitische Sakramententheologie im 13. Jahrhundert* (Münster, 1959), pp. 33–6, 97–9. Cp also his *Nomocanon* (ed. Bedjan), ch. 2 (pp. 20–8).

[57] Quoted by Dionysius bar Salibi, *Comm. on Baptism* §2; an abbreviated version appears in the West Syriac *Synodicon* (ed. Vööbus) §45 = pp. 228–30.

[58] I use British Library Add. 12165, ff. 258b–262b. The work has now been published, with German translation, by J. Martikainen, *Johannes I. Sedra* (GOFS 34; 1991), pp. 170–209.

[59] I use Add. 12165, ff. 249a–251b. This is now published, with English translation, in *Oriens Christianus* 63 (1979), pp. 20–36.

[60] In Add. 12165, ff. 262b–66a; ed. V. Ryssel in *Atti della R. Accademia del Lincei*, IV. 9 (1892), pp. 46–80.

(ii) East Syriac commentators[62]

Of particular importance is the anonymous ninth-century work (sometimes known as Ps. George of Arbela), published by Connolly in *Anonymi auctoris Expositio Officiorum Ecclesiae* II (CSCO 72, Scr. Syri 29). This contains (pp. 96–116) a full description of the baptismal service, the importance of which is enhanced by the fact that no early manuscripts of the East Syriac rite survive; the section dealing with the anointings is translated in my 'The baptismal anointings according to the anonymous Expositio Officiorum,' in *Hugoye* 1:1 (1998). See also C. Leonhard, 'Die Initiation nach der Expositio Officiorum Ecclesiae,' in M. Tamcke (ed.), *Syriaca* (Münster, 2002), pp. 321–54.

There are a number of unpublished works on baptism which I have not consulted for the present work; these include tractates by Emmanuel bar Shahhare (10th century),[63] Iohannan bar Zo'bi (13th century)[64] and Timothy II (14th century).[65]

---

[61] Ed. W. Strothmann, *Moses bar Kepha, Myron-Weihe* (Göttingen Orientforschungen I. 7; 1973).

[62] See in general W. de Vries, *Sakramententheologie bei den Nestorianern* (OCA 133; 1947), chapter III.

[63] Available in a photographic edition, ed. J. Ishaq in *Bayn al-Nahrain* 14 (42) (1983), pp. 33–66; French translation by V. van Vossel, in his 'Quelques remarques en marge du Memra sur le Baptême d'Emmanuel bar Shahhare,' *Questions liturgiques* 82 (2001/2), pp. 128–47.

[64] Available in a photographic edition, ed. J. Ishaq, in *Bayn al-Nahrain* 16 (61/2) (1988), pp. 108–31; French translation by A. Khoraiche, 'Explication de tous les Mystères divins par Yohannan bar Zo'bi selon le ms Borg.sir. 90,' *Euntes Docete* 19 (1966), 386–426.

[65] Edited with English translation by P. Kadicheni, *The Mystery of Baptism* (Bangalore, 1980).

4 THE GIFTS OF THE SPIRIT

(1) THE VEHICLE OF THE GIFT

All Syriac writers on the subject are agreed that at baptism the newly baptized receive the Holy Spirit, but the sources are far from united when they come to define more precisely the point at which the Spirit is received, and it is clear that opinions on the subject were more fluid than some modern writers would like to allow. Indeed confusion has been added to the situation by western scholars who have tried to read the evidence in the light of the very different western tradition on the subject, either by forcing the evidence available into the straight-jacket of that tradition, or unconsciously interpreting it from an essentially western standpoint. My aim here is to attempt to avoid these pitfalls, and to let the evidence speak for itself as far as possible.

In the first place it is quite clear that we must abandon any hope of discovering some unified teaching on the subject: the evidence from different writers of different periods, and from the liturgical texts themselves, is definitely contradictory from a strictly logical point of view, and it is not possible to reconcile the conflicting views on the subject—above all if we look at the texts with the presuppositions of western liturgical tradition where Baptism and Confirmation have become separated in time. The gift of the Spirit is essentially conferred by the rite *as a whole*, and within the rite the anointing and the baptism in water form an inseparable unity.

Nevertheless, while admitting the basic unity of the baptismal rite, it is still possible to extricate, for the purposes of formal analysis, three different traditions that find expression in the liturgical texts and the literature on baptism, whereby the gift of the Spirit is focussed on one of the anointings, or on the water, or on an imposition of hands.

While in some cases the variety of views will reflect different lines of thinking in the early church, it should also be kept in mind that, because Christian baptism is a single unit, as it were, in sacred time, its salvific effect can be localized simultaneously at different points in historical time; in other words, if a writer states that the gift of the Spirit is conferred by the water, this does not exclude the fact that it is just as much conferred by the anointing(s). Moreover, it must be remembered that the term *ma'mudita*, sometimes used in this connection is ambiguous, since it can mean either

the font, or the rite as a whole. Thus, when Aphrahat states that 'we receive
the Spirit of Christ from *ma'mudita (Dem.* 6–14)[1] it is not certain whether he
is referring to the water or to the service as a whole (in fact a little later on
he is specific, when he says '…when they come to the rebirth of water, they
receive the Holy Spirit').[2]

One should be aware, too, that there are a number of different factors
which lead writers, often subconsciously, to localize the gift of the Spirit to
one particular part of the service; two are of particular importance, namely
the choice of a conceptual model, and the choice of particular imagery. It
would seem that basically it was a shift in conceptual models that lay behind
the change in people's understanding of the prebaptismal anointing, or
rushma, that we noted in the previous chapter, away from a charismatic experience towards a purely cathartic rite. The original Antiochene pattern of
rushma followed by baptism is definitely modelled on the Jewish initiation
rite of circumcision followed by baptism. That circumcision lies behind the
rushma is something that all early writers are very much aware of, and it is
from this background that cutting imagery, which might otherwise have
been thought very unsuitable, came to be applied to the oil. But in addition
to circumcision, the *rushma* corresponds to another Old Testament rite as
well, namely the anointing of priests and kings, For baptism proper it is
Christ's own baptism, with its public proclamation of Sonship, that provided the dominant model from the beginning; here the emphasis at first
was just on rebirth, and at this early stage there is little hint of the Pauline
teaching of baptism as a death and resurrection. It was only towards the end
of the fourth century that the Pauline view of baptism begins to catch on in
the Antiochene area, and the logical consequences of this new conceptual
model are obvious: if baptism is a death and resurrection, then the gifts of
the Spirit can hardly be conferred before it; instead, they now have to be
transferred either to the baptism proper (as happens in John Chrysostom)
or to the post-baptismal anointing introduced into the area around 400. The
introduction of the Pauline concept thus necessitates a new, cathartic and
protective, interpretation of the *rushma*. It is significant that only now is specific attention paid to the fact that in the Gospel narratives the Holy Spirit
appears at Christ's baptism only *after* he has gone up from the water. This,
somewhat literalist, view of the old conceptual model of Christ's baptism

---

[1] *PS* I col. 292.
[2] col. 293.

again points to the need for a new, post-baptismal, anointing to take on the role formerly held by the *rushma*.

An analogous application of a new and literalistic understanding of the archaic imagery of 'putting on' the Spirit led in exactly the same direction. As we shall see later in chapter IV, the imagery of 'putting on the robe of glory' is intimately tied up with the recovery of the royal and priestly robe of glory that Adam and Eve lost at the Fall. Since one of the most important aspects of the pre-baptismal anointing was the conferring of the royal priesthood, the imagery of 'putting on the robe of glory' and 'putting on the Spirit' was necessarily associated with the *rushma*, and not the water. Later, however, the 'putting on of the robe of glory' came to be understood in a more literal manner: the water which covered the whole body in the baptismal immersion was obviously a more suitable 'garment' than the oil, applied originally only to the head.[3] Thus once again, attention comes to be focussed on the water, rather than on the oil. In both cases the reasons can be described as purely accidental, the consequences of shifts of emphasis, and certainly not integral to the understanding of the place of the gift of the Spirit in the rite as a whole.

With these preliminary considerations we may look briefly at each of these vehicles of the Spirit.

(a) The Oil and Myron

As we have seen in chapter II, oil is one of the more important symbols of the Holy Spirit in early Syriac tradition. The original Antiochene prebaptismal anointing of the head represented two main themes, the marking or 'branding' of the newly baptized as sheep in Christ's flock (corresponding to Old Testament circumcision), and secondly, the conferring on them of the royal priesthood (based on the Old Testament anointing of kings and priests). The latter is definitely charismatic in nature, and tends to be pushed into the background once baptism came to be more formalized, from the mid-fourth century onwards. Where the idea does survive, it gets transferred to the post-baptismal anointing; this, for example, happens in *Timothy* § 45, quoted below.

One important gift of the Spirit is still associated with the prebaptismal anointing in many of the surviving liturgical texts, namely Sonship. This is

---

[3] The anointing of the whole body, of course, was more suitable, and 'putting on the oil' is a phrase used in *Acts of Thomas* § 157, Ephrem, *H. Fid.* 82.10; cp Theodore *Cat. Hom.* 14.8.

of particular importance here, since sonship implies the gift of the indwelling Spirit, in view of Romans 8:15: 'The Spirit whom you have received is a Spirit that makes us sons, enabling us to cry 'Abba, Father'.'

Sonship is specifically mentioned in the formula at the pre-baptismal anointing (position II) in the oldest manuscripts of *Severus*, but this is no longer the case in the printed editions.[4] Likewise in both the Maronite and East Syriac services 'sonship' is again specifically associated with the oil.[5] Since the gift of sonship confers on the newly baptized the authority to utter the Lord's prayer, it is very significant that in both the Maronite and East Syriac services (as well as in a few old manuscripts of the Syrian Orthodox one[6]) the Lord's Prayer is placed *before* the baptism proper—a position which implicitly implies the conferring of the Spirit and of sonship at the pre-baptismal anointing. In the printed texts of *Severus*, as well as in *Timothy* and the Melkite *Basil*, the Lord's Prayer follows the post-baptismal anointing, historically a secondary development. This is just one more example of the general trend which transfers to the post-baptismal anointing the benefits conferred by the Spirit that were originally associated with the pre-baptismal *rushma*.

The association of the Spirit with the post-baptismal myron requires no special comment here; reference may be made to chapter V (2) (c) below.

The pouring of oil/myron on the baptismal water provides a good example of the combining of the two traditions in a prayer at this point to be found in the Syrian Orthodox service preserved in Add. 14518:

> We pour this holy oil on this water for the *gift of sonship* and the preserving and watchfulness of the souls and bodies of those who are being baptized. (§ 40).

(b) The water

As we have seen, the introduction of the Pauline theology of baptism, and strict adherence to the sequence of events at Christ's own baptism, led many writers of the late fourth century onwards to transfer to the water gifts of the Spirit formerly associated with the pre-baptismal anointing. As a good example of this process, and by way of contrast to the views outlined above, we may take Theodore of Mopsuestia's discussion of the 'grace of

---

[4] For details, see 'Studies,' p. 30.
[5] JS II, p. 330; U, p. 67–8.
[6] See 'Studies,' pp. 61–3.

sonship.' For Theodore this gift is conferred, not by the oil, but by the baptismal formula, N. is baptized...' The passage is worth quoting at some length:[7]

> When the priest says 'In the name of the Father' he recalls the Father's words, 'This is my beloved Son in whom I am well pleased,' and here you should understand the sonship which is thereby given you. And when he says 'of the Son,' you should understand him who was present in that he was baptized, and you should recognize that he is the cause of your sonship. And when he says 'of the Holy Spirit,' remember him who descended in the form of a dove and remained upon him; you too should expect thence the confirmation of sonship, since 'those who are led by the Spirit of God are the sons of God' as Paul says (Romans 8:14). True sonship is conferred by the Holy Spirit.

From this it is clear that Theodore's view that the Holy Spirit conferred the gift of sonship at the baptism, rather than at the *rushma*, was due to the strict parallelism he wants to see between Christ's baptism and Christian baptism. In the same way the descent of the dove *after* Christ's baptism provides Theodore with an explanation of the post-baptismal anointing:[8]

> (The priest signs (*rashem!*) you) because Jesus, having gone up from the water, received the grace of the Holy Spirit, who, in the form of a dove, came and remained upon him. Thus it is said that he was anointed by the Holy Spirit: 'The Spirit of the Lord is upon me, as a result of which the Lord has anointed me' (Luke 4:18), and 'Jesus of Nazareth, whom God anointed with the Holy Spirit and power' (Acts 10:38), to show that the Holy Spirit was completely inseparable from him.

Theodore has been quoted at some length here, since he illustrates the process of how writers came to localize the gifts of the Spirit in specific parts of the baptismal rite. In subsequent writers the gift of the Spirit is fairly regularly associated with the water (while the myron of the post-baptismal anointing is understood as 'perfecting' or ' sealing' it),[9] the same

---

[7] *Cat. Hom.* 14.25 (Tonneau, pp. 452–5).

[8] *Cat. Hom.* 14.27 (Tonneau, pp. 456–7) if this section belongs to Theodore (see chapter III (2) (c)). It is interesting that Luke 4:18 is quoted in the Peshitta Old Testament form (Isaiah 61:1), with 'Lord' as the subject of 'anoint' (cp chapter II (c)).

[9] A rather individual point of view is put forward by the annonymous East Syriac commentator (ed. Connolly II, p. 106): 'baptism in the font ('Jordan') is the

view is implied in many of the liturgical texts themselves, but explicit statements there are not common.

(c) Laying on of hands

John Chrysostom, like Theodore, sees the Spirit conferred in the baptismal water, but he specifies that it is in conjunction with the priest's laying his hand on the candidate's head:[10]

> ..It is the grace of the Spirit which sanctifies the nature of the water and touches your head with the hand of the priest.

And a little later on:[11]

> It is at this moment (of baptism) that, through the hand of the priest, the Holy Spirit descends upon you.

That John is using Christ's own baptism as a model here is clear from a passage in a later homily where the Trinitarian formula at baptism is linked with the activities of the three Persons of the Trinity at Christ's baptism.[12] In this connection it is interesting that in early Christian art John is often depicted as placing his hand on the head of Jesus, and it is very possible that this is tied up with the tradition that John conferred the Levitical priesthood on Jesus at baptism (familiar to several Syriac writers, including Aphrahat, Ephrem and Jacob of Serugh).[13] Once again a desire for strict parallelism between Christian baptism and Christ's own baptism helps explain why John transfers the idea of the conferring of priesthood on the Christian from the *rushma*, with which it had originally been associated, to the baptism proper.

The presence in the East Syriac rite of an imposition of hands, separate from, and subsequent to, the baptism, has attracted a lot of attention from European scholars, for obvious reasons. As a matter of fact there are

---

baptism of John, for the forgiveness of sins; the final seal (*huttama*) is the baptism of our Lord, which is completion in the Holy Spirit.'

[10] *Cat.* II. 10 (= ET p. 47). 'Touching' is a characteristic word of John's: at the consecration of the bread and wine in the Eucharist the Holy Spirit 'touches' the elements, e.g. *Cat.* III. 26 (= ET p. 65).

[11] *Cat.* II. 25 (= ET p. 52.)

[12] *Cat.* XI. 13 (= ET p. 165). The point is often taken up in the later commentators.

[13] Cp Murray, *Symbols*, pp. 178–80 and my 'Baptismal themes'; also below, (2) (b) (iii).

three places where the priest lays his hands on the candidates, and so it is important to see the post-baptismal one in a proper perspective. In the East Syriac service a first imposition of hands comes immediately before an anointing in position I; the rubric here reads (p. 56):

> The priest recites this *syamida* (lit. 'imposition of hand') in an audible voice, placing his hand on the head of each of them.

The prayer itself has no reference at all to the Spirit, and must be a comparatively late composition since its theme is that of the 'door being opened' to those who are small children: the time when adults were baptized is clearly long past.

The next *syamida* described in the rubrics comes after the baptism (p. 72):

> The priest recites this *syamida*, passing his right hand over the heads of all of them, saying in a audible voice...

The ensuing prayer recounts in general terms the disobedience of the human race, and its deliverance from destruction through the events of the Incarnation: it speaks of 'the grace of the Spirit' as already having been received.

The third *syamida* corresponds to the consignation in position IV, and so is of particular interest. The prayer (described as a *syamida*) immediately before the consignation reads as follows, (p. 73):

> The pledge of the Holy Spirit that you have received, the mysteries of Christ of which you have partaken, his living sign (*rushma*) that you have received, the new life that you acquired, the armour of righteousness that you have put on—may (all) this preserve you from the evil one and his powers...

Once again the 'pledge of the Holy Spirit' is described as having already been received—which is not surprising since the mention of the 'mysteries' indicates that this prayer originally belonged to a post-communion context, and is quite out of place here.[14]

The rubrics in the Urmia edition (likewise those in *Codex Liturgicus*) do not mention oil in connection with the accompanying consignation, although the East Syriac commentators, and some manuscripts, do specify

---

[14] Cp Raes in *L'Orient Syrien* 1 (1956), p. 249.

it.[15] There can be little doubt that the consignation in position IV in the
East Syriac rite was originally with oil. The wording of the accompanying
formula is of interest, in that (alone of all the formulae) it employs past
tenses:[16]

> N has been baptized and perfected in the name...

Clearly this consignation in position IV is not of great importance in the
service as a whole.

Thus it would seem that the three impositions of hands in the East
Syriac rite do not have—or perhaps one should say, were not intended by
the compiler to have—any special link with the actual transmission of the
gift of the Holy Spirit.

Before leaving the East Syriac rite we should consider for a moment a
metaphorical extension of the idea of laying on of hands, based on Ps.
138:8; this is to be found in an alternative prayer that leads into the *syamida*
before the anointing in position I, discussed above. This reads (p. 56):

> Our Lord and our God, cause your right hand from your holy height to
> overshadow[17] these souls which expect to receive the gift of your grace,
> O Lord of all, Father, Son and Holy Spirit.

This is of course entirely appropriate, coming before the priest's laying on
of hands before the first consignation. The same idea interestingly enough
also occurs in a *sedro* at the very beginning of the Homs edition of *Severus*
(the early manuscripts sometimes provide other *sedre*), where there is no
context of any laying on of hands. In this prayer, after mention of Christ's
inclining his head before the Baptist's hand, we find:

---

[15] Diettrich, pp. 83–92; anonymous commentator (ed. Connolly) II, p. 108; cp
Raes in *L'Orient Syrien* 1 (1956), p. 247; W. de Vries, 'Zur Liturgie der
Erwachsentaufe bei den Nestorianern,' *OCP* 9 (1943), pp. 467–8; L. Ligier, 'La
Confirmation en Orient et en Occident. Autour du nouveau Rituel romain,'
Gregorianum 53 (1972), pp. 291–2.

[16] Raes (p. 251) suggests that 'perfected' has an auxiliary sense, i.e. 'N has now
(by this consignation) been completely baptized...,' but this seems to me to force
the Syriac: perhaps one should rather compare the consignation formula, using past
tenses, in the Melkite 'loosing of the crown' on the seventh day (Assemani III, p.
236).

[17] Ps. 138:8.

Do you, O Lord, cause your merciful right hand to overshadow this
your servant who has been prepared for holy baptism, and sanctify him,
purify him, and cleanse him with your hyssop that absolves all...

As a matter of fact there are, in the West Syriac services, some interesting traces of the idea that the Holy Spirit was conferred by the imposition
of hands.[18] Thus the prayer immediately before the anointing in position II
in *Severus* reads as follows:

Holy Father, who gave your Holy Spirit to those who were baptized by
the hands of your holy Apostles, do you now too, using the shadow of
my hands, send your Holy Spirit upon those who are about to be baptized so that, being filled with him and his divine gifts, they may pro
duce fruit thirtyfold and sixtyfold and a hundredfold.

The compiler of *Severus* has quite clearly adapted a prayer that was originally
connected with an imposition of hands to a consignation with oil. That this
was the case is in fact demonstrated by the situation in the Melkite *Basil*,[19]
where virtually the identical prayer is used in conjunction with an actual
imposition of hands, immediately before the anointing in position II:

You gave your Holy Spirit to those who were illumined with the light of
your holy baptism by means of the imposition of hands of your holy
Apostles; do you now too, O Lord, as I through a gift employ the imposition of my hand, send your living and holy Spirit upon those who are
about to be illuminated with the grace of holy baptism, so that, being
filled with your Holy Spirit, they may produce fruit for your kingdom
thirtyfold and sixtyfold and a hundredfold; for you are the God who
alone performs wonders, and to you praise and honour are fitting...

The same prayer (which must have originated in a Greek milieu)[20] has been
adapted (rather more drastically) in *Basil* for the brief service of 'loosing the
crown' on the seventh day after baptism; there it accompanies a 'signing' of
the child.

In the Maronite *Jacob* there is just possibly another echo of a pre-
baptismal imposition of the hands connected with the gift of the Spirit. This
is to be found in the prayer, asking for the coming of the Spirit 'upon the

---

[18] Cp Ligier, *art. cit.*, pp. 451–3.

[19] Cp Ligier, *art. cit.*, pp. 448–51.

[20] It is evidently modelled on a prayer in the Anaphora of St Mark; cp 'Studies,'
p. 29 note 1. The prayer has been adapted yet again for the 'loosing of the crown'
in the Melkite service, Assemani III, p. 236.

head' of the candidate, to be found immediately after the anointing in position II, with which the compiler of the service certainly intended it to be
connected.[21]

Finally, it is worth observing that an imposition of hands is implied in
a very different, exorcistic, context in a prayer that immediately precedes the
awe-inspiring invocations of the exorcism itself; this is to be found in the
Melkite and in several of the Syrian Orthodox services. Here I follow the
rather longer form of the text in the anonymous service preserved in Add.
14518;[22]

> O God of angels and archangels, of principalities and powers, of domin-
> ions and splendour, who sits upon the cherubim and who is glorified by
> the cherubim, at the presence of whose might everything trembles and
> quakes, because of whom every action of the enemy is subdued and the
> accuser lies fallen, the serpent trampled on, and the dragon slain; we call
> upon the name of your divinity which is obeyed, against the unclean
> spirits, and, as we lay our hand upon this your creature and sign him in
> the name of the Father and of the Son and of the Holy Spirit, we ad-
> monish every wicked, unclean and rebellious spirit which has taken its
> abode, or has laid ambush, or has overshadowed, or tempted, from the
> very first breath until this present hour, that it flee and remove itself
> from your creature and your image, the work of your hands.

Such an exorcistic laying on of hands is found in the New Testament (Luke
4:40–1) and in the document from Qumran known as the *Genesis Apocryphon*, dating from a little before the Christian era. In the latter, Pharaoh, af-
flicted because of Sarah (Gen. 12, but influenced by the similar story of
Abimelek in Gen. 20), asks Abraham to pray for him:[23]

> 'Pray then for me and for my house, so that this evil spirit may be re-
> buked from us.' So I (Abraham) prayed...and I laid my hands on his
> head. The affliction was removed from him and the spirit rebuked, and
> so he recovered.

(2) THE NATURE OF THE GIFT

The Syriac texts speak of both the 'gift' and the 'gifts' of the Holy Spirit as
being conferred at baptism. These are complementary: the baptized receive
both the Holy Spirit himself, who henceforth will 'dwell in him,' and the

---

[21] JS II, p. 334 (cp Ligier, *art. cit.*, p. 453).
[22] D. §4; cp B III, p. 205, T § 11.
[23] *Genesis Apocryphon* col. 20, lines 28–9.

varied gifts of the Spirit, in other words the consequences that follow from this supreme gift.

The indwelling presence of the Holy Spirit above all makes us into the children of God and brothers of Christ, it effects in us a 'new creation,' makes us into 'temples,' confers on us priesthood and kingship, brings us healing and forgiveness, provides us with protection against the powers of darkness, wipes out for us the 'document of debt' incurred by Adam at the Fall, restores to us the 'robe of glory' that he thereby lost, and gives us re-entry into Paradise. We are given the 'pledge of the Spirit,' in other words we are given the potential of entering, in sacred time, the kingdom of heaven while still on earth.

The way that the nature of the gift or the gifts is described depends a great deal on the imagery or the biblical models used; this gives rise to some apparent contradictions, but it is important to realise that behind the variety of metaphor, the reality that is being described remains the same. Ephrem has some eminently wise words that are applicable in this context:

> If someone concentrates his attention solely
> on the metaphors used of God's majesty,
> he abuses and misrepresents that majesty
> by means of those metaphors with which God has clothed
> himself for man's benefit,
> and he is ungrateful to that Grace
> which bent down its stature to the level of man's childishness:
> although God had nothing in common with it,
> He clothed himself in the likeness of man
> in order to bring man to the likeness of himself.
> Do not let your intellect be disturbed by mere names,
> for Paradise has simply clothed itself in terms that are familiar to you:
> it is not because it is poor that it has put on your imagery,
> rather, your nature is far too weak to be able
> to attain to its greatness, and its beauties are much diminished
> by being depicted in the pale colours that you are familiar with.

> *(H. Parad.* 11.6–7)

In the present chapter we shall concentrate on those themes that are most prominent in the early Syriac writers. Thus we shall first look at the two main ways of describing the nature of the gift, one in terms of the Spirit 'dwelling within us' as in a 'temple,' the other in terms of us 'putting on the Spirit'; then we shall turn to the gifts that are resultant upon this 'gift,' and here we shall find that the dominant themes are those of re-entry into Paradise (expressed in many different ways) and 'sonship.'

(a) THE GIFT OF THE SPIRIT

Acts 10:45 speaks of the 'gift of the Spirit' in connection with baptism and the actual phrase is found several times in the Syriac services, most frequently in the Melkite and East Syriac ones. Thus in *Basil* the deacon prays that 'they may receive the gift of the grace of the Holy Spirit'[24] and that the Father may 'grant them the gift of his living and holy Spirit.'[25] Similarly in a prayer associated either with the pre-baptismal anointing (position II) (so *Severus*), or a laying on of hands at the same point (so *Basil*), the priest asks that, as the Spirit had been given through the hands of the Apostles, he now be sent upon those being baptized.[26] In the East Syriac service, too, he prays for 'the sending of the gift of the Holy Spirit which will strengthen the weakness of their nature' (p. 59).[27]

The 'gift of the Spirit' is also specifically mentioned in connection with the post-baptismal anointing where, in most of the West Syriac services, the formula employed is:[28] 'N. is imprinted with the holy myron of Christ God, the pleasant scent of the holy faith, the imprint and perfecting of the gift (some texts here read 'grace' or 'gifts') of the Holy Spirit.'

(i) The indwelling of the Spirit

Paul speaks of the body as a 'temple of the Holy Spirit' (I Cor. 6:19) and of the Holy Spirit as 'dwelling in' Christians (Rom 8:11; 2 Tim. 1:14). His imagery continues to enjoy popularity in Syriac writers of all periods, although it is the clothing imagery, to be described in due course, that is much more characteristic of Syriac Christianity.

In the priest's solemn adjurations in the course of the exorcism in *Severus* he proclaims that 'this is not the dwelling place for demons, but the temple and dwelling place of the living God'[29] (in the *Julian Romance* the emperor Julian is actually described as a 'temple of Satan' on several occa-

---

[24] B III, p. 216.

[25] B III, p. 217.

[26] Quoted above in (1) (c).

[27] Compare D § 27, quoted below.

[28] See my commentary to T § 47.

[29] Similarly in JS II, p. 323 (exorcisms): '... he has come so that he may become the dwelling place of the Holy Spirit'; likewise Severus, *Hymn* 95 (*PO* 6, p. 135): 'they are now become the dwelling place of the Holy Spirit.'

sions).[30] In the East Syriac service the imagery features in the following prayer (p. 61):

> Praise to you, who healed the sickness of our body through the oil and water which you poured on our wounds (cp Luke 10:34), and through your Spirit you wiped off, as though with a sponge, the filth (or pus) of sin from our soul, so as to make us pure temples for your honour, O Lord of all, Father, Son and Holy Spirit.

In the Maronite *Jacob* it is the oil that is specifically described as being the means for effecting this; there the deacon prays:[31]

> May the oil make them pure temples for the dwelling of the Holy Spirit.

In keeping with the early Syriac emphasis on the priesthood conferred on the newly baptized, Ephrem implies in the following passage that the baptized have now become priests ministering to the temple of the divinity who dwells within them:

> Our Lord has renewed your 'oldness' in baptism:
> he is the Carpenter of salvation, who has fashioned with his own blood,
> and built himself a temple to dwell in.
> Do not let the 'old man' dwell in his stead
> in that temple he has built.
> O body, if you allow God to dwell in your temple
> you too will become his royal sanctuary. *(H. Virg.* 1.2)

Both Ephrem and Aphrahat feel a sense of urgency when they stress that the new 'temple' must be kept pure; as Aphrahat puts it:

> Let him who has been called the temple of God purify his body from all that is unclean, for he who 'grieves' the Spirit of Christ will not be able to raise his head above misery. Let him who has received the body of Christ preserve his own body from all that is unclean, let him who has stripped off the old man, not return again to his former ways... *(Dem.* 6.1)

A little later in the same homily Aphrahat reveals why there is this urgent need to keep the 'temple' pure:

> Let us prepare our temples for the Spirit of Christ, and let us not 'grieve' the Spirit lest he depart from us. *(Dem.* 6.14)

---

[30] Ed. Hoffmann, p. 247 etc.
[31] JS II, p. 331.

It is not clear exactly what Aphrahat understands by 'grieving' here. Two centuries later Philoxenus deals with much the same topic in his fine *memra* on the indwelling of the Holy Spirit;[32] he is very emphatic that the Holy Spirit resides permanently in the baptized, and the only occasion when he envisages the departure of the Spirit is apostasy. This was certainly the traditional view, but throughout this homily Philoxenus is arguing against people who held that the Spirit departed from a man whenever he sinned, and returned on his repentence. The fact that Aphrahat specifically quotes the case of Saul in 1 Sam. 16[33] as a parallel to the Spirit's coming and going suggests that Aphrahat may have held a similar view. It may be, however, that the difference between Aphrahat and Philoxenus is only apparent and not real. 'Grieving the Spirit' to both men implies failure to allow the Spirit to work with oneself, in other words failure to co-operate with the Spirit; the resulting absence of the 'fruits of the Spirit' are described by Aphrahat in terms of the Spirit's departure, whereas for Philoxenus the Spirit is still present, but rendered inactive. Repentence for Aphrahat means the return of the Spirit, whereas for Philoxenus the Spirit's presence manifests itself again by activity. In any case Aphrahat would certainly agree with Philoxenus that it was only apostasy, the renunciation of the 'covenant' entered into at baptism, that results in the *permanent* departure of the Holy Spirit.

How the Spirit departed from the baptized Christian if he apostasized is illustrated in a vivid way in a narrative describing some conversions to Islam in the mid eighth century in north Mesopotamia:[34] just after a man had renounced Christ 'his body shook, and there went forth from his mouth what looked like a beautiful white dove, which was raised up to heaven.' The man thereupon gave a piercing wail of lament, thus brought to the sudden realisation that 'the Holy Spirit, the mistress, had left him, and a servile unclean spirit had instead entered him.'

Before we turn to the clothing imagery two further ways of describing the relationship of the Holy Spirit to the baptized Christian should be mentioned. In his homily on the indwelling of the Holy Spirit, already quoted, Philoxenus speaks of the 'Holy Spirit whom we receive from God' at bap-

---

[32] Ed. Tanghe, *Le Muséon* 73 (1960), pp. 39–71.

[33] Whether the 'spirit' in this passage was the Holy Spirit or not was the subject of much controversy in the early church.

[34] Ps. Dionysius of Tellmahre, *Chron.* (ed. Chabot) II, p. 391. For the episode and the surrounding context see now A. Harrak, 'Piecing together the fragmentary account of the martyrdom of Cyrus of Harran,' *Analecta Bollandiana* 121 (2003), pp. 297–329.

tism as 'the soul of our soul': 'for this reason,' he continues, 'the Spirit was given to the Apostles by means of anointing, and through them, to all of us. For instead of our original soul we have received the Spirit, with the intention that he should be a soul to our soul, just as our soul is the soul to our body.'[35]

Paul uses the phrase 'union of the Spirit' in Eph. 4:3, and this finds its way into all the West Syriac baptismal services in association with the post-baptismal anointing:[36]

....grant through this imprint the union of your living and holy Spirit...

What is meant by this is well elucidated by Sahdona, who explains that 'the Holy Spirit effects in their limbs all his fruits, and he unites them with God in love, mingling them with Christ.'[37] This particular phraseology is not very common in Syriac writers, and it is clear that this emphasis was only introduced into the Syriac services with the insertion of the post-baptismal anointing. The fact that the prayer quoted employs a rendering of the Greek *henotes* (Eph. 4:3) that is different from the Peshitta is simply another indication that this theme is imported into the Syriac world from a Greek milieu.

(ii) Putting on the Spirit:

Go down, my brethren, and put on the Holy Spirit from the water

(H. Epiph. 5.1)

We receive the Spirit of Christ from the baptismal water, for the moment the priest invokes the Spirit, the heaven opens and the Spirit descends, hovering over the water, and those who are being baptized put on the Spirit. (Aphrahat, *Dem.* 6.14)

Early Syriac writers revel in the theological imagery of clothing. In his letters Paul had already set an example for this type of language when he spoke of us 'putting on Christ' at baptism (Rom. 13:14; Gal. 3:27). The precise phrase is echoed in another of the Epiphany hymns:

---

[35] Ed. Tanghe, pp. 52–3.

[36] See my commentary to T § 45. Ps. Dionysius the Areopagite says that the myron 'unites to the supremely divine Spirit those who have been perfected' (*Eccl. Hier.* II. 8).

[37] Ed. de Halleux I, p. 29. Whereas 'unites' belongs to a Greek background, 'mingling' is essentially Semitic (as Philoxenus points out in *Tractatus tres de Trinitate et Incarnatione* (ed. Vaschalde), p. 40); cp also above, chapter I (b).

Go down, my brethren who are marked, and put on our Lord.

(H. Epiph. 4.1)

As so often in early Syriac literature, 'Christ' and 'Spirit of Christ' are used more or less interchangeably: in the Chaldean Breviary the baptized are described as putting on both Christ and the Holy Spirit:[38]

> You have risen from the water, you have risen from the dead, you have put on Christ, you have put on the Holy Spirit.

Ephrem already speaks of the 'robe of the Spirit' which is put on at baptism; it provides adornment for the soul, according to Narsai, while Jacob of Serugh writes that 'Fire and Spirit are woven for you as an all-luminous garment.'[39] It is indeed normally the 'robe of light' or (above all) the 'robe of glory' that we find the baptized putting on at their baptism, as a Syrian Orthodox *sedro* addressed to Christ puts it:

> You have clothed us in the robe of glory of the gifts of your Holy Spirit, and you have granted that we should become spiritual children to the Father in the second birth of baptism.' (SH, p. 19)

This 'robe of glory' or 'light' plays a very important role in early Syriac literature, and it has its origins in Jewish interpretations of Gen. 3:21;[40] here, although the Hebrew, Greek and Syriac all speak of 'garments of skin' being provided for Adam and Eve, the Aramaic targums interpret these as 'garments of honour,' while a copy of the Law belonging to the famous Rabbi Meir was reputed to have read 'garments of light.' These garments were understood by one strand of Jewish tradition as belonging to Adam and Eve *before* the Fall, and not after (following the usual interpretation). Thus the 'robe of glory, or light' was in origin the clothing of Adam and Eve in Paradise, of which they were stripped at the Fall. At baptism this robe is once again restored; as Jacob puts it:[41]

> You have put on in the water the robe of glory which was stolen (from Adam and Eve) among the trees.

---

[38] *Brev. Chald.* I. p. 400.

[39] Ephrem *Sermo de Domino Nostro* § 55; Narsai (ed. Mingana) I, p. 344 (ET p. 49); Jacob of Serugh (ed. Bedjan) I, p. 173.

[40] For details see my 'Some aspects of Greek words in Syriac,' *Abhandlungen der Akademie der Wissenschaften in Göttingen* 96 (1975,) pp. 98–104; reprinted in *Syriac Perspectives on Late Antiquity* (London, 1984), chapter IV.

[41] Ed. Bedjan I, p. 209.

Ephrem describes how, in the new paradise of the Church, 'none of the saints is naked—they are all clothed in glory...our Lord himself has caused them to rediscover Adam's former robe' *(H. Parad.* 6–9). The same idea is still reflected in Moshe bar Kepha's commentary on the baptismal service; the white robe that the newly baptized puts on indicates, among other things, that 'after the resurrection he will receive a robe of immortality and incorruption, and will put on the glory which Adam wore before he transgressed the commandment' (§19). In both the East and West Syriac baptismal services the phrase 'put on the robe of glory' occurs a number of times, alongside 'robe of incorruptibility' and 'robe of immortality' based on I Cor. 15:53.

When the author of the Odes of Solomon says, 'I was covered with the covering of your Spirit and I removed from myself the garments of skin' (25:8), he is extending his interest to a subject on which Greek writers loved to speculate, but one which Syriac authors normally pass over in silence; if they do have anything special to say about the 'garments of skin' that are stripped off, they do not follow the Origenist interpretation of these as the body, but rather identify them as much the same as the fig leaves. Ephrem, for example, associates them with the withered fig tree of Matt. 19:21 (and parallels):

> When Adam sinned and was stripped of the glory in which he had been clothed he covered his nakedness with fig leaves. Our Saviour came and underwent suffering in order to heal Adam's wound and provide a garment of glory for his nakedness. He dried up the fig tree to show that there would no longer be any need of fig leaves to serve as Adam's garment, since Adam had returned to his former glory, and so no longer had any need of leaves, or 'garments of skin.' *(Comm. Diat.* 16.10)

Exactly how Adam is himself baptized and so receives back his lost 'robe of glory' is delightfully described in the *Cave of Treasures*, where we learn that Adam is buried on Golgotha, and that the water and blood from Christ's pierced side (John 19:34) flowed down on to his skull.

The 'robe of glory' put on at baptism sums up the effects of the various gifts of the Spirit in terms of a re-entry into Paradise,[42] a restoration to the pre-Fall state of Adam who reflected the image, as yet uncorrupted, of

---

[42] See my 'World and Sacrament in the Syrian Fathers,' *Sobornost* VI. 10 (1974) pp. 685–96.

Christ the Second Adam. As the Maronite *Jacob* actually puts it, baptism 'brings the baptized into glorious Paradise, that is, his faithful Church.'[43]

The robe imagery is essentially based on a cyclical view of salvation history centred on Adam/Christ typology; the aim of the Incarnation is regarded as being the restoration of the primordial Paradise. Once restored, however, Paradise will not be the scene of a second Fall, and a repetition of the whole cycle; rather, at this point salvation history becomes linear, as it were; the potential with which Adam and Eve had been created now becomes realized, in their divinization. This is something to which we shall return shortly.

The restoration of Paradise is seen as being fully achieved only at the end of time, at the *eschaton*; nevertheless the newly baptized are described as potentially anticipating the *eschaton*, by their entry into Paradise already, in sacred time, even though they are still living in the world in historical time. It is the presence of the Holy Spirit in the individual which effects this potential entry into Paradise; depending on whether he allows the Holy Spirit to work within him, or whether he 'grieves' the Spirit, he will experience this anticipation of the *eschaton* to a greater or lesser degree.

The same concept of baptism restoring the original condition of Paradise is brought out in a number of other different ways as well. The rich typology surrounding John 19:34, the piercing of Christ's side, is particularly suggestive in this context.[44] Important too is the imagery of re-creation, implied by the parallelism seen between the Holy Spirit's hovering over the baptismal water and over the primordial water, and that of the restoration of the divine image, marred by sin.

Later writers, who perhaps understood the Paradise of Genesis in a less elevated, and more literalist, manner, preferred to contrast the Paradise of Adam with 'Heaven.' Thus in one of his homilies Severus contrasts Christ with Adam and says 'instead of Paradise he is now opening up heaven, showing clearly that baptism constitutes for us the opening of heaven.'[45]

In fact the Paradise regained, evoked by the robe imagery, is something much more than a mere return to the past. Adam, in whom mankind

---

[43] JS II, p. 331.

[44] See my 'The mysteries hidden in the side of Christ,' *Sobornost* VII, (1978), pp. 462–72.

[45] *Homily* 85 (*PO* 23, p. 34).

as a whole is represented, now at last realizes his true goal—divinization. As Ephrem puts it:

> The Exalted one knew that Adam desired to become a god,
> so he sent his Son, who put him on, in order to give him his desire.

(*H. Nisib.* 69.12)[46]

When the Spirit confers sonship on the newly baptized they become sons of God, in other words, potential divine beings.

The robe imagery lent itself in other ways to describe this enriched understanding of Paradise, for the robe of glory is also the robe of royalty, the robe of priesthood, and at the same time, the robe of the just and the 'wedding garment' of Matt. 22:12. The first pair are essentially tied up with Adam/Christ typology, and may be said to look backwards to 'Paradise regained,'[47] while the second pair is forward looking, and eschatological in character.

The Peshitta translation of 1 Peter 2:9, in Greek 'a chosen race, a royal priesthood,' is illuminating in this connection, for it reads 'a chosen race which serves as priests for the kingdom.' As we shall see, priesthood and kingship are among the gifts of the Spirit received at baptism, both having their basis in the Old Testament practice of anointing kings and priests. Besides being anointed, however, kings and priests were also invested with the robe of office, and in Jewish tradition this robe is once again described as 'the robe of glory.' In Ben Sira 50:11 for example, the high priest Simon's garments are described as a 'robe of glory,' and in later tradition Adam's own 'robe of glory' or 'honour' is interpreted as being the robe of kingship and priesthood. This dual role exercised by Adam in Paradise is still very much in the background of the early Syriac Adam/Christ typology: by incorporation into Christ's own kingship and priesthood (in Syriac terms, by putting on the robe of glory at baptism) the baptized realize Adam's original intended role in Paradise.

The Syriac translation of Ps. 132:16 reads 'I will clothe her priests in salvation and her just in glory' (both the Hebrew and the Greek have '…and her just shall rejoice'). Thus right at the source of Syriac tradition we

---

[46] Cp *H. Virg.* 48.15–18; cp also below (b) (iv) with note 97.

[47] Adam is often described as priest prophet and king: e.g. *Cave of Treasures* (ed. Bezold) pp. 20–2 (ET Budge, pp. 62–3); *Chron. anon, ad annum* 1234 (ed. Chabot) I. p. 29; Adam is 'king' in Ephrem *H. Nisib.* 74.10. All this goes back to Jewish sources.

can see that the garment of glory has yet a further dimension, this time eschatological, for the just will put it on at the resurrection. In Jewish texts of
the early post-biblical period this idea is particularly prominent in Enoch,
where we find (En. 62:15): ' The righteous and the elect will have risen from
the earth...and will be clothed with garments of glory.'

It is again already in the Syriac translation of the Old Testament that
we discover yet another extension of the imagery: in Dan. 10:5 and 12:7 the
'garment of glory' is what Daniel's angelic interlocutor wears. Given this
background it is easy to see how early Syriac writers came to describe baptism as an entry into the angelic life,[48] thus providing them with further justification for their ideal of virginity: as Jacob of Serugh puts it in his description of the blessing given by the Apostle Thomas to the Indian royal couple
(based on the *Acts of Thomas*):[49]

> he did not bless them with sons or daughters,
>> but so that they might be like angels, without intercourse.

In the early church the guest who was thrown out from the wedding
feast for having no wedding garment (Matt. 22:12) was regularly understood
as a reference to the baptized Christian who had spoiled his wedding garment, the robe of glory, with which he had been provided by Christ the
Bridegroom at his baptism (cp chapter VI). From early on in Syriac tradition Christ's own baptism was regarded as the betrothal of the Church to
Christ, and Christian baptism as the betrothal of the soul of the baptized to
Christ. This was certainly one of the concepts which gave rise to the hostile
attitude to marriage that characterized the very earliest Christian communities
in the Syriac-speaking area (still exemplified in the *Acts of Thomas*). As Aphrahat
put it, in a passage already quoted in another context,

> As long as a man has not taken a wife he loves and reveres God his Fa-
> ther and the Holy Spirit his Mother, and he has no other love.

> *(Dem.* 18.10)

The imagery of the heavenly bridal chamber, *gnona*, is much loved by
the Syriac poets such as Ephrem and Jacob, and baptism appears as 'the
bridal chamber' or 'wedding feast' in several of the surviving baptismal services, but above all in the Maronite, where the baptized are described as
'entering the bridal chamber of Life (or Salvation),' and as being 'betrothed

---

[48] See my 'Early Syrian Asceticism,' *Numen* 20 (1973), pp. 1–19.
[49] Ed. Strothmann, p. 276 (II, lines 679–80).

to the living God.'[50] The 'betrothal' of the baptized tends to fall into the background in later writers, but Moshe bar Kepha still speaks of the entry of the newly baptized into the church for communion as signifying their spiritual betrothal.[51]

Elsewhere in the baptismal services we find a slightly different emphasis: the baptized are *guests*, invited to the wedding feast. Thus in the Maronite service the newly baptized are counted blessed 'because you have been invited to the wedding feast of the royal Bridegroom.'[52] This wedding feast is envisaged as being between Christ and his Church, which took place, as we have just seen, at Christ's own baptism. Because each individual baptism is understood as being contemporaneous with Christ's own baptism in sacred time, the baptized are thus indeed participating as guests in that event. In this context Ephrem recalls the parable of Matt. 22;

> The Firstborn wrapped himself in a body, as a veil to hide his glory;
> the immortal bride shines out in that robe.
> Let the guests in *their* robes resemble him in his;
> let your bodies, which are your clothing, shine out.
> for they bound in fetters that man whose body was stained.
> Do you whiten my stains at your banquet with your radiance!

> (H. *Nisib.* 43.21)

In his homily on John 1:16[53] Severus describes this robe as 'the glorious garment of sonship' and he cautions the newly baptized 'not to strip off the tunic which saves you from sins, this tunic which resembles snow' (cp Ps. 51:7); rather, recline with confidence at the royal feast, as you eat this spiritual banquet, *and so* you will not have to hear those gloomy words 'Friend, how did you enter here without a wedding garment?' (Matt. 22:12).

This extract provides a good transition to our next section, on the resultant gifts of the Spirit, where 'sonship' and 'confidence' *(parrhesia)* feature prominently.

---

[50] JS II, p. 323; cp U. p. 57 'the gates of the spiritual bridal chamber are opened.' Similarly Jacob of Serugh (ed. Bedjan) I, p. 210 etc.; Narsai (ed. Mingana) I, p. 346 (ET p. 52). At end of note 50 add: For the imagery of the bridal chamber, see my 'The Bridal Chamber of Light: a distinctive feature of the Syriac liturgical tradition,' *The Harp* 18 (2005), pp. 179–91.

[51] §23.

[52] JS II, p. 345; cp T § 13.xi.

[53] *Homily* 43 (PO 36, pp. 84–6).

(b)   The gifts of the Spirit

Employing the imagery of Christ as the Rock, so much favoured by Syriac writers,[54] Aphrahat explains Zech. 3:9, 'on the rock will I open up seven eyes,' in the light of Isaiah 11:2:

> What, then, are these seven eyes which have been opened up on the Rock, if not the Spirit of God who resided on Christ with seven opera-tions as the prophet Isaiah said: 'There shall rest and reside upon him the Spirit of God, of wisdom, of understanding, of counsel, of might, of knowledge and of the fear of the Lord.' These are the seven eyes which were opened up on the Rock.

(Dem. 1.9)

Ephrem also speaks of the Spirit as being 'sevenfold,' alluding to the same passage of Isaiah.[55] There, in the Peshitta as in the Hebrew and Targum, the number seven can only be reached by including the 'Spirit of God' in the enumeration; in the Septuagint, however, there are seven, rather than six, attributes listed in apposition to the 'Spirit of God,' thanks to a double translation of 'the fear of God.' Yet despite this early interest in the number seven in this passage of Isaiah, Syriac writers never tried to limit the gifts of the Spirit to a particular group of seven, and in the following pages I have selected for discussion only those gifts which feature most prominently in the texts themselves.

(i)   Sonship

> The Father sent the Spirit of his Son into men's hearts,
> and through the Spirit we truly call the Father 'our Father.'

Jacob of Serugh is here[56] expressing one of the most important aspects of the gift of the Spirit, as far as Syrian tradition is concerned. It is this gift of 'sonship' or 'adoption as sons' that confers on Christians the authority to use the Lord's Prayer. Theodore, quoting the Pauline basis for this teaching (Rom. 8:15) addresses the newly baptized as follows:[57]

> You have received the Spirit of sonship, as the result of which you are enabled to address God as 'Father.'

---

[54] Cp Murray, *Symbols*, chapter 6.
[55] *Comm. Diat.* 3.15.
[56] Ed. Bedjan I, p. 203.
[57] *Cat. Hom.* 11.7 (Tonneau p. 296).

Philoxenus likewise states:[58]

> Indeed we are quite unable to employ this term of address and call God
> 'Father,' except through the authority of the Holy Spirit who is within
> us, for it is well known that those who have not yet become God's chil-
> dren by the holy rebirth of baptism are not authorized to use this term,
> and they are not permitted to say 'Our Father who art in heaven, hal-
> lowed be thy name.' The manifest reason for this is that the Holy Spirit
> is not yet within them.

Before baptism man can only legitimately call Adam his 'father,' as Jacob of
Serugh points out in a passage where he also draws on the typological contrast between Eve, sprung from Adam's rib, and Baptism, the 'new mother'
who springs as 'the water' from the side of Christ on the Cross (John
19:34):[59]

> Baptism has become for us a new mother, and through her we become
> children to the Father, who may call him 'our Father' lovingly...
> From Eve we were of dust, and children of death,
> from this new mother we are children of God.
> From now on we have a Father in heaven,
> whom we can in confidence address as 'our Father'...
> If Eve's birthgiving was still operative,
> our 'father' would be in Sheol, and not in heaven.

In the light of this emphasis given to sonship it is not surprising to
find that the 'Our Father' plays a prominent part in all the baptismal texts,[60]
and in a number of services the phrase 'gift of sonship' specifically occurs.[61]
It has already been pointed out that in the baptismal services themselves
there is considerable ambiguity over precisely when and how this and other
gifts are conveyed. In the oldest texts of the Syrian Orthodox *Severus*, for
example, the gift of sonship is clearly associated with the pre-baptismal
anointing, or *rushma*, while in the anonymous service of Add. 14518 it is
linked rather with pouring of the myron on to the water. Once again it is
important to stress that the baptismal rite was essentially seen as a whole,
whose total effects can be focussed on any of a number of different points,

---

[58] Ed. Tanghe, p. 44. The point is often made by Jacob of Serugh (e.g. Bedjan
III, p. 656).

[59] Ed. Bedjan I, p. 198.

[60] Sadly omitted in the Syrian Catholic edition of 1922 (French translation by
G. Khouri-Sarkis in *L'Orient Syrien* 1 (1956)).

[61] E.g. D § 40; B III, p. 221 etc.

in particular the various anointings and the baptism proper. Looked at historically, we can discern how shifts of emphasis were caused once again by the changing biblical models and imagery that were uppermost in the minds of different writers. Thus, in the case of sonship, earlier writers most frequently associate this gift with the pre-baptismal *rushma*, but with the development of the mother imagery in connection with the font, very popular from the fifth century onwards, it was considered more 'logical' to associate 'sonship' with baptism proper, in the 'womb of the font.'

Two related aspects of sonship are important in the Syrian tradition: the *parrhesia* that we acquire, and the fact that we thus become 'brothers' to Christ the Only-Begotten, and thus co-heirs.

The Greek *parrhesia* is as difficult to express in Syriac as it is in English. 'Uncovering of the face,' *galyut appe*, was one solution of the early translators, but more frequently the Greek term itself was taken over as a loanword. In a baptismal context the word means 'freedom to speak to God,' 'confidence,' and above all the freedom to address God as 'Father.' Immediately following on the words already quoted, Theodore says '...you have been made worthy of sonship, and you have the freedom (*parrhesia*) to address God as 'Father.'

In many of the Syriac anaphoras the prayer introducing the Our Father specifically makes mention of the *parrhesia*: '...grant us therefore, O Lord, your Holy Spirit, so that we may be bold, with *parrhesia* and fearlessness, to address you, the heavenly God, saying 'Our Father..!'[62] We find exactly the same in the prayer introducing the Our Father in East Syriac baptismal service:[63]

> Make us worthy, our Lord and our God, to stand before you continually, without blame, with a pure heart and openness of face, and with that *parrhesia* which has been granted to us by you in your mercy, so that we may all together address you and say 'Our Father...'

Parrhesia also has eschatological connotations, which are introduced into several anaphoras, as well as into the final prayer of the Syrian Orthodox baptismal service attributed to Timothy:[64]

---

[62] Anaphora of Timothy of Alexandria (*Anaphorae Syriacae* I, p. 42). On *parrhesia* and baptism see R. G. Coquin, 'Le thème de la *parrhesia* et ses expressions symboliques dans les rites d'initiation, à Antioche,' *Proche Orient Chrétien* 20 (1970), pp. 1–17.

[63] U, p. 69.

[64] T § 55.

...Sanctify them in your truth, fill them with the gi'
so that, as they travel on the paths of righteousr
fidence (*parrhesia*) to stand before the fearful judgeme
Christ...

'Baptism makes us children so that we become brothers of the Only-
Begotten.'[65] Jacob of Serugh is particularly fond of this title of 'brother'
conferred on the baptized (based on passages such as Matt. 12:50, and de-
duced from the fact of their becoming sons of the Father); it is, however, a
theme familiar to most Syriac writers, from Aphrahat on.[66] The baptized
become 'brothers to Christ' only because Christ first of all 'condescended to
become a brother to bad servants,' as Jacob puts it.[67]

As 'children of God' the baptized are also heirs (Rom. 8:17; Gal. 4:7),
and this is an idea which is found in most of the baptismal services. In the
Syrian Orthodox *Timothy*, for example, at the invocation of the Holy Spirit
over the water, the priest asks the Holy Spirit that the water may be for the
baptized 'for the absolution of wrong doings and the forgiveness of sins,
for the keeping of your holy commandments...and for the inheritance of
the kingdom of heaven.'[68]

(ii) Membership

At the same time as conferring 'sonship' on the baptized, the Holy Spirit
makes them members of Christ's Church. Paul's imagery of 'members' or
'limbs' of Christ's body (Rom. 12:4; I Cor. 6:14) features in several of the
baptismal services, in particular the East Syriac, where it recurs three times
in the course of the prayers: 'may they receive the purification that cannot
be altered, and become limbs of Christ, growing up at the table of his mysteries., (p. 56) '...putting their hope in the holy *rushma* and baptism that
brings forgiveness, may they become limbs and imitators of him who is the
head of the Church...' (p. 57); and '...they have put on this your gift, and
through it they have been freed from the passions of their sins, and they
have become pure limbs in the body of Christ, the head of our salvation' (p.
73).

---

[65] Jacob (ed. Bedjan) I, p. 161.
[66] *Dem.* 6. 1 (*PS* I, col. 240).
[67] Ed. Bedjan I, p. 194.
[68] T § 36.

Although early Syriac writers make use of Paul's concept of the Church as Christ's mystical body in other contexts,[69] its baptismal implications are not developed. Much more characteristic, however, of Syriac tradition is the pastoral imagery of entry of (lost) sheep into Christ's fold. Already in the *Acts of Thomas* there is a strong emphasis on this aspect:[70] '…unite them to your Fold and anoint them; purify them from their uncleanness and guard them from the wolves, feed them in your pastures, and let them drink from your fountain which is never turbid and whose stream never fails.'

The pre-baptismal anointing provides the *rushma*, or mark of identity, the brand that shows that the new sheep now belong to Christ:[71]

> He makes him to stand as a sheep at the door of the sheep-fold;
> and he signs his body and lets him mix with the flock.
> The *rushma* of the oil he holds in his hand before the beholders,
> and with things visible he proclaims the power of things hidden;
> as by a symbol he shows to the eyes of the bodily senses
> the secret power that is hidden in the visible sign.

Besides ensuring that the new sheep now become 'mingled' or 'mixed' in the flock of Christ, the mark of ownership also acts as a protection against the power of darkness, an aspect we shall return to later, in our discussion of the oil.

All the baptismal services are extremely rich in this pastoral imagery, and a few examples must suffice to illustrate this. In the introductory prayer of the Syrian Orthodox *Severus* we have the sheep motif side by side with that of the 'limbs' of Christ:[72]

> .. may he be made worthy of rebirth from above which comes through water and the Spirit, effecting him a sheep of that true Shepherd, imprinted with the imprint of your Holy Spirit, an honourable limb in the body of your holy Church.

The archaic Syrian Orthodox service in Add. 14518 has a particularly fine prayer, just before the pre-baptismal anointing (in position II);[73]

---

[69] See Murray, *Symbols*, pp. 86–93.
[70] § 25. For the contrast with wolves, see chapter V note 128.
[71] Narsai (ed. Mingana), I, pp. 363–4 (ET p. 40); see also below, chapter V (2).
[72] SH, p. 18.
[73] D 11; cp JS II, p. 347.

O good Shepherd and finder of those who are lost, who by the sign of your Trinity signed your sheep that they might be preserved from ravening wolves, by your glorious name, O Father, Son and Holy Spirit, may they be signed lambs in your flock, that they may be numbered among your holy flock and be mingled with your sheep, and enter your sheepfold and belong to you; preserve them by your sign from all evil things, and give them repose with your fragrant oil, and sanctify them with the sign of your Trinity, that they may come to second birth, singing praise to your Trinity, Father, Son and Holy Spirit, for eternal ages.

In the Maronite service the formula for this pre-baptismal anointing actually reads:[74]

N is marked a new (or pure) lamb in the flock of Christ,

Finally, here is an example from the East Syriac service;[75]

. . . may the angels in heaven have joy over them, and likewise your whole Church, because they have been mingled in the flock of Christ.

In the third of the Epiphany hymns attributed to Ephrem, the unknown author dwells on the paradox of the Shepherd who himself became food for his sheep;[76]

The crowds in the wilderness
were like sheep who had no shepherd;
the merciful one became their shepherd,
multiplying bread as their pasturage,
Blessed are you, innocent
lambs of Christ who are signed,
for you have been made worthy of the Body and Blood:
the Shepherd himself has become your food.

Much less prominent than the pastoral imagery is that of 'planting.' Once again various passages in the New Testament provide the starting point, and Romans 6:5 is particularly influential, forming the basis of part of the long consecration prayer common to the Syrian Orthodox and Melkite services:

---

[74] JS II, p. 332.
[75] U, p. 61.
[76] *H. Epiph.* 3.21.

grant that those who are planted together (Greek *sunphutoi*) in the likeness of the death of your Christ through baptism may also become partakers of the resurrection...

and earlier in the service, associated either with the consignation in position
I, or that in position II, we have:

Fashion your Christ on those who are about to be reborn through the
agency of my weakness; confirm them on the foundation of the apostles
and the prophets, plant them as a true plant in your catholic Church...

Most early Syriac writers associated the idea of planting with that of vines in
the vineyard. 'Let us be planted as vines in his vineyard,' says Aphrahat,
with the Diatessaron reading of John 15:1 in mind, 'I am the vineyard
(*karma*) of truth' (instead of the later Peshitta 'I am the vine (*gpetta*) of
truth').[77]

The Syrian Orthodox pre-baptismal anointing is accompanied by the
formula[78] 'N is signed *with the oil* of gladness to be armed against every
working of the adversary, and for a grafting into the good olive of the holy
catholic and apostolic Church.' The New Testament basis is here Romans
11, a chapter which is only very rarely used in a baptismal context by Syriac
writers;[79] it features prominently, however, in the Mystagogic Catecheses
attributed to Cyril of Jerusalem, in connection with the pre-baptismal
anointing of the Jerusalem rite:[80]

Stripped of your clothes you have been anointed with the exorcistic oil
from the top of your head downwards, and you have become sharers in
the good olive of Jesus Christ; for you have been cut off from the wild
olive and grafted on the good olive, and become sharers in the fatness
of the true olive.

---

[77] *Dem.* 6.1 (*PS* I, col. 244); cp Murray, *Symbols*, pp. 95–6.
[78] In position II or III; see ' Studies,' pp. 30–2, 38–9.
[79] Aphrahat uses the verse, emphasizing that if we sin, we shall be cut off again
(*Dem.* 16.8=*PS* I, col. 784). Ephrem seems to transfer the grafting from the olive to
the vine in *H. Haer.* 39. 10; in *Sermo de Domino Nostro* § 57 and *H. Nisib.* 50.6.1 he
mentions 'grafting' without reference to the olive. In his commentary on the
Pauline Epistles he expands Romans 11:23 as follows : '...for God is able, through
the absolution of baptism, to graft them in again' (Armenian, p. 42=Latin translation, p. 37). cp also chapter V (2) (b) (i).
[80] *PG* 33, col. 1080.

Very probably the imagery was taken over into the Syrian rite from the Jerusalem liturgy, perhaps at much the same time as the introduction of the post-baptismal anointing.[81]

(iii) Priesthood and kingship

These two gifts of the Spirit have rather fallen into the background in the extant texts, but there is strong evidence to suggest that at an early date they played a much more prominent role. One of the few places where they still feature in the baptismal texts themselves is in the prayer before the post-baptismal anointing in the Syrian Orthodox *Timothy* and the Melkite *Basil:*[82]

> O God, whose gifts are very great, Father of our Lord and our God and our Saviour Jesus Christ, who raises up to adoption by yourself these men who are being filled with the scent of your Christ, of whom you have given a symbol in this myron which you are wont to sanctify through invisible power; grant through this imprint the union of your living and holy Spirit, and the honour of priesthood and the heavenly kingdom to those who are sanctified; and grant, in the coming of your Christ, glorious honour and priestly produce, since to you all things are simple and easy; and may they be made worthy to offer up, together and in company and companionship with us, praise for your mercies towards us, Father Son and Holy Spirit, now and always and for eternal ages, amen.

Although priesthood and kingship are here associated with the postbaptismal anointing, it was originally with the pre-baptismal *rushma* that these gifts were connected. Indeed, at the earliest stage of Syriac tradition it would appear that these two elements represented, along with mark of ownership, the chief symbolic content of that anointing. The concept is based on Exodus 19:6 ('You shall be for me a kingdom, and priests, and a holy people') and 1 Peter 2:9 ('You shall be a chosen race, serving as priests for the kingdom').

Since Old Testament prophets as well as kings and priests were also sometimes anointed, this role too may be added as belonging to the newly-baptized. Aphrahat speaks of[83] '...the illumination of the mind and the fruit-bearing of the light-giving olive, with which the *rushma* of the mystery of salvation takes place, and by which Christians are perfected as priests,

---

[81] See above, chapter III (1) (b).

[82] See my commentary to T § 45.

[83] *Dem.* 23.3 (*PS* 2, col. 9).

kings and prophets.' Severus, commenting on 1 Peter 2:9, explains why it is that Christians take on these roles:[84]

> We who believe in Christ receive the same things that he did: since he was of royal stock and high priest by birth, we have received the same dignities, by his grace.

Severus takes back both Christ's kingship and his priesthood to his nativity, but native Syriac tradition prefers to see the priesthood (and prophecy) as conferred on him at his baptism by John. As Ephrem puts in his *Commentary on the Diatessaron* (4.3):

> The Spirit who rested on him at his baptism testified that he was the Shepherd (i.e. king, following Old Testament language), and that he had received the roles of prophet and priest through John. He had already received the kingship belonging to the house of David by being born 'of the house of David' (Luke 2:4); he received the priesthood from the house of Levi at his 'second birth' conferred on him at his baptism at the hand of the descendant of Aaron.

The importance of this early tradition, known to Aphrahat, Jacob of Serugh and others, lay in its provision of an unbroken chain of priests, from Moses' time to the Christian priesthood. This comes out very clearly in another passage from Ephrem:

> The Most High decended on Mount Sinai
> and stretched forth his hand over Moses. Moses laid it on Aaron
> and so it continued till John. Therefore did our Lord say to him
> 'It is right that I be baptized by you, that the Order may not perish.'
> Our Lord gave it to the Apostles, and behold, in our Church is its hand-
>   ing-on.
> Blessed be he who gave us his Order. (*H. Haer.* 22.19)

The wording of John of the Sedre (died 648) in his treatise on the myron shows very clearly, by the use of the term *rushma*, that this gift of the Spirit, which he associates with the post-baptismal anointing, was originally linked to the pre-baptismal one:[85]

> With the imprint of this holy oil you are inscribed into the sonship of the heavenly Father; through the mark *(rushma)* or imprint of this heav-

---

[84] J. A. Cramer, *Catenae Graecorum Patrum* VIII, p. 54; cp John Chrysostom *Hom. on 2 Cor.* (PG 61, col.417) : 'by baptism you too are made king, priest and prophet.'
[85] British Library Add. 12165, f. 261b.

enly oil you became the sheep of Christ, a priestly kingdom (I Pet. 2:9), a holy people…

The prayer common to *Timothy* and *Basil*, quoted above, is the only one in the baptismal services which speaks directly of the 'priesthood' being conferred on the newly baptized. Quite a number of other texts, indeed, mention the anointing of Old Testament prophets, priests or kings as the antecedent for the baptismal anointing, but a slightly different a slant is given; thus in *Timothy* we also find the following prayer, which comes immediately before the anointing in position III.[86]

> O God, Father Almighty, you set up of old priests, Levites and kings for your people, and commanded that the sons of Aaron be anointed with oil; now, because we have been called by your great name, and you have appointed us, although unworthy, as priests, through the heavenly grace of our great God and our Saviour Jesus Christ, and you have commanded us through your apostles to anoint with oil the lambs of your flock, with it do we sign (*rashminan*) and anoint these your servants and maidservants, and we ask and beseech that, being anointed and baptized, they may be partakers in your beloved Son, through your Holy Spirit, and be united to your true flock, so that the power of the adversary may have no dominion over them; for you are mighty and have dominion over all, and to you is fitting praise and honour, and to your only-begotten Son our Lord Jesus Christ, and to your living and holy Spirit, now and always and for eternal ages, amen.

In other words, whereas in the Old Testament oil anointed priests, in the New Covenant priests anoint lambs of Christ's flock. A similar relationship is expressed in a *qolo* found in *Severus* and *Basil* at the anointing in position III:

> God ordered Moses to anoint Aaron with holy oil so that he might thus be consecrated. With oil too are the innocent lambs, who have come to baptism, anointed.

---

[86] T § 39. 'Priests': in *Timothy*, *Basil* and *Severus* associated with the anointing in position III; 'prophets, priests': in *Jacob* (JS II, p. 330) associated with the anointing in position II; 'priests, kings and prophets': in *Jacob* (JS, II, p. 344), position III; 'priests, kings': East Syriac (U, p. 68), position II. JS II, p. 344, in particular, is worth quoting: 'Moses the prophet was bidden to make fine oil out of sweet unguents, for priests, kings and prophets. For God would not allow a king to rule until he had been anointed, nor is anyone allowed to enter the kingdom on high without baptism that gives forgiveness.'

The idea that, whereas oil anointed priests and kings in the Old Testament, it now serves to anoint lambs, is a recurrent one in Syriac writers, and is already found in Ephrem, who says, in one of his most important hymns on the subject of baptism

> This oil is the dear friend of the Holy Spirit,
> it serves him, following him like a disciple.
> With it the Spirit signed priests and anointed kings;
> for with the oil the Holy Spirit imprints his mark on his sheep.
> Like a signet ring whose impression is left on wax,
> so the hidden seal of the Spirit is imprinted by oil
> on the bodies of those who are anointed in baptism;
> thus are they marked in the baptismal mystery.

(H. Virg. 7.6)

Likewise in the Epiphany hymns attributed to Ephrem the contrasting relationship between Jewish and Christian baptismal anointing is again brought out:

> When Moses signed and anointed the sons of the Levite Aaron
> fire consumed their bodies, fire preserved their clothes.
> Blessed are you, my brothers, for the fire of mercy has come down,
> utterly devouring your sins, purifying and sanctifying your bodies.
>
> Aaron's anointing, my brothers, only sprinkled ordinary blood
> of animals on altar horns,
> but this is the true anointing that sprinkles on your bodies
> the living blood that gives life to all,
> mingling it in your minds, sprinkling it in your chambers.
>
> The anointed priests offered up the slain corpses of animals.
> But you, who are gloriously anointed,
> have your own bodies as your offerings;
> the anointed Levites offered up the entrails of beasts,
> you are more glorious than the Levites,
> for you have consecrated your own hearts.
>
> The Jewish people's anointing is a shadow of Christ's;
> its rod is a symbol of the cross,
> its paschal lamb a type of the Only-begotten:
> its Shekhina a symbol of your churches,
> its circumcision a type of your faith being signed
> under the shadow of your beauties did that first people sit
>
> At David's anointing, my brothers, there came down the Spirit
> who gave scent to his heart.

for the scent of David's heart pleased him,
just as the scent of the oil;
the Spirit dwelt in him and sang in him, but your anointing is greater,
for Father, Son and Holy Spirit have come down to dwell in you.

(H. Epiph. 3.10–14)

Circumcision (stanza 13) as an antecedent to the *rushma* has already been considered above [cp also chapter V(2)(b)(i)]. In the East Syriac service it is likewise put into the context of Old Testament anointing (p. 68):

For you gave holy oil to men of old as a mark (*rushma*) and token of temporal priesthood and transient kingship, but now you have transmitted it to be a symbolic mark for those who move from things earthly to things heavenly, with an immortal body and incorruptible soul, being circumcised with a circumcision without hands, stripping off the flesh of sin at the circumcision that belongs to Christ…

In the later commentaries 'kingship' (associated with the myron) is understood as the ability to rule over the passions; the words of Moshe bar Kepha, in the proem of his treatise on the myron,[87] are characteristic of this later type of interpretation:

Kings used to be anointed with this oil, a symbol that everyone who is anointed with it would rule over all the passions, if he so wills.

(iv) Purification and Sanctification

Just as the coming of the Holy Spirit on the baptismal water provides purification and sanctification, so too his presence in the hearts of the baptized provides both purification and sanctification. In the *Acts of Thomas*[88] Judas Thomas prays at the pre-baptismal anointing 'Come, Spirit of sanctification, and purify their inmost hearts.' Exactly the same idea is expressed in the old Syrian Orthodox service in Add. 14518:[89]

To you, God of the fathers, and giver of light to souls and purification to bodies, are our eyes raised and our hands stretched out, and we beseech you that you give us from the heights of your holiness the granting of the gift of your all-holy Spirit, who gives blessed purification and divine holiness; and sanctify and unite us all into communion with you, by the grace and mercy and loving-kindness of your only-begotten Son,

---

[87] Ed. Strothmann, p. 32.
[88] § 27.
[89] D § 27; cp JS II, p. 334, T § 27.

along with whom to you is fitting praise and honour and power, together with your all-holy Spirit, now and always and for eternal ages,
amen.

We find numerous ways of expressing how this purification takes place: it
involves the expulsion of all evil influences, the forgiveness or removal of
sin by means of 'washing away,' as in *Severus*:[90]

> He has cleansed us today from the filth of our sins…in the washing that
> comes from water and the Spirit.

Or the imagery is of burning off the dross of sin in the 'furnace' of baptism,
as we have again in *Severus*:[91]

> Make him shine anew in the furnace of the holy font.

Or it may be of wiping off sin as with a sponge, as we find in Narsai:[92]

> He willed to wipe away the rust (or pus) of iniquity from mortals; his
> providence put the sponge of the Spirit into the hand of our body.

Or again purification may be seen in terms of healing, a theme developed at
length by both Aphrahat and Ephrem; such healing was needed because, as
Timothy puts it,[93] 'our wickedness had become strong and entrenched, reach-
ing the heart, and not able to be healed by man.' Further examples of these
and other images will be found in chapter V.

All writers are emphatic that the purification brought about by the
Holy Spirit as baptism cannot be repeated: baptism is once and for all, and
so we find dire warnings to the newly-baptized not to return to their old
sinful ways. But the problem of post-baptismal sin is not seen as an insolu-
ble one in the early Syriac church, and Ephrem gives advice on the matter:

> Because we cannot be baptized again, we should not sin again.
> Nevertheless there is another kind of 'sprinkling' too (Ps. 51:9):
> He who gave hope in baptism provided a further means of forgiveness,
> so that this hope should not be in vain,
> But the toil required for this, after you have been baptized,
> is harder than that needed before it.
> Sins committed before baptism

---

[90] SH, p. 18.
[91] SH, p. 19; cp below, chapter V (1) (h) (v).
[92] Ed. Mingana 1, p. 357 (E1 pp. 33–4). cp U, pp. 60–1 (see also chapter V,
note 155).
[93] I N, 44

can be absolved easily, in baptism,
And even if the mark of sin's wounds is deep,
yet baptism will whiten and wipe them away;
But post-baptismal sins can only
be reversed by means of doubled labours. *(H. Virg.* 46.21–26)

In his hymns on the ascetic Abraham Qidunaya, Ephrem describes this arduous repentance for post-baptismal sin as the 'baptism of tears':

Even though there is only one baptism for the whitening of stains,
yet there are two eyes which, when filled with tears,
provide a baptismal font for the limbs.
For the Creator knew well beforehand that sins multiply in us at all
    times,
and though there is only a single baptism,
he fixed in the single body
        two fonts that give absolution.   *(H. Abr. Qid.* 4.2–3)

In later writers tears are often spoken of as 'a second baptism.'[94]

The close association of the baptismal water with the water which issued from the side of Christ (John 19:34) accounts for the ability of the former to absolve sins. This is brought out well in the epiclesis over the water in the Syrian Orthodox *Timothy*:[95]

May your living and holy Spirit come, O Lord, and dwell and rest upon this water, and sanctify it and make it like the water which flowed from the side of your Only-Begotten on the cross; that it may be for the absolution of wrongdoings, and the forgiveness of sins, of those who are baptized in it...

In the *Syrian Orthodox* exegetical tradition Gabriel's words to Mary at the Annunciation (Luke 1:35) are understood as reflecting a twofold process of purification and sanctification; in readiness for her conception of Christ:[96]

It was necessary that the Holy Spirit should come before the Only-begotten: first the Spirit, then the Power resided in the pure one.
...Mary is called to be mother to the Son of God;
once the Spirit had sanctified her, then the Power overshadowed her:
the Spirit freed her from (Eve's) debt, so that she might be
above sin when Christ dwelt in her in holy fashion.

---

[94] E.g. Sahdona (ed. de Halleux) I, p. 51.
[95] T § 36; cp also chapter V (1) below.
[96] Jacob of Serugh (ed. Bedjan) S, pp. 631–2; cp chapter I note 11.

In an analogous way the purification effected by the Holy Spirit at baptism initiates the process of sanctification. In Mary's case this was brought about by the Word (or Power) dwelling in her very womb, in the Christian's case it is the indwelling Spirit who can bring it about, provided he is not 'grieved' or constrained. As we shall see, the Eucharist plays an essential role in this on-going process of sanctification.

Greek writers speak of the 'divinisation' of man as the aim of the Incarnation, or 'hominisation' of God. Early Syriac writers use somewhat different language, but the underlying idea is the same, and it should be remembered that in the Semitic languages the term 'son of' 'sons of,' often denotes membership of a specific category of person; thus in the Old Testament 'sons of God' are divine beings (often interpreted 'angels' in the early biblical translations), and the fact that the newly baptized become 'sons of God' will consequently imply that they are, or rather, have the potential of becoming, divine beings. In his *Commentary on Genesis* Ephrem states that Adam's fall was the result of his trying to grasp divinity for himself.[97] This is taken up in the *Hymns on Virginity* and expanded in an interesting way:

> Divinity flew down and descended
> to raise and draw up humanity.
> The Son has made beautiful the servant's deformity,
> and he has become a god, just as he desired. (*H. Virg.* 48.17–18)

The same idea of the conveying of divinity to mankind recurs in one of the *Hymns on Faith*;

> He gave us divinity,
> we gave him humanity. (*H. Fid.* 5.17)

But, just as Christians are 'sons of God' only by grace, and not by nature, so too 'God in his mercies called mortals 'gods' through grace' (*H. Fid.* 29.1).

It is only in later writers, influenced by Greek phraseology,[98] that the verb 'divinise' is used. Sahdona, for example, sees the divinisation of man as a direct consequence of the hominisation of God the Word:[99]

---

[97] *Comm. on Gen.* 3.26.

[98] Thus Ps Dionysius (*Eccl. Hier.* II. 8) speaks of 'the sacred and deifying participation of the Holy Spirit.'

[99] Ed. de Halleux II, p. 19. Elsewhere (III, p. 20) Sahdona urges his readers 'to carve out the full beauty of the soul, so that we appear like glorious statues of the divinity in the world.'

Because God the Word was united in nature and person to man and became man…so too man, because he has been truly united in his nature
to God the Word and so been divinised, appears in the guise of a god,
as though that were his own.

The absence of this bold language from the baptismal services themselves is not surprising, but the underlying concept of a radical change in
the mode of existence, brought about at baptism, is indeed present, though
expressed in different terms. Thus, in a prayer common to the Maronite
Jacob and the anonymous Syrian Orthodox service in Add. 14518, we
have:[100]

> Instead of the womb of Eve which produced children who were mortal
> and corruptible, may this womb of water produce children who are
> heavenly, spiritual and immortal; and as the Holy Spirit hovered over the
> water at the establishment of created things, do you, O Lord, be present
> in this baptismal water, which is the spiritual womb that gives birth to
> spiritual beings; and may it produce, instead of the Adam made of dust,
> the heavenly Adam, and may those who are baptized in it receive in you
> the lasting changes that will not be made ineffective: instead of corpo-
> rality, spirituality; instead of visibleness, communion with the invisible;
> and instead of the weak soul, your Holy Spirit,

(c) The Pledge of the Spirit

In 2 Cor. 1:22 Paul speaks of the 'pledge' of the Holy Spirit in our hearts;
the Spirit is the 'pledge' of the inheritance which the Christian is to receive
(Eph. 1:14). This language is echoed in several of the baptismal services,
above all in the East Syriac rite, as for example,

> …in the oil and water is perfected the type of death and resurrection,
> together with a pledge of the kingdom of heaven, (p. 59)

Likewise the oil with which they are anointed is 'a pledge of the resurrection
from the dead' (p. 67); in the anonymous Syrian Orthodox service in Add.
14518 the same phrase is used of the oil that is poured on to the water.[101]

We have seen that baptism is frequently viewed as a re-entry into
Paradise: the baptized are able, provided they allow the Holy Spirit to work
within them, to live in Paradise while still on earth: 'you have entered Eden
before the resurrection,' Ephrem says of Juliana Saba.[102] Such people have

---

[100] D § 36; JS II, pp. 339–40.

[101] D § 40.

[102] H. *Jul. Saba*, 21.14.

effectively yoked together 'sacred' and 'historical' time as far as they themselves are concerned, and so they can be described as anticipating the resurrection. This anticipation of resurrection is precisely what the early Syriac
writers mean by the 'pledge' of the resurrection; as Ephrem puts it,[103] 'in the
hope of the resurrection we await the life that is to come, and indeed we
already walk in this new life, in that we have the pledge of it.'

Other writers, who prefer a linear, rather than a cyclical, model, see the
new life of baptism as an anticipation of the end of time. Thus Theodore,
having quoted Phil. 3:21, says:[104]

> It is in the hope of these good things that we have been called, and have
> been reborn in baptism through the power of the Holy Spirit; as though
> in a type, and as a pledge of what we shall receive, we have received the
> first-fruits of the Spirit...

This is echoed by Narsai:[105]

> In symbol the baptized dies and is resurrected and adorned:
> symbolically he imitates immortal life.
> The rebirth of his baptism is a symbol of the rebirth
> that takes place at the end of time.

In East Syriac sources in particular baptism is sometimes specifically described as the pledge of salvation.[106] But this sort of language is by no
means confined to East Syriac writers; in several of the West Syriac
anaphoras, for example, the gift of 'sonship' which allows Christians to say
the Our Father, is described as 'the pledge of sonship which you have given
us.'[107]

In short, then, the 'pledge' that the Holy Spirit gives to the newly baptized can be described as the potential for the realization of the manifold
gifts of the Spirit.

---

[103] *Comm. Diat.* 21. 25.
[104] *Cat. Hom.* 9.17 (Tonneau, p. 242.)
[105] Ed. Mingana I, p. 317 (ET p. 52).
[106] E g Bahai, *History of Ginwargis* (ed Bedjan), pp 419, 433, 489
[107] De, Iohn Chrysostom (, Anaphoras Syriaca T ii, 161). Dionysius (, Anaph. Syr.
I, p. 201).

5 THE INVOCATIONS TO THE SPIRIT

The Holy Spirit effects our entry into and participation in sacred time, and thus the invocation to the Holy Spirit, or epiclesis, is as essential a part of the baptismal service as it is of the eucharistic liturgy. Actually a close examination of the various Syriac baptismal services will reveal that they all incorporate several different epicleses.[1] The most important of course, is the one (and sometimes there are more than one) uttered in the course of the consecration of the baptismal water. In some of the services (the East Syriac, Maronite and Melkite) there is, in addition, an epiclesis over the oil which is to be used in the pre-baptismal anointing. We also find, in some services, an epiclesis over the baptismal candidates, or indeed one uttered by the priest on his own behalf. All these we shall look at in turn.

(1) THE INVOCATION OVER THE WATER

(a) Historical Development

If we read carefully the present-day prayers of consecration for the water we will discover that the wording of the epiclesis takes on one of a number of different forms: in most of the West Syriac services the Father is addressed, and he is asked to *send* the Holy Spirit, while in the Maronite and East Syriac traditions the invocation takes the form 'may the Spirit *come...*,' which represents the more archaic of the two phrases. We will also find differences in the description of what the Holy Spirit will effect: the Spirit is asked to 'bless' or 'sanctify'[2] or 'perfect' the waters, or to 'rest and reside' upon them, or to 'make' them into the Jordan waters, or the water from the side of Christ (John 19:34).

With the Syrian Orthodox and Melkite services the matter becomes even more complex, since their prayers of consecration (both going back to an original Greek text, for the most part still preserved in the Byzantine and Ethiopic rites) contain several different epicleses which have been accumulated over the course of time.

---

[1] See also 'Epiklesis,' where further secondary literature will be found.

[2] Or 'consecrate': the Syriac *qaddesh* covers both English terms.

Clearly, behind this rich profusion of different types of epiclesis, there lies a long history, of which we can only sketch the bare outlines here. But before we do this, it will be helpful to have the texts of the various invocations before our eyes:[3]

East Syriac: …the Spirit who came down and remained upon our Saviour, (thus) depicting the type of this holy baptism: may that same Spirit come, O Lord, upon this water, so that it may receive power for the help and salvation of those who are baptized in it.

Maronite Jacob: …may the Holy Spirit come, Lord, and reside upon this water and drive from it every power of the enemy and kindle it with his invincible power, and bless and sanctify it, in the likeness of the water which flowed from the side of the Only-Begotten on the cross…

Syrian Orthodox Severus: (A comparison of the texts of the long consecration prayer common to *Severus*, the Melkite *Basil* and the Greek Constantinopolitan rite will show up the presence of a number of interpolated epicleses in these different rites; in the various texts of *Severus* there are as many as three such additional epicleses inserted at various points into the wording of the consecration prayer; the added wording is given in italics).

a   (found in one early manuscript, British Libr. Add. 14494) …But do you, Lord of all, send your Holy Spirit and sanctify this water and appoint this water the water of rest…

b   (for the origin of this interpolated prayer, found in several early manuscripts (Add. 17218, 14493, 14499 (mg) and two of the services printed in *Codex Liturgicus* (SA II, III), see below) …*Have mercy on us, God the Father Almighty, and send upon this water which is being sanctified…the Paraclete, your Holy Spirit…*

c   (found in several early manuscripts (Add. 14494, 14495, 14499, 17218, 14500) and printed editions (SA I IV VI, SH))…appear, O Lord, on this water, *and sanctify it by the overshadowing of your Holy Spirit* and grant that those who are baptized in it may be changed…

Syrian Orthodox Timothy:

(a) § 33 Yea, we beseech you, Father of mercies and God of all comfort, send your living Spirit and sanctify this water, and may it become the womb of the Spirit that gives rebirth anew to mankind who are baptized in it…

---

[3] The Syriac texts are given in 'Epiklesis,' pp. 217–8.

(b) § 36 ...and may your living and Holy Spirit come, O Lord, and reside and rest upon this water, and sanctify it and make it like the water that flowed from the side of your Only-Begotten on the cross . . .

Syrian Orthodox, short service (Severus): Yea, Lord, send your Holy Spirit on this water and bless and sanctify it, so that it may be for him who is baptised in it saving water, water of joy...

Syrian Orthodox, short service (Philoxenus): Shine forth, O Lord, on this water, and may your Holy Spirit stir it in the power of its might, and do you be mingled in it, and may the all-worshipful Trinity too be mingled in it...

Melkite Basil: (the corresponding part of the prayer in *Severus* is an invocation over the candidates; the added words on the epiclesis over the water in *Basil* are italicized) Do you now too, Lord God, *send upon this water by means of this sanctified oil of true unction your dove which is beyond all ages, namely your living and holy Spirit, and bless and sanctify* and perfect *it and* those who are baptized in it, and make them associates of your Christ...

Melkite, Short service: May your Spirit, living and holy, be sent, and may he come and reside and rest and dwell on this water, and sanctify it and make it like the water which flowed from your side on your cross.

In order to illustrate the main developments that lie behind this profusion, it will be best to take a brief look at the most complicated situation of all, that of the consecration prayer in the Syrian Orthodox *Severus* and Melkite *Basil*.[4] The manuscripts and editions of *Severus* provide an invocation to the Holy Spirit in various different places, and this alone is enough to show that they represent later additions: the corresponding Greek text and that of *Basil* know nothing of them, adding instead their own epicleses at yet other points in the prayer. Usually these later epicleses take the form of an added phrase, but in some texts it is as a whole prayer; thus the following prayer, found in some of the Syrian Orthodox services given in Assemani's *Codex Liturgicus* and in the Charfet edition (but not that of Homs), actually has its origin in the Eucharistic liturgy, and has been borrowed from the Anaphora of St. Mark:[5]

Have mercy on us, O God the Father almighty, and send upon us and upon this water that is being consecrated, from your dwelling that is

---

[4] For details, see 'Studies.'
[5] See 'Studies,' pp. 54–6.

prepared, from your infinite womb, the Paraclete, your Holy Spirit, the
established Lord and life-giver, who spoke in the Law and in the prophets and apostles, who everywhere is close at hand, who fills all things;
with authority does he act authoritatively, and not like a minister, with
those whom he wishes, through your good will; who is simple in nature
and many-sided in action; the source of divine gifts; who is consubstantial with you, who proceeds from you, who is equal on the throne of the
kingdom that belongs to you and your only-begotten Son, our Lord and
our God and our Saviour, Jesus Chirst.

This prayer is also employed as an epiclesis in the rite of the Consecration
of the Myron.[6]

If for the moment we ignore all the secondary epicleses in *Severus*, the
original (Greek) prayer of consecration will still be found to contain as
many as three different epicleses.[7]

(i) Look, Lord, upon this your creature, this water, and grant it the grace of
redemption, the blessing of the Jordan...

(ii) But do you, O Lord of all, appoint this water the water of rest... (cp Ps.
23)

(iii) Appear, O Lord, upon this water and grant that those who are baptized
in it may be changed so that they may strip off the old man...

In its present form in our texts the long consecration prayer is addressed to
the Father, and it will seem surprising that these three vestigial epicleses
contain no reference to the Holy Spirit. There are several indications, however, that make it clear that in its original form the prayer of consecration of
the water was addressed, not to the Father, but to Christ.[8] In other words,
Christ, or the Spirit of Christ, was asked to come and 'reactivate' the Jordan
water in the form of the baptismal water of the font: the Spirit of Christ
effects, in sacred time, the identity of the water in the font with the water of
the Jordan, consecrated once and for all at Christ's own baptism.

This address, made directly to Christ, or the Spirit of Christ, conforms
with the practice of the early Church, where we find the liturgical phrase
Marana tha, 'our Lord, come,' quoted both in the New Testament itself (I
Cor. 16:22; Rev. 22:20) and in the *Didache* (10:6). Precisely such an epiclesis,

---

[6] See Simon *I 'Euphémion*, pp. 777 0

[7] See 'Epiklesis,' pp. 186–7.

[8] See 'Epiklesis,' p. 197: the epiclesis is still addressed to Christ in the archaic short Melkite service.

addressed to Christ and asking him to 'come,' exists in a baptismal context in the *Acts of Thomas*:

> Yea, Lord, come, abide on this oil, as you abided on the tree, and they who crucified you were not able to bear your word… (§ 157)

Elsewhere in the archaic baptismal epicleses preserved in the *Acts of Thomas* it is the 'Power of Christ' which is asked to come:

> …come, power of grace…(?§ 27)

or

> May your power come and rest on this baptismal oil… (§ 121)

In the New Testament 'Power' and 'Spirit' are sometimes more or less synonyms, and the actual transition to an epiclesis addressed to the Spirit is also found in the *Acts of Thomas:*

> Come, Spirit of holiness, and purify their reins and hearts…(§27)

As a result of this excursion into the prehistory of the epiclesis, we can see that of the two basic types of epiclesis, 'send your Spirit' and 'may your Spirit come,' the latter is the more archaic, and it is clear on other grounds too that it once predominated in the whole Syrian area, both in the baptismal and in the eucharistic liturgy. It is interesting too that this type of epiclesis was widely known in the early church as an alternative reading for the second clause of the Lord's Prayer: instead of 'May your kingdom come,' the wording 'May your Holy Spirit come upon us and purify us' was also current.

Before we close this introductory historical section, it is worth looking briefly at the other type of epiclesis, 'send your Spirit,' predominant in the West Syriac services, with the exception of the Maronite. This is the wording of all the Greek eucharistic epicleses, apart from that in the Anaphora of St. Basil, and the same applies to the majority of the numerous Syrian Orthodox anaphoras (although at least fifteen of the fifty I have examined use the wording 'come').

An examination of the various epicleses, addressed to the Father, which employ the imperative 'send,' highlights a further distinction; in some epicleses (and this applies to all those of the 'send' type which occur in our baptismal services) the imperative 'send your Spirit' is followed by another imperative ('and sanctify' etc.); in other words, the action is closely linked with the Father, although it is effected by the Spirit. In a second pattern we have 'send your Spirit and *may he* sanctify etc,' giving the Spirit a much more direct role.

The background of the type of epiclesis which requests the Father to
'send' the Spirit would appear to belong to the eucharistic, rather than the
baptismal liturgy, and the biblical antecedents to the phraseology suggest
that its original context was that of the acceptance of a sacrifice: the Spirit is
sent under the symbol of fire to consume the sacrifice.[9] The request made
to Christ, or the Spirit, to *come* and reactivate the Jordan water would thus
appear to belong to the earliest stages of Syrian tradition.

One final point requires notice. A feature found in all the Syriac baptismal services is the pouring on to the water of the holy oil or myron,
shortly after the epiclesis to the Holy Spirit. The myron[10] is of course itself
consecrated, in Syrian Orthodox tradition on another occasion and by the
Patriarch, but there is nothing in any of the baptismal services apart from
the Melkite *Basil* that specifically links the sanctifying activity of the Holy
Spirit with the pouring of the myron. The Melkite service interpolates its
own epiclesis right at the end of the long consecratory prayer common to it,
the Syrian Orthodox and Constantinopolitan rite, at a point where the three
services part company to a considerable extent. The Melkite insertion
comes at a suitable point, for, in common with the Constantinopolitan (but
not Syrian Orthodox) service, mention has just been made of the dove
bearing the olive branch to Noah's Ark[11]

> Giver of all illumination of souls and bodies, Creator of every creature,
> who sent to those who were protected from the Flood in Noah's Ark
> the dove that bore in its beak the branch of olive, which is the symbol
> of reconciliation and of deliverance from the flood, and through them
> you designated for us the type of this hidden grace, and you perfected
> in hidden fashion the mystery of this anointing of the body of your
> holy and only-begotten one and you gave to those who believe in
> you invisible cleansing by means of water and the Spirit, and you
> sanctified the streams of the Jordan. Do you now too, Lord God,
> send upon this water, by means of this consecrated oil of true
> anointing, your dove that is beyond all ages, that is to say, your holy
> and living Spirit, and bless and sanctify and perfect the water and

---

[9] See chapter II. Jacob of Serugh (ed. Bedjan V, p. 8) is interesting in this connection: artificial fire came down from on high, and distinguished between the
two offerings, seeing which was good…the fire *hovered* over the burnt offering that
shot through.'

[10] See above, chapter III, note 15.

[11] See *Studies*, p. 51f. for the dove; compare chapter II (4).

those who are baptized in it, and make them associates of your Christ in this saving laver…

The nearest that one has to this idea of the myron as the means of consecrating the water, outside this prayer, is in the statement by the Syrian Orthodox Moshe bar Kepha to the effect that the myron represents the Holy Spirit hovering over the water.[12]

(b) The imagery of the baptismal water

Behind the many epicleses over the baptismal water lies a rich variety of imagery, focussing on particular aspects of the baptismal mystery, and drawing on different biblical passages in order to express them. As many as eight different sets of reference can be isolated in the various epicleses:

(i)   The Jordan waters are seen as being reactivated in the font.

(ii)   The baptismal water is 'water of rest' (Ps 23:2).

(iii)   Baptism is a representation of the death and resurrection of Christ (Rom. 6:5)

(iv)   Baptism is a type of our own resurrection,

(v)   The baptismal water represents the primeval water (Gen. 1:2).

(v)   The baptismal water represents a spiritual womb (cp John 3:4).

(vii)   The baptismal water is prefigured in the water of the pool of the Bethesda (John 5:4, 7).

(viii) The baptismal water is the water which flows from the side of Christ on the cross (John 19:34).

Let us look at each of these in turn.

(i) The Jordan waters are reactivated in the font

In one of the vestigial epicleses in the Syrian Orthodox *Severus* and Melkite *Basil*, Christ is asked to give the baptismal water the 'blessing of the Jordan,' that is to say the sanctification that the Jordan itself received at Christ's descent into it. The Jordan water and the consecrated water of the font, though separate in historical time, are effectively brought together in sacred time in every baptismal service that takes place; 'Like angels you have gone up from the Jordan, my beloved,' says the author of the Epiphany hymns ascribed to Ephrem (13.2), addressing the newly baptized, and Severus in a homily speaks of the rebirth given by 'the mystical fount of the Jordan.'[13] In East Syriac tradition the font is actually called the 'Jordan.'

Underlying this conception is the understanding, familiar to all Syriac writers, that Christ purified and sanctified the Jordan waters—and potentially all baptismal water—at his own baptism. The earliest writer to express this idea is St Ignatius of Antioch, who in his letter to the Ephesians (18:2) states that 'Christ was baptized in order that by the experience he might *purify* the water.' Later writers often use the word 'sanctify/consecrate' alongside 'purify.' It will be sufficient to give a few quotations to illustrate this widespread view. Addressing the Jordan, Ephrem writes:

> Blessed are your streams which were made clear
> by the descent of the Holy One
> who turned aside and washed in you.
> By his descent at his baptism
> he opened up baptism for the forgiving of sins. (*H. Virg.* 15:3)

And in Hymn 32.5.7. of the same collection we have:

> The river which received him was sanctified.

Jacob of Serugh, in his *memra* on our Lord's baptism, addresses Christ and says[14]

> By your hovering, the entire nature of the water was stirred,[15] since by your baptism you made it worthy to purify all.

In an Epiphany hymn Severus states that Christ was baptized 'so that he might purify and sanctify the water by his own baptism.'[16]

In the baptismal services themselves we find the same idea expressed in several places, such as the following:[17]

> (Christ was baptized, not because he was in need of cleansing), but for the benefit of us who are soiled in sin; he came to sanctify the water by his holy baptism, so that those who are baptized in it in faith should be wrapped in the hidden power and armour of the Spirit...

or[18]

[13] *Hom.* 66 (PO 13, p. 95); cp. *Hom.* 90 (PO 23, p. 140) and 117 (PO 36, p. 66).
[14] Ed. Bedjan 1, p. 188.
[15] For the two terms 'hover' and 'stir,' see below (v) and (vii).
[16] PO 6, pp. 59–60.
[17] U. p. 66.

O Lord, who effected the economy of baptism on earth and who sent your Holy Spirit in the form of a dove upon your only-begotten Son, God the Word, and who sanctified the streams of the Jordan, do you now too be pleased to make your Holy Spirit rest upon your servants who are being baptized…

or again in two beautiful prayers in the Maronite Jacob:[19]

Praise to you, our Lord, who became the Shepherd who gathered us in; you were baptized and purified us, you were a teacher and instructed us, you were called needy, yet you enriched us, seating us at the right hand of your Father. Your mercy bent down, O Lord, your compassion urged you to put on our body and be baptized in the Jordan by John, and to sanctify for us, by your own baptism, this holy baptismal water…

and

To you, the God who is praised in his majesty, who is both hidden in the wealth of his being, and revealed in his miracles, and fearful in the might of his works; to you do we offer prayer and supplication at this time, for you receive the penitent and you work wonders by your might, you cause the weak to approach yourself by means of your own self-abasement towards us; your greatness, O Lord, was willing to save us by your unsparing love, and you sent for our salvation your only-begotten Son and your everlasting Child, who was born of you without a beginning, and he left his hidden abode, descended and dwelt in the virgin's womb, so as to come to the open by means of bodily birth; he remained entirely with you, and he came entirely unto us, and, though he was not wanting or lacking in anything, he was baptized in the river Jordan and sanctified for us the womb of water, to be a womb full of health and power.

The Holy Spirit effects, in the course of the consecration prayer, the coming together, in sacred time, of the baptismal water and the Jordan water, but at Christ's own baptism the Spirit descends *after* Christ has gone up from the Jordan water. It has already been pointed out that the sequence, Christ's baptism followed by the descent of the Spirit, has served as a model in another context, influencing some writers' understanding of the post-baptismal anointing.[20] Here and there a reverse situation can be observed:

---

[18] SH, p. 39. In the present form of the prayer the Father is addressed, but originally it must have been Christ; cp also SH, p. 19.

[19] JS II, pp. 328–9, 337—8 (=D §31).

[20] See chapter III (1) (b) and IV (1).

since in the baptismal service it is the Holy Spirit who sanctifies the water, the Spirit is occasionally given in the same role in descriptions of Christ's own baptism. Thus, in one of the Epiphany hymns attributed to Ephrem, we find:

> The Spirit descended from on high
> and sanctified the water by her hovering *(H. Epiph.* 6.1)

—where the water is evidently the Jordan as well as the baptismal water. Quite explicit are a number of passages in the *Fenqitho*, such as the following:[21]

> Let us give thanks to the Holy Spirit who appeared above the Son at the baptism in the form of a dove and sanctified for us the baptismal water in which our faults and sins are forgiven.

In some heretical circles in the early church it was held that Jesus himself received the Sonship of God and became the Christ, or anointed one, at his baptism, and this is a view against which another passage in the *Fenqitho* polemicizes.[22]

> Who will dare to say, and not tremble, that our Lord received the Holy Spirit when he was baptized in the Jordan?

It was presumably as a result of such abusive views of the Holy Spirit's role at Christ's baptism that we frequently find writers emphasizing that the Spirit appeared there, not to sanctify Christ or the water, but merely to bear witness, and as proof of this the fact that the Spirit only appeared after Christ had gone up from the water is adduced:[23]

> The Holy Spirit stirred and came down on the Only-Begotten
> so that the Father and Spirit should be witnesses at the baptism.
> The Spirit did not come down to sanctify the water for the Holy Son to
>   be baptized in,
> because the sanctification proceeds from him.
> After Christ had washed and gone up from the water
> the Spirit descended, to show who this was, not to sanctify.

---

[21] *Fenqitho* III, p. 284b–5a; similarly John of Apamea, *On baptism* (ed. Rignell) p. 32. Actually as respectable a writer as Aphrahat can say *(Dem.* 21.9 = *PS* I, col. 956) 'at the age of thirty Jesus came to the Jordan to be baptised and *he received the Spirit* and went forth to preach.' Aphrahat in fact just sees the Baptism as the beginning of Jesus' public ministry.

[22] *Fenqitho* III, p. 273a.

[23] Jacob of Serugh (ed. Bedjan) I, p. 159.

Ephrem already makes the same point in his Commentary on the Diatessaron:

> The Spirit who rested on him at his baptism bore witness that he was the Shepherd, for through John he received prophethood and priesthood. (4.3)

We find the same thing in the Maronite *Jacob*, where the deacon states that:[24]

> the Holy Spirit descended (at Christ's baptism) upon him from the uppermost heights, not to sanctify him, but to bear testimony concerning him.

We have already quoted some passages from the baptismal services themselves where direct expression is given to this basic understanding that Christ's own baptism sanctifies the water for Christian baptism. Since, however, this concept is pushed somewhat into the background in the actual consecration prayers, it tends to be preserved chiefly in poetic texts (usually more archaic), among which the following might further be adduced. In the East Syriac service the deacon proclaims,[25]

> It was not that Christ's lucid purity required any baptism in water; rather, it was to sanctify, at his own holy baptism, the waters for us, impure and stained with sin.

Similarly in the Maronite *Jacob*,[26]

> You (Christ) shone forth from the Father and opened up baptism; exalted, you abased yourself and sanctified the water at your baptism.

In the Syrian Orthodox *Severus*, just before the consecration prayer, there is a *qolo* also occurring in the *Fenqitho* at Epiphany.[27]

> John mixed the water of baptism, but Christ sanctified it when he went down and was baptized in it. At the moment he went up from the water, heaven and earth accorded him honour, the sun inclined its rays, the stars worshipped him who had sanctified all rivers and springs.

---

[24] JS II, p. 333.
[25] U, p. 70.
[26] JS II, p. 314.
[27] *Fenqitho* III, p. 259b; SH p. 35.

(ii) The baptismal water becomes the 'water of rest' (Ps. 23:2)

Psalm 23, 'The Lord is my shepherd…,' was frequently given a baptismal interpretation by the early fathers, from Origen onwards:[28] the 'shadow of death' in verse 4 corresponds to the baptismal water seen as the grave (see below, (iii) and (iv)), while the 'table spread' and the 'oil' in verse 5 reflect the Eucharist that culminates the baptismal service, and the baptismal anointing. It is very probable that the description of the baptismal candidates as 'sheep,' regular in all the Syriac traditions, is in part at least influenced by the psalm.[29]

(iii) Baptism is a representation of the death and resurrection of Christ

The third of the archaic epicleses in *Severus* is followed up by allusions to the 'old man' and 'being planted in likeness of the death of Christ,'[30] taken from Romans 6:5–6. In the previous verse Paul states that 'we have been buried in Christ by baptism into death, so that, as Christ was raised from the dead by the glory of the Father, we too might walk in newness of life.'

Curiously little emphasis is given to this Pauline teaching in Syrian tradition, at least until a fairly late date. In the services themselves the water is never described as the 'grave' or the baptized as 'being buried,' perhaps because of the dominance of the image of the font as a womb (see below). Likewise early Syriac writers such as Ephrem and Aphrahat, give little attention to this aspect of baptism. Aphrahat indeed quotes Romans 6:4, but in connection with a tradition, quite widespread in the early Syriac church, that Christ instituted baptism at the washing of the feet before the Last Supper.[31] For the fourth-century writers baptism is primarily to be seen in Johannine terms, as a rebirth (John 3:3), and not as a death followed by resurrection (Romans 6). Such an outlook has its parallel in the use to which they put the imagery of the 'robe of glory': whereas Greek writers liked to speculate what garment was first stripped off, Syriac ones are almost exclusively interested in the robe that is put on.

---

[28] See 'Epiklesis' p. 207; in later Syriac writers Jacob of Serugh, for example, calls baptism 'the restful water' (ed. Bedjan IV, p. 902).

[29] Another important biblical passage will be Matt. 25:33.

[30] Displaced in the Homs edition; see 'Consecration,' p. 325 ('notes to 1') and 'Studies,' pp. 26–7.

[31] Aphrahat, *Dem.* 12.10 (*PS* I, col. 529); cp E. J. Duncan, *Baptism in the Demonstrations of Aphraates* (Washington, 1945), pp. 67–71.

In contrast to this native Syriac lack of interest in the Pauline teaching, Theodore, in his *Catechetical Homilies*, lays considerable emphasis on Romans 6, although it should be stated that his main interest is in Christ's ensuing resurrection serving as a pledge of our own resurrection, a slant that we shall shortly meet, in the next section.

Both Jacob of Serugh and Narsai speak of the 'grave of the water.' In it, Narsai says 'the priest buries the whole man' and 'resuscitates him by the saving power concealed in his words' (i.e. the baptismal formula).[32] Jacob has a very similar passage in his homily on our Lord's baptism:[33]

> (Christ speaks) I bring men down to the grave of the water so that I may make them immortal at the resurrection.

Later writers associate the threefold immersion at baptism with the three days Christ spent in the grave. Severus tells his congregation:[34]

> You bury the old man in the baptismal water; for this reason by means of the threefold immersion we indicate the three day burial and ensuing resurrection.

This is a point already made in Pseudo-Dionysius' *Ecclesiastical Hierarchy*,[35] and it is taken up in most of the later Syriac commentators.[36]

(iv) Baptism as a type of our own resurrection

This extension seems to be the prime interest of Theodore when he quotes Romans 6:3–4.[37]

> For we know that death has already been dissolved by our Lord Jesus Christ. In this faith, then, do we approach and receive baptism, for we desire henceforward to be associated in his death, in the hope that by the same means we may participate in the resurrection from the dead, in that he too rose.

---

[32] Ed. Mingana I, p. 345 (ET p. 51).

[33] Ed. Bedjan I, p. 181.

[34] *Hom.* 90 (*PO* 23, p. 160).

[35] *PG* 3, col. 404.

[36] E.g. Moshe bar Kepha § 14.

[37] *Hom.* 14.5 (ed. Tonneau, p. 412/3); a little later in the paragraph he says 'by the ascent from the water I consider that I have already, in type, risen from the dead.' Cp also pp. 155, 333, 429; *Comm. John* (ed. Vosté), pp. 66–7, 79, 215, 320; Cyrus of Edessa (ed. Macomber), p. 8.

Precisely this idea features in the consecration prayer of the East Syriac service, with a further shift backwards, from Christ's death to his baptism.[38]

> ...our Lord Jesus Christ who, by the type of his baptism, signified the resurrection from the dead, and commanded us that in the mystery of his baptism we should make a new and spiritual birth for those that believe.

Two passages earlier in the service reflect the same interest; in the first the eschatological concern is very clear.[39]

> ...Christ approached baptism in the River Jordan that was mediated by John the herald; he showed forth and depicted as though in an image that by means of his holy baptism true resurrection and real renewal is given to us at the end of this world.

The same view point is taken up again in an 'onitha [40]

> Your baptism with water, O Christ, has sanctified our souls and proclaimed our resurrection.

In the later commentators the ascent from the font is seen as a symbol of the resurrection of both Christ and the Christian; as Dionysius bar Salibi puts it:[41]

> The ascent from the font signifies three things: first, the ascent and resurrection of Jesus from the grave; second, that we shall have an ascent and resurrection from the grave at the last day; and third, that we shall have an ascent above the heavens if we preserve baptism undefiled.

(v) The baptismal water represents the primordial water

In the consecration prayer of the Maronite service the activity of the Holy Spirit over the baptismal water is paralleled with that of the 'Spirit of God' over the primordial waters in Gen. 1:2:[42]

> As the Holy Spirit hovered over the waters at the establishment of creation, so may your Holy Spirit, O Lord, hover over this baptismal water which is a spiritual womb, and may he rest upon it and sanctify it and make it fruitful with the heavenly Adam, in place of the earthly Adam.

---

[38] U, p. 70.
[39] U, p. 58.
[40] U, p. 66.
[41] Dionysius bar Salibi, Comm. Bapt. § 9.
[42] JS II, pp. 339–40 = D § 36.

The same parallelism is made in one of the Epiphany hymns attributed to Ephrem:

> At creation the Spirit hovered over the waters.
> they conceived and gave birth to reptiles, fishes and birds;
> the Holy Spirit hovered over the baptismal water
> and it gave birth to symbolic eagles—the virgins and leaders,
> and to symbolic fishes—the chaste and the intercessors,
> and to symbolic reptiles
> — the cunning who have become as simple as doves (cp Matt. 10:16)
>
> (*H. Epiph.* 8.15)

Aphrahat has the same thing in mind:[43]

> At that moment when the priest invokes the Spirit, she opens the heavens, descends and hovers over the water, and those who are baptized put her on.

Modern scholars are divided between those who take the *ruah elohim* of Gen. 1:2 as a 'divine Spirit' and those who prefer to translate 'a mighty wind,' giving a purely elative sense to *elohim*. Curiously enough, exactly the same sort of division of opinion was to be found in the Syriac fathers, some of whom took the *ruah* or *ruha* to be the Holy Spirit, while others saw it simply as the wind.[44] The former view was taken by most Syrian Orthodox writers, while the latter became the traditional East Syriac exegesis, based probably on Theodore of Mopsuestia's *Commentary on Genesis* (although the same view is also found earlier, in Ephrem's *Commentary on Genesis*, as well).[45]

It is interesting that the epiclesis proper in the Maronite service actually drops all reference to the parallelism, adopting instead the motif of the water and blood from the side of Christ (see below); it might be suggested that the typological parallel with Gen. 1:2, which had clearly once been popular, was deliberately dropped in most circles, due to the domination of the Antiochene exegesis of the passage, and as a result of this the idea has only survived here and there in the texts on baptism.[46] The situation in Nar-

---

[43] *Dem.* 6.14 (*PS* I, col. 291/4).

[44] Cp T. Jansma, 'Some remarks on the Syro-hexaplaric reading of Gen. 1,2,' *Vetus Testamentum* 20 (1970), pp. 16–24. See also *Fire from Heaven*, chapter XIV.

[45] Cp *H. Haer.* 50.8. This interpretation was adopted by a few West Syriac writers (notably Jacob of Serugh in his homilies on Creation: Jacob had been trained at the Persian School).

[46] See below.

sai's commentary on the baptismal service is intriguing in this connection, for on two occasions he does mention the primordial waters as a parallel to the baptismal water, but significantly all reference to the Spirit is dropped:[47]

> The priest imitates the fashion of him who brought the world into being, and he makes heard a voice similar to that which cried out in the world at the beginning. Like the Creator, he too commands the ordinary water, and instead of light there shines out from it the power of life... The Creator's word which the primordial waters heard and then brought forth creeping things, this the baptismal waters hear from the mouth of the priest, and they bring forth men.

Since Narsai knows an epiclesis of the Spirit at the consecration of the baptismal water, the absence of all reference to the Spirit here is remarkable and it indicates that he is utilizing a piece of traditional catechesis which originally brought out the role of the Spirit at creation, but has suppressed this reference under the influence of Theodore's exegesis.

Even in places where Theodore's exegesis has been adopted, other traces of the older interpretation are frequently left in the phraseology employed for the Spirit's activity. In Gen. 1:2 the Spirit 'hovers (*mrahhfa*) over the water, and as a result of this passage the verb *rahhef* early became a technical term for the Spirit's activity; thus Ephrem, who in his *Commentary on Genesis* did not take the Spirit of Gen. 1:2 to be the Holy Spirit, nevertheless in his *Hymns on Virginity* (and elsewhere) speaks of

> The Holy Spirit hovers over the streams (of the baptismal water)

> (*H. Virg.* 7.8.2)[48]

Likewise Jacob of Serugh, who was educated at the School of Edessa, follows Theodore's exegesis of Gen. 1:2 in his *memre* on Creation, but elsewhere frequently employs *rahhef* and its derivatives in connection with baptism.[49]

It was no doubt because of this use of *rahhef* as a technical term of the Spirit's activity that East Syriac writers like Narsai prefer the passive verb of the Septuagint at Gen. 1:2, *epefereto* 'was carried,' which they took over from Theodore.

---

[47] Ed. Mingana I, pp. 344–5 (ET pp. 49–50); cp I, p. 341 (ET p. 46).
[48] Cp *H. Fid.* 18.16.2; 38.12.2; 51.7.6; 77.22.1 etc.
[49] Ed. Bedjan I, p. 173 and often.

In the baptismal services the term *raḥḥef* significantly occurs only in the West Syriac services; thus in some texts of *Severus* the deacon says at the epiclesis:[50]

> How fearful is this hour…when the living and holy Spirit circles down from the uppermost heights and hovers and dwells on the water, sanctifying it, just as the Jordan's streams were sanctified.

The post-communion prayer in *Timothy* opens with the words:[51]

> The power of God which has overshadowed you, and the Holy Spirit who has hovered over your bodies, be with you…

The significance of the reminiscences here of the wording of the Annunciation (Luke 1:35) will be considered later (chapter VII).

It is, however, in the Maronite service that we find the term *raḥḥef* used most freely, for outside the consecration prayer already quoted it occurs in two further passages in conjunction with exorcism.[52]

Among later writers who explicitly make the parallel between Gen, 1:2 and the baptismal water, we may quote John of Dara, who says[53]

> 'The Spirit of God hovering over the face of the water': so it is also he who descends on the holy font, and through him all who are baptized have life.

As a bye-product of the parallelism between the Spirit of Gen. 1:2 and the Holy Spirit at baptism mention should be made of the association of the baptismal water with the primordial abyss, or *thoma*, which features at the beginning of the long consecration prayer in *Severus* and *Basil*.[54]

> O Lord God almighty, creator of all creation, both visible and invisible, who made the heaven and the earth, the water, and all that is in them, who gathered the water into a single mass and the dry land appeared, who bound the abyss (*thoma*) and who confines it, who separated the water that is above the heaven; you established through your might the sea, you are to be feared, and who can withstand you? Do you look upon this your creation, upon this water, and grant it the grace of your salvation, the blessing of the river Jordan, the holiness of the Spirit…

---

[50] Assemani II, p. 292 (SA I).

[51] T § 53.

[52] JS II, pp. 325, 326.

[53] *De Oblatione* III. 4w (ed. Sader, p. 58).

[54] The abyss is also mentioned in the exorcisms in *Severus*. Cp in general, P. Lundberg, *La typologie baptismale dans l'ancienne église* (Uppsala, 1942), p. 68.

In this passage, as elsewhere in the services, baptism is understood as a new creation: the baptized is a new creature. It is easy to see how this imagery merges into the Adam typology, so prominent in the metaphor of the 'robe of glory,' and elsewhere. There is a further link, too, between the new creation of baptism and the creation of Adam, and this is provided by Gen. 2:7, 'The Lord God breathed into his nostrils the breath (*mappuhita*) of life.' An allusion to this passage is obvious in the following words, by Jacob of Serugh:[55]

> Instead of a soul, the Holy Spirit is breathed (*metnafha*) into the newly baptized.

The verb is also used in John 20:22, and this passage provides the prime reference for a prayer in the Syrian Orthodox *Severus*:[56]

> Grant them, Lord, your holy breath (*mappuhita*) which your Only-Begotten Son breathed into his disciples...

(vi) *The baptismal water represents a spiritual womb*

One of the two epicleses over the baptismal water in *Timothy* prays:[57]

> We request you, Father of mercy and God of all comfort, send your living Spirit and sanctify this water, and may it become the spiritual womb which gives rebirth anew to mankind who are baptized in it.

The origin of this very popular motif is to be found in John 3:4, where Nicodemus asks 'can a man enter his mother's womb a second time and be born again?' It is almost always the Holy Spirit who activates this 'womb' of water,[58] as can be seen, for example, in a prayer common to the Syrian Orthodox and Maronite services:[59]

---

[55] Ed. Bedjan, I, p. 162.
[56] Prayer before consignation in position I (SH, p. 25).
[57] T § 33.
[58] Rare exceptions are to be found where Christ does this at his baptism: thus in JS II, p. 338 = D § 31 we have 'Christ sanctified this womb of baptism for us,' and in the Chaldean Breviary at Epiphany (I, p. 421), 'At your baptism, O Saviour, the springs of water were sanctified and became a spiritual womb for our race .' (Curiously enough the imagery of the womb is absent from the Syrian Orthodox *Fenqitho* at Epiphany). See also note 65.
[59] Introducing the Our Father in S; JS III, p. 185; T § 43. For the various positions, see 'Studies,' p. 63.

Blessed are you, Lord God, through whose great and indescribable gift this water has been sanctified by the coming of your Holy Spirit so that it has become the womb of the Spirit that gives birth to the new man out of the old.

Very similar wording is found in the East Syriac service, where the oil is the medium through which the Spirit works:[60]

This water is signed with holy oil to become a new womb that gives birth spiritually…

This is actually one of the few places where the imagery occurs in the East Syriac rite which prefers, as we have seen, the Pauline themes of Romans 6. In the West Syriac services, however, this sort of phraseology is common.

The imagery of the baptismal womb is already well known to Ephrem, and it is in his poetry that we first come across the phrase 'womb of water,'[61] later to become a commonplace alongside 'womb of the font.'[62] Even Theodore, with his stress on Romans 6, uses the imagery in connection with the baptismal epiclesis:[63]

(the priest asks) that the grace of the Holy Spirit come upon the water and make it…a womb of sacramental rebirth.

The wording is interestingly somewhat reminiscent of *Timothy*, quoted above. The baptismal womb is sometimes contrasted with that of Eve:[64]

Instead of the womb of Eve which produced children who are mortal and corruptible, may this womb of water produce children who are heavenly, spiritual and immortal.

Very similar wording is used by Jacob of Serugh:[65]

Christ came and opened up baptism on his cross (John 19:34) so that it might be a 'mother of life' in place of Eve.

---

[60] U, p. 70 (immediately after the epiclesis).

[61] *H. Crucif.* 3.7.4.

[62] E.g. Narsai (ed. Mingana) I, p. 358; Jacob of Serugh (ed. Bedjan) I, p. 168; John of Apamea (ed. Rignell), p. 21* etc.

[63] *Hom.* 14.9 (ed. Tonneau, p. 420/1). Theodore goes on immediately to quote John 3 :5.

[64] T § 35 = JS II, pp. 339–40.

[65] Ed. Bedjan, I, p. 162. Elsewhere Jacob says the baptismal womb was already sanctified by Christ's baptism; '(the Jordan water) embraced him so that its womb might be sanctified by him' (Bedjan I, p. 174). Cp also note 58.

Besides these references to Eve's womb we also find a straightforward parallelism between Mary's womb and the womb of the Jordan brought out in a prayer in the Maronite *Jacob* and anonymous Syrian Orthodox service in Add. 14518:[66]

> Christ came down and dwelt in the womb of the virgin, to become bodily manifest in birth; while remaining entirely with you, he came entirely to us, and though he had no need and lacked nothing, he was baptized in the river Jordan, and so sanctified for us the womb of water, to be a womb that gives health and strength.

The connotations of the links with Mary will be brought out in chapter VII.

This sort of imagery readily lends itself to further developments: the font takes on the role of 'mother,' or even furnace.[5] 'Mother' is found in the baptismal services themselves only rarely; in the Maronite rite the font is described as 'a new mother, a spiritual mother giving birth to spiritual children who enter the bridal chamber of life filled with joys,'[67] while in a response to be found in some texts of *Severus* we have.[68]

> O Christ God, who at his baptism sanctified for us the baptismal water,
> the mother who gives birth to spiritual children...

The patriarch Severus himself, in one of his hymns,[69] also describes the font as 'the new and spiritual mother who gave birth spiritually, from her womb, to the people of the Christians,' while in Jacob of Serugh it is 'the mother who daily gives birth to immortals.'[70]

The *Fenqitho*, which surprisingly has no specific womb imagery at Epiphany, does speak of Christ as having 'sanctified the font for us, as a mother who gives birth to spiritual children for the kingdom of high.'[71]

In a Syrian Orthodox prayer the 'womb of the font' is further linked with the idea of a furnace:[72]

> Mix, O Lord, into this water, the power and working of your Holy Spirit so that it may become a spiritual womb and a furnace that pours out incorruptibility.

---

[66] JS II, p. 338 = D § 31.

[67] JS II, p. 333.

[68] In Assemani II, p. 263 (lower text, = SA II).

[69] *Hymn* 90 (*PO* 6, p. 131.)

[70] Ed. Bedjan, I, p. 194.

[71] *Fenqitho* III, p. 279b.

[72] SH p. 31; likewise in the *sedro* on p. 19.

The Syrian Orthodox service is in fact the only one to make use of this image, but it is popular with both East and West Syriac writers outside the services themselves; no doubt the concept of the Spirit as fire, who set the Jordan waters aflame, helped to suggest it. In the Epiphany hymns attributed to Ephrem the 'womb of flame' (i.e. baptism) is compared with the Fiery Furnace of Dan. 3:91–2,[73] and the same reference is to be found in the *Fenqitho* at Epiphany.[74] Dionysius bar Salibi also makes use of the same combination of images in his commentary on the baptismal service:[75]

> In the midst of the water there dwells a hidden fire which burns up sins while preserving the features of the body—just as iron is preserved unharmed in fire, while its rust in purged away. You should be convinced of this by the fire of the Babylonians which consumed the bonds but left behind the hair, as a symbol of baptism which consumes sins, but preserves the body.

More frequently, however, the furnace imagery is used in connection with metallurgical language, as in the prayer from *Severus*, quoted above. Narsai is particularly fond of this imagery, using it on several occasions in his two homilies on baptism:[76]

> He recast our image in baptism as in a furnace;

or[77]

> The furnace of the waters did his purpose prepare mystically,
> instead of with fire he heated it with the Spirit of the power of his will,
> He made his own handiwork into a craftsman for his creation
> so that it should recast itself in the furnace of water and the heat of the
> Spirit.

The Spirit is the source of the heat in this furnace, as Narsai brings out in another passage too:[78]

---

[73] *H. Epiph.* 8. 6; cp Dionysius b. Salibi, *Comm. Bapt.* § 4, where baptism burns off sin as the furnace burnt off the fetters of the three young men.

[74] *Fenqitho* III, pp. 254b, 282b (in neither place, however, is the Jordan water itself described as a furnace).

[75] § 4.

[76] Ed. Mingana I. p. 356 (ET p. 33); cp also John of Apamea (ed. Rignell), p. 20*.

[77] Ed. Mingana I, p. 364 (ET p. 41.)

[78] Ed. Mingana I, p. 343 (ET p. 48–9).

> The drug of the Spirit he casts into the water as into a furnace, and he
>   purifies the image of men from uncleanness.
> By the heat of the Spirit he purges the rust of both body and soul.

The 'recasting of the spoiled image' is also found in the East Syriac Breviary
at Epiphany:[79]

> He who is good saw his image made ugly by sin; he recast it in the fur-
> nace of the water and scoured off its ugliness, plating its shape with the
> gold of the Holy Spirit.

We may conclude with a passage from Jacob of Serugh where he introduces
yet a further element into this phraseology, that of the stamp, or die, that reforms the 'image':[80]

> (Christ speaks): Though I need nothing, I enter the furnace of the water
> so that men who have grown old may be recaste with that stamp of
>   mine.

As we shall see, the stamp has been borrowed from quite a different context, that of the oil at the anointing.

(vii) *The baptismal water is prefigured in the water of the pool of Be-thesda*

The pool of Bethesda, *kolymbethra* in 'Greek *ma'muditha* in Syriac, is quite
often found as a type for baptism in early Christian writers in Greek and
Latin,[81] and this episode lies behind the wording in the epiclesis of the
shortest of the Syrian Orthodox services, attributed to Philoxenus:[82]

> Shine forth, O Lord, on this water, and may your Holy Spirit stir it with
> the power of his might; and may your Trinity, worshipped by all, be
> mingled in it, your Trinity which gives birth to spiritual beings and pro-
> duces new children, O Father Son and Holy Spirit, for eternal ages,
> amen.

---

[79] *Brev. Chald.* I, p. 411.

[80] Ed. Bedjan I, p. 181 (cp 197).

[81] E.g. Tertullian, *On Baptism* V. 5; Ambrose, *On the Mysteries* IV. 22; Didymus,
On the Trinity II. 14. In a 6th cent. Peshitta Gospel manuscript (Pierpont Morgan ms
783 f. 68b) John 5 is given as the lection for baptism.

[82] Assemani II, p. 308.

The allusion to John 5:7 is provided by the word 'stir,' and there are parallels for such an allusion in this context in both Latin and Ethiopic baptismal texts.

The one Syriac writer who makes special use of John 5 as a baptismal type is Jacob of Serugh, in his homily on the healing of the paralytic in the pool of Bethesda. The following passages are worth quoting fairly extensively:[83]

> Because he could not gain life (*or* salvation) from the Law,
> mercy had compassion on him so that his very birth was altered;
> he entered the moist womb of the pool (*ma'mudita*)
> and came forth clean, in a spiritual second birth.
> The Son of the God has descended and stirred the baptismal water
>   (*ma'mudita*),
> so that it might give healing birth to all kinds of beautiful creatures each
>   day,
> a new creation has begun, having come from our Lord,
> a new world which does not become corrupted, as did the former.

and a little later on,[84]

> Your Child shall cause his power to overshadow the fountains,
> and see, the infirm world is healed of its sickness...
> That mighty one, who was born of you (the Father) in a divine way,
> will stir the fountain so that the whole world may be healed by it...
> Urged by Grace the Father sent his Son
> who came down and trod out the great path of baptism;
> he caused his Shekhina to reside upon fountains and rivers,
> so that all water might receive the power to be healed;
> he opened up at his baptism the great gate to forgiveness.

In *Philoxenus* it is the Spirit of Christ who stirs the baptismal water (the epiclesis is addressed to Christ, rather than to the Father). In many Latin liturgical texts of the West it is the 'angel of holiness,' while for Jacob it is Christ himself.

(viii) The baptismal water is the water which flows from the side of Christ

What is basically the same epiclesis is found in four different West Syriac services, *Jacob*, *Timothy*, Add. 14518, and the short Melkite service; in the

---

[83] Ed. Bedjan IV, p. 702. Cp also *H. Epiph.* 7.22.
[84] Ed. Bedjan IV p. 707.

last, Christ himself is addressed, while in the others it is the Father, following the later norm. In accordance with the archaic Syrian pattern, request is made that the Spirit 'come and reside and rest (cp Isaiah 11:2) and dwell upon the water and make it in the likeness of the water which flowed from your side on your cross' (John 19:34).[85]

This frame of reference, centred on John 19:34 is a particularly suitable one with which to conclude this section, for the lance and the pierced side of Christ have gained for Syriac writers perhaps richer connotations than any other single verse in the whole bible. It serves both as the hall-mark, and at the same time, the focal point of Syriac typological interpretation in general, and in particular, along with Christ's baptism, his pierced side provides the second main source of the sacrament of baptism.

A number of points require elucidation if we are to appreciate the amazingly rich overtones that this baptismal epiclesis carries.

First we need to pay attention to some details of wording. In the original biblical text, it is 'blood and water' which 'come forth' from the pierced side of Christ. Because the blood and water were taken as symbols of baptism and the eucharist[86] from a very early date, there is always a strong tendency on the part of writers to quote them in the reverse order, giving the sequence 'water-blood,' more logical for such a sacramental interpretation of the verse. Another small, but significant, alteration to the wording that is frequently found is the substitution of 'flowed' for 'came forth.' The purpose of this alteration was to link John 19:34 with John 7:37–38. This latter passage was taken in two different senses by early Christian writers, depending on the way in which the verses are punctuated. What has now become the traditional way of taking the verses is: 'If anyone thirst, let him come to me and drink. He who believes in me, as the scripture has said, 'Out of his belly shall flow living water.'' Here the 'belly' is that of the believer: this is the effect that the coming of the Spirit has on him (cf verse 39). The other

---

[85] For the sequence 'come, reside and rest,' compare 'come, rest and reside' in the *Acts of John* (ed. Wright, p. 58). The texts of the three epicleses are set out together in my 'A short Melkite baptismal service in Syriac,' *Parole de l'Orient* 3 (1972), pp. 119–30.

[86] As a typical example of this interpretation we may take Philoxenus' *Letter to the monks of Senun* (ed. de Halleux, p. 6); 'It is written that from Christ's side 'there came forth blood and water'—baptism and the saving blood: by 'water' baptism was indicated, by 'blood' the holy mysteries, which purify us from sin when we partake of them continually.'

way of dividing the phrases understands the 'belly' as Christ's:[87] 'If anyone thirsts, let everyone who believes in me come to me and drink: as the scripture has said, 'Out of his belly shall flow rivers of living water.''

It is in order to link John 19:34 with this Christological interpretation of John 7:37–38 (known to several early Greek and Syriac fathers) that the verb 'go forth' in 19:34 has been altered to 'flow' in many quotations of that verse. It is characteristic of the essentially undogmatic nature of typology that Ephrem and Aphrahat make use of both interpretations: they are both valid in that they both convey deep spiritual meaning.

All symbols and types point to Christ and the piercing of his side serves as the focal point, the pivot, between the Old and the New Covenants.[88] Within this single verse there are four main starting points for typological interpretation:

(1) the side
(2) the blood and water
(3) the lance
(4) the action of piercing.

Just as there is a certain freedom in the wording used for the 'blood and water which came forth,' so there is considerable flexibility in the use of the words for 'side,' 'lance' and 'pierce,' in order to highlight the typological associations.[89]

What are these associations? The one which we come across most frequently in early Syriac literature is the contrast with Gen. 3:24, 'He cast him out, and to the east of the Garden of Eden he stationed the cherubim and a sword whirling and flashing to guard the way to the tree of life.' Ephrem explains the typological connection in the following words:

> Blessed is the Merciful one who saw the lance
> beside Paradise barring the way
> to the Tree of Life; and he came and took for himself
> a body which was wounded so that, by the opening of his side,
> he might open up the way into Paradise. (H. Nativ. 8.4)

---

[87] Cp 'Epiklesis,' p. 211; Murray, Symbols, p. 213.

[88] Cp R. Murray, 'The lance which reopened Paradise: a mysterious reading in the early Syriac fathers,' OCP 39 (1973), pp. 224–34, 491, and my 'The mysteries hidden in the side of Christ,' Sobornost VII. 6 (1978), pp. 462–72.

[89] The Old Syriac is unfortunately missing for John 19:34. The Peshitta uses lukita for the weapon, 'lance,' dapna 'side' and mha 'strike.' It is likely that the Old Syriac used rumha 'sword' (cp Gen. 3:24) and setra 'side.'

The 'opening up' of Christ's side with the lance removes the flaming and revolving weapon of the cherubim which excludes mankind from the Garden of Eden. The effects of the Fall are reversed, and mankind can once again approach the Tree of Life (which here also points forward to the Eucharist.)

A slightly different, and more specifically baptismal slant, is given to the typology by Ephrem in another passage; speaking of the piercing of Christ's side he says:

> There went forth from it water and blood;
> Adam washed, was given life, and returned to Paradise.
>
> (*H. Nisib.* 39.7)

How the piercing of Christ's side provides Adam's 'baptism' is given a rather quaint and literalistic explanation in the anonymous *Cave of Treasures*.[90]

> The blood and water flowed from the side of Christ and came down into the mouth of Adam (buried immediately below the cross on Golgotha) and they constituted for him the baptismal water, and he was baptized.

Another typological pattern, which has profound and far-reaching consequences, is the contrast drawn between Christ's side and Adam's side: the first Adam gives birth, from his side, to Eve, through whom sin enters the world; the second Adam, Christ, gives birth from his side to the sacraments which wipe out sin's 'document' (Col. 2:14.) This contrast between the 'sides' of the two Adams is notably brought out by Jacob of Serugh in his famous homily on the veil of Moses:[91]

> The groom's side has been pierced, and from it the bride has come out,
> fulfilling the type provided by Adam and Eve;
> for from the first he knew and depicted
> Adam and Eve in the likeness of the image of his Only-begotten:
> he slept on the cross as Adam had slept his deep sleep,
> his side was pierced and from it there came forth the Daughter of Light
> —water and blood as an image of divine children
> to be heirs to the Father who loves his Only-Begotten.
> Eve in prophecy is the mother of all that lives—

---

[90] Ed. Bezold, p. 263. That Adam's body was buried on the Temple site is well known from Jewish tradition; Christian tradition from Origen onwards transfers the site to Golgotha.

[91] Ed. Bedjan III, pp. 299–300.

what, if not baptism, is the mother of life?
Adam's wife bore human bodies subject to death,
but this virgin bears living beings who are spiritual.
Adam's side gave birth to a woman who gives birth to mortals,
while our Lord's to the Church who gives birth to immortals.

The typology is already familiar to Ephrem, who uses it, for example in his *Commentary on the Diatessaron*:

'There came forth blood and water': that is, his Church, which is built on his 'side.' Just as in the case of Adam, his wife was taken from his side. Adam's wife is his 'rib,' so our Lord's 'blood' is his Church. From Adam's rib issued death, from our Lord's rib life.

(Comm. Diat. 21.11)

Typology involving Adam:Eve and Christ:the Church/sacraments inevitably introduces Mary, the new Eve who miraculously gives birth to the second Adam, thus reversing the effect of the (equally miraculous) birth of Eve from the first Adam. Ephrem expresses this in two tightly packed stanzas in the first of his Nativity Hymns:

Adam brought travail upon the woman who sprang from him,
but today Mary, who bore him a Saviour, has redeemed that travail.
Adam, the man who himself knew no birth, bore Eve the mother:
how much more should Eve's daughter Mary be believed
to have given birth without the aid of a man.

(H. Nativ. 1.14–15)

Jacob of Serugh makes the same point, in a more straightforward way:[92]

As our father Adam begot our mother without intercourse,
so did Mary give birth, just as Adam did before he had sinned.
The Holy Spirit blowed upon Adam's face,
and he gave birth to Eve: this Spirit did Mary too receive,
and she gave birth to a son.
Adam gave birth to the 'mother of all living beings' without intercourse,
   so depicting the birth of our Lord, who is the fountain of all life.

In this intricate typological web we can see how Mary and the Church play very similar roles; thus Jacob can take a further step and say:[93]

Through Mary the path to Eden, that had been shut, was trod again,

---

[92] Ed. Bedjan, S, p. 634. Cp chapter VII, where the passage is quoted again.
[93] Ed. Bedjan, S, p. 637.

the serpent fled, and men could pass over to God.
Through Mary the cherub turned aside his sword,
to guard no more the Tree of Life (i.e. Christ),
which had now given itself over to be eaten.

In other words, Christ's 'giving birth' to the sacraments (John 19:34), which
effects the reentry into Paradise, is anticipated here by Mary's giving birth to
Christ.

Jacob's rather bold interpretation is actually based on a very individual
understanding of Simeon's words to Mary in Luke 2:35. The normal text of
this verse reads 'a sword shall pass through your soul,' but from Ephrem's
Commentary on the Diatessaron, it would appear that Tatian's Diatessaron
treated the sword as object of the verb and Mary as subject: 'you shall cause
the sword to pass...' Thus in his *Commentary* Ephrem writes:

> Simeon also said 'You shall cause the sword to pass':—the sword which
> guarded Paradise as a result of Eve's action was removed by Mary.

> *(Comm. Diat.* 2.17)

We may draw together the various strands of this extended discussion
by considering the more specifically baptismal interpretation given to John
19:34. In one of the Epiphany hymns we find the baptismal water called
'the fountain which flowed from the side of the Son of God.'[94] No Syriac
writer, however, is closer in feeling to our four baptismal epicleses than
Jacob of Serugh:[95]

> Christ came and opened up baptism by his cross
> so that it might be a mother of life for the world in place of Eve;
> water and blood for the fashioning of spiritual babes
> flowed forth for it, and baptism became the mother of life.
> No previous baptism (i.e. of Moses or John) ever gave the Holy Spirit,
> only the baptism which was opened up by the Son of God on the cross;
> it gives birth to children spiritually with 'the water and the blood,'
> and instead of a soul, the Holy Spirit is breathed into them.

---

[94] *H. Epiph.* 13.13. In passing it is worth noting the absence of allusions to
John 19:34 in Theodore and Narsai.
[95] Ed. Bedjan I, p. 162.

We can now see how intimately linked with the epiclesis is the immediately preceding part of the consecratory prayer to be found in all these services, apart from the short Melkite one:[96]

> Instead of the womb of Eve which produced children who were mortal and corruptible, may this womb of water produce children who are heavenly, spiritual and immortal, and as the Holy Spirit hovered over the water at the establishment of created things, do you, Lord, be present in this baptismal water, which is the spiritual womb that gives birth to spiritual beings; and may it produce, instead of Adam, made of dust, the heavenly Adam, and may those who are baptized in it receive in you lasting changes that will not be made ineffective: instead of corporality, spirituality; instead of visibleness, communion with the invisible, and instead of the weak soul, your Holy Spirit.

By opening up baptism and the eucharist, the lance of John 19:34 effects our own reentry into Paradise at baptism, as Ephrem points out:[97]

> To the gentiles the Lord of the Tree
> has given himself as Life. By the point of the sword was barred
> the way to the Tree of Life; as the trees of Eden were given
> to Adam the First for food, for us its very Planter
> has become food for our souls. As we left Paradise with Adam,
> who from Paradise had to depart, now that the lance is removed,
> through the lance let us gird ourselves and go hence.

Something of the depth of meaning that the verse contained for Ephrem can be seen from the following lyrical passage, taken from his *Commentary on the Diatessaron*:

> I ran to all your limbs, and from them all I received every kind of gift. Through the side pierced with the sword I entered the garden fenced in with the sword. Let us enter in through the side that was transfixed, for we were stripped naked by the counsel of the rib that was extracted. For the fire that burnt in Adam, burnt him in that rib of his. For this reason the side of the second Adam has been pierced, and from it comes a flow of water to quench the fire of the first Adam. (*Comm. Diat.* 21.10)

Ephrem's introduction of burning imagery has an interesting parallel in a prayer common to the Syrian Orthodox *Timothy* and Maronite *Jacob*.[98]

---

[96] JS II, pp. 338–9 = D § 36: abbreviated in T § 35 (but keeping the reference to Eve).

[97] Armenian hymns no 49 (translation by R. Murray).

[98] T § 27, JS II, pp. 334–5.

Towards you, O God of Abraham and of Isaac and of Israel, are the
eyes of our mind raised up and the hands of our heart stretched out; and
like the stag that yearns for the spring of water (Ps. 42:1), so do our
souls, Lord, yearn for you, so that living and spiritual water may flow for
us from the fountain on high, and so through it our thirst that results
from the burning of sin may be assuaged...

The eschatological dimensions of John 19:34 are brought out in a remarkable way in one of the *Hymns on Virginity*; in contrast to the bitterness
with which Christ's crucifiers are usually regarded, Ephrem here links
Christ's own words, asking for their forgiveness, with this verse:

> They pierced you with the lance, and water gushed forth
> as though meant to wipe away their sins.
> There came forth water, and blood too, to inspire awe in them,
> so that they might be able to wash their hands of your blood.
> The slain one gave water to his slayers,
> so that through his blood they might be cleansed and have life.

(H. Virg. 30.10)

(2) The invocation over the oil

(a) Introductory

An epiclesis over the oil is found only in the East Syriac, Melkite and Maronite services, but it is clearly an ancient feature, since it also finds a place
in the *Acts of Thomas* and in the service described by Narsai. In two of the
accounts of baptism in the *Acts of Thomas* Judas Thomas takes oil and utters
the following prayers over it.

> §121 Holy Oil, which was given to us for unction, and hidden mystery
> of the Cross, which is seen through it; you are the straightener of
> crooked limbs, our Lord Jesus, life and health and forgiveness of
> sins; may your power come and dwell upon this oil and may your
> holiness reside in it.

> §157 Fair fruit that is worthy to become glowing with the word of
> holiness, so that men may put you on and conquer through you
> their enemies, once they have been cleansed of their former works;
> yea, Lord, come and abide on this oil as you abided on the tree
> and those who crucified you could not endure your word; may
> your gift come, which you breathed upon your enemies and they
> turned backwards, falling on their faces, and may it abide on this
> oil, over which we utter your name.

In both cases the invocation is addressed to Christ (the first puns on *meshha* 'oil' and *mshiha* 'Christ'); in the former the oil is primarily seen as healing, in the latter as apotropaic. These are themes to which we shall return below.

Narsai specifically mentions the epiclesis in passing, in the course of his description of the *rushma*.[99]

> The three names (of the Trinity) he casts upon the oil and consecrates it, so that it may be sanctifying the uncleanness of men by its holiness.

In the Maronite service the oil is sanctified in a prayer shortly before the anointing in position II:[100]

> Holy and glorious (Lord), who through your symbolic anointing anointed for yourself prophets and priests, so that it might be a mark *(rushma)* for the sheep of your flock; may your power come, O Lord, from the uppermost heights, and rest on this oil, and may the mysteries of your Christ be imprinted in it and may it be a mark for the sheep of your flock, and hyssop that whitens, and a pledge of sanctification for the bodies of your faithful; and may your mysteries be perfected in it, and may your divinity be depicted in it; may everyone who is held worthy to be anointed with it be accounted a son, and may the sheep of your flock which has been held worthy of your heavenly gift grow rich in it.

Although the prayer is here addressed to the Father, the phrase 'may your power come...' harkens back to the wording of the epiclesis in Acts of Thomas § 121. Also archaic is the specific mention of 'prophets and priests.'[101]

The East Syriac epiclesis over the oil speaks of its role as imparting to those anointed the pledge of their resurrection,[102] an emphasis that this rite also gives to the baptismal water, following the lead of Theodore of Mopsuestia.[103]

> May the grace of the Holy Spirit come...and be mingled with this oil, and may it (sc. the grace) grant to those who are anointed with it a pledge of the resurrection from the dead; for it is given as the fulfilment

---

[99] Ed. Mingana I, p. 365 (ET p. 42).

[100] JS II, pp. 330–1.

[101] See chapter IV (2) (b) (iii).

[102] Also associated with the Eucharist in U, p. 61. The phrase 'pledge of the resurrection' is used by Ephrem of the olive leaf carried by the dove at the flood (*H. Virg.* 6.3).

[103] U, pp. 67–8. Cp above (1) (b) (ii) and (iii).

of sonship, deliverance from the sufferings of sin, and the enjoyment of
heavenly repose; . . . and may it rest and dwell in this oil, bless, sanctify
and seal it in the name of the Father, Son and Holy Spirit...

The 'pledge of the resurrection from the dead' is also associated with the
'holy oil of anointing' which the priest pours on the water in the archaic
Syrian Orthodox service in Add. 14518:[104]

> We pour this holy oil on this water for the remission of sins and the
> forgiveness of wrongdoings, for the wiping out and dissolution and an-
> nulling of the whole work of the adversary, in the name of the Father;
> halleluia; we pour this holy oil on this water for the gift of adoption and
> the preserving and watchfulness of the souls and bodies of those who
> are being baptized, in the name of the Son, halleluia; we pour this holy
> oil on this water for the pledge of resurrection from the dead, and for
> life everlasting for those who are being baptized, in the name of the
> Holy Spirit, halleluia.

The East Syriac and Maronite prayers both employ the verb 'come,'
whereas the only other service, the Melkite, with a prayer over the oil, has
the verb 'send,' using, not the more usual imperative, but an imperfect; once
again the prayer comes immediately before the anointing in position II.[105]

> We invoke your great and fearful and all-holy name, that you send your
> Spirit of might (or fearful Spirit) upon this oil, and perfect it so that it
> may become armour that terrifies away every working of the accuser; for
> the expulsion of all hostile powers, and for the punishment and burning
> and destruction of all evil spirits, for the driving out of all demons, for
> the cleansing of all remains of idolatry and all demonic worship; and
> may it be, Lord, to these your servants, for salvation, for protection, for
> refuge, in that they have taken refuge in the holy washing; for the build-
> ing up of reverence of you, and for glory, and for sharing in the faith in
> you, through Jesus Christ, along with whom you are blessed and glori-
> fied, together with your Holy Spirit.

Here we may briefly notice the contrast in themes between these various prayers over the oil. In the Melkite prayer it is the idea of protection
which predominates, and this is an element that is already present in *Acts of
Thomas* § 157; the other aspect, however, that of ownership, which features
so much in the *Acts of Thomas* is absent from the Melkite prayer, whereas it
is prominent in the Maronite service, which also preserves the archaic refer-

---

[104] D §40.
[105] B III, p. 213.

ence to 'priests and prophets.' The East Syriac service, on the other hand, rather goes its own way, and abandons these more traditional associations of the oil. It is to these associations that we now turn.

(b) Symbolism of the oil

The Spirit's effect on the oil is seen in a number of different ways. Some of these are associated with the idea of sharpness and incision of some sort or another, whether it be in terms of circumcision, or of imprinting a mark of ownership; in other cases the concept of cleansing, or (less frequently) healing, is uppermost, notably in connection with the restoration of the 'image' (Gen. 1.26), seen as a badly preserved painting; or the oil is protective, serving either to dazzle the opponent, or to render combat (seen as a wrestling match) more difficult for the enemy. Protection gives rise to the imagery of armour, and the associated rich symbolism of putting on and off, which in turn is intimately connected with the important baptismal motif of the 'robe of glory.' Last but not least, the oil is sometimes linked with the anointing of priests, prophets and kings in the Old Testament, a theme we have already discussed above[106] and to which there is no need to return again here.

(i)   The mark of ownership

Absolutely fundamental in the Syriac tradition of the *rushma* is the idea that it provides a mark of ownership, and by far the most frequent image is that of the newly baptized being 'branded' as sheep. In the Maronite service all the anointings are accompanied by the formula 'N is signed a lamb in the flock of Christ.'

Pastoral imagery is recurrent in almost all services. The Maronite *Jacob* asks that the consecrated oil may be the identity mark (*rushma*) of the lambs in Christ's flock, and a preliminary prayer in *Severus* reads 'may he be worthy of the rebirth from on high that comes through water and Spirit, so that he may become a sheep of the true shepherd, imprinted with the imprint (*tab'a*) of the Holy Spirit.' Likewise in the East Syriac service we find 'Gather us to you, bring us into your fold, receive us with your mark (*rushma*),' after the anointing in position I.[107] Curiously enough the Melkite *Basil* has this pas-

---

[106] Chapter IV (2) (b) (iii). For the theme of 'robe of glory,' see ch. IV (2) (a) (ii).

[107] U, p. 57.

toral imagery in the same place, even though in this service no oil is used for this consignation.[108]

This role of the oil at the *rushma* is already prominent in the *Acts of Thomas*, and evidently goes back to the very oldest strata of Syriac tradition. Judas Thomas prays for the king and his brother with the words[109] 'unite them to your fold and anoint them.' They in turn, beg the apostle that they may receive the *rushma*, 'for we have heard that all the sheep of the God whom you preach are known to him by the *rushma*.'[110]

Narsai's commentary on the baptismal service elucidates the imagery. The 'king of the height' reaches out 'the hand of the Spirit' to the priest and gives him the signet (*tab'a*) of his name in order to imprint his sheep.[111] The imprint, or branding, is effected by the oil, to which the epiclesis confers a 'sharpness,' so that 'the sharp power of the name enters the soul.'[112]

In Narsai the 'name' is imprinted first on the oil, and then, through the oil, on the baptismal candidate. This idea helps to illustrate the Maronite prayer over the oil, already quoted:[113] '...may your power come...and reside in this oil, and may the symbols of your Christ be *depicted* in it, so that it becomes a *rushma* for the lambs of your flock.' Traces of this same concept survive in the Syrian Orthodox and Melkite services, in a prayer of Greek origin, 'Giver of light and illuminator of souls,' where we find the words '...let the light of your presence be marked (*rsham*) on him, and let the cross of your Christ be fashioned in his heart.' Likewise in another one, before the anointing in position II, we have '...sign your Christ on those who are now being reborn...'[114]

In the third of the Epiphany hymns attributed to Ephrem, Christ himself, rather than the Spirit, is seen as effecting this imprint of ownership through the oil:

Christ and the oil participate in each other:

---

[108] 'N is signed so as to be a new lamb in the flock of Christ' (B III, p. 205) The formula at the anointing (with oil) in position II has no pastoral imagery, however.

[109] § 25.

[110] § 26; cp § 131 etc.

[111] Ed. Mingana I, pp. 358–9 (ET pp. 35–6).

[112] Ed. Mingana I, pp. 365–6 (ET p. 42).

[113] JS II, p. 330.

[114] Cp also 'Studies,' p. 35. Likewise the Egyptian Euchologion of Serapion speaks of those 'anointed with oil with the imprint of the sign of the cross'; cp also T § 15.

the Hidden one is mingled with the visible: the oil anoints visibly,
Christ marks hiddenly, the new and spiritual sheep
—a doubly wondrous flock, for it was conceived in the oil
and born in the water. (*H. Epiph.* 3.1.)

In John Chrysostom, Theodore and Narsai there is a tendency to put
the image of 'branding sheep' into the background, giving prominence instead to that of providing the newly-enrolled soldier of Christ with an identity mark (also envisaged as a brand mark). Here the idea of baptism as a
battle with Satan will be very much in the foreground: 'The priest traces the
standard of the King on their foreheads,' says Narsai, and 'with the King's
name is he branded so that he may serve as a soldier.'[115]

Ephrem compares the action of the oil on those anointed to that of a
signet ring on wax:

> The Holy Spirit incises[116] his mark (*rushma*) on his sheep, like a signet on
> wax, he incises his imprint: the hidden seal of the Spirit is imprinted by
> the oil on the bodies which are anointed at baptism. (*H. Virg.* 7.6)

From here there is no great step to the idea of the Christian as a coin
which is stamped with the imprint of the portrait, or 'image' of Christ. Thus
Ephrem speaks of the Christian as a *moneta*, or coin, on which the portrait
of the King (Christ) has been imprinted, and ends up with the exclamation
'Blessed is he who has imprinted us with his name' (*H. Haer.* 22.9).

Closely linked with the concept of the oil leaving an incision in the
form of a brand mark is that of the oil effecting a spiritual circumcision.
Circumcision, the initiation rite of the Old Covenant, was replaced by 'a
circumcision not made with hands' (Col. 2:11) under the Christian dispensa-
tion, and in the Antiochene area it was the later Jewish initiation rite for a
convert, consisting of circumcision followed by baptism, that provided the
model for the new Christian rite, in which anointing took the place of circumcision. It was very probably this exact parallelism between circumcision
and anointing that gave rise to the imagery, otherwise surprising, of the
'sharpness' of the oil. In the baptismal services themselves the oil's association with circumcision is preserved only in the East Syriac rite, where it is
found in the prayer over the oil:[117]

---

[115] Ed. Mingana I, p. 367 (ET p. 44).

[116] *ktm* 'scar, mark, defile,' usually in a bad sense, hence Beck emends to *htm*
'seal,' but the manuscript reading is probably to be preferred.

[117] U, p. 68.

...being circumcised by it *(sc.* the oil) with 'a circumcision not performed
by hands,' stripping off the flesh of sins with Christ's circumcision...

But the idea was well known to early Syriac writers; Ephrem speaks of 'the
hidden circumcision' replacing the 'manifest one' (*H. Virg.* 9.1), and in the
Epiphany hymns Jewish circumcision is specifically described as a 'symbol'
of your mark (*rushma*),[118] while earlier in the hymn the anonymous author
writes:

> He separated out the Jewish nation from the gentile nations by the for-
>   mer mark (*rushma*) of circumcision,
> with the mark of anointing
> he separated out the nation from the nation.

(H. Epiph. 3.4)

Throughout this hymn there is an intriguing play on words between *gzurta*
'circumcision' and *gzara* 'flock':

Narsai's description of the action of the oil has the same background,
although he only uses the verb *gzar* 'cut away, circumcise,' and not the
noun: thanks to the Spirit's inner working the priest 'cuts away iniquity of
body and soul by the word of his mouth.'[119] A little later the role of the oil
here is made more explicit:[120]

> The priest holds the iron of the oil on the tip of his finger and marks the
> body and the senses of the soul with its sharpness; the mortal priest
> sharpens the oil with the word of his mouth (*sc* at the epiclesis), sharp-
> ening it like iron to cut away iniquity.

Later writers mostly drop the imagery of circumcision, once the importance
of links with Old Testament Judaism had faded into the background.[121]

Before leaving the theme of circumcision we should consider a passage
in the Odes of Solomon which has usually been interpreted in this sense; it
occurs in Ode 11, now known in both Greek and Syriac, and the verb *gzar*
(Greek *peritemno*) used twice, is ambiguous. I give both possible interpretations:

---

[118] *H. Epiph.* 3.13 ('symbol' is here *ata*, lit. 'sign'). The passage is used in the
Fenqitho at Epiphany (III, p. 266b).

[119] Ed. Mingana I, p. 364 (ET p. 40).

[120] Ed. Mingana I, p. 365 (ET pp. 41–2).

[121] Though see, for example, Philoxenus, *Letter to Patricius* § 10 (PO 30, p.
752/3); Ishobarnun (ed. Clarke), p. 31 etc.

My heart has been pruned/circumcised and its bloom has appeared, and grace has sprung up within it, providing fruit for the Lord: the Most High has pruned/circumcised me with his Holy Spirit.

Although 'circumcise' is the translation favoured by most commentators, the imagery of the plant would seem to demand 'prune' as the proper rendering,—or perhaps one should say, the uppermost meaning, for the resonances of 'circumcision' are likely to be present as well. In any case the passage is interesting from our point of view because of the connection between the Holy Spirit and the idea of cutting.

A related agricultural image is that of grafting, and in the printed texts of the Syrian Orthodox *Severus* the formula at the anointing in position II actually reads:[122]

N is signed with the oil of gladness to be armed against every work of the adversary, and for a grafting into the good olive of the holy catholic and apostolic church.

This theme, borrowed from Romans 11, is extremely rare in early Syriac writers,[123] and as we have seen it is likely that it reached *Severus* by way of the influential Jerusalem catechetical tradition, where it is very prominent in the mystagogic catecheses attributed to Cyril of Jerusalem; there too it is associated with the pre-baptismal anointing. It is worth quoting the passage again:[124]

Then, when you were stripped, you were anointed with exorcized oil, from the very hairs of your head to your feet, and were made partakers of the good olive tree, Jesus Christ. For you were cut off from the wild olive and made to share in the fatness of the true olive.

Several of the Syrian Orthodox commentators describe the anointing in position II in a similar vein; thus Dionysius bar Salibi explains the meaning of the anointing (evidently he has the formula just quoted in mind):[125]

He is anointed with oil—first because he is entering into the contest and fight against Satan; for the man who enters a contest or battle is anointed with oil so that the hands of those fighting with him will slip off him. So the baptismal candidate is anointed so that he cannot be

---

[122] The oldest manuscripts, however, use this formula in position III (see 'Studies,' pp. 29–33.)

[123] See chapter IV, note 79 for references.

[124] *PG* 33, col. 1080.

[125] § 7; cp Moshe bar Kepha § 10.

seized by the demons. Secondly, by being anointed he acknowledges
that he was the wild olive, alien to God, but now he is anointed with oil
so that he may be grafted into the olive of the faith of the Father Son
and Holy Spirit, in whom he is about to be baptized; and that he may
become like the tree planted by the stream of water (Ps. 1:3), and that he
may say openly that 'I, like an olive tree, am glorious in the house of
God' (Ps. 52:10). For just as a farmer, when there is a tree that does not
produce fruit, brings part of another tree that does yield fruit, makes a
split in the one that does not bear fruit, inserts the part from the fruit-
bearing tree, and so grafts it; just so does the priest do with the baptismal candidate: because he was the wild olive which did not bear the
fruits of righteousness, he anoints him with oil, and so grafts him, in order that he may confess the Trinity, that is the Father Son and Holy
Spirit, and thus produce the fruits of righteousness, either thirty-fold, or
sixty-fold, or a hundred-fold.

The final words pick up the ending of the prayer in *Severus* which introduces
the anointing in position II.[126] A beautiful Epiphany *qolo* in the *Fenqitho*[127]
describes Christ himself as the tree of Ps. 1, ' planted by the streams of water':

Come, my brethren, let us go and see
that Tree planted by the streams of water
whose leaves never drop;
At its crown the heavenly Eagle (i.e. the Father) nests,
in its branches the Dove, the Holy Spirit,
while from its roots
flows forth the baptismal water
in which sinners go down to be baptized
and come up all pure.

(ii) Protection

The idea of the oil providing protection is already present in some of the
earliest texts on baptism, and the transition between this and the idea of the
rushma as a mark of ownership put on sheep is to be found in passages such
as the following, from the *Acts of Thomas* (§25):

Unite them to your fold and anoint them; purify them from their uncleanness, and guard them from the wolves...

---

[126] See chapter IV note 20.

[127] *Fenqitho* III, pp. 259b–60a (already quoted in another context in chapter II
(b)).

It is very clear, too, in a prayer in the archaic Syrian Orthodox service in Add. 14518 (immediately preceding the anointing in position II):[128]

> O Good Shepherd and finder of those who are lost, who with the mark (*rushma*) of the Trinity marked your sheep so that they might be preserved from ravening wolves, by your glorious name, O Father Son and Holy Spirit, may they be marked as lambs of your flock, so that they may be numbered among your holy flock and be mingled with your sheep, enter your sheepfold and belong to you; and do you preserve them by your mark from all evil things, give them repose with your fragrant oil, and sanctify them with the mark of your Trinity, so that they may come to second birth, singing praise to your Trinity, Father Son and Holy Spirit, for eternal ages, amen.

The protection afforded by the oil is described in three different ways in the baptismal texts: it is an apotropaic sign on the forehead, at which the demonic powers take fright and depart; it is the spiritual armour in the contest against the forces of evil; and it corresponds to the athlete's anointing before the wrestling contest. The first of these clearly has its origin in the Old Testament (Exodus 12:23, Ezekiel 9:4), and obviously belongs to an anointing of the forehead alone. The second and third have as their biblical basis imagery used by St Paul (Romans 13:12;[129] cp I Corinthians 9:24–7),[130] but essentially they belong to a Greco-Roman, rather than a Jewish, milieu; for both of them, an anointing of the whole body would be appropriate. Perhaps further in the background, behind these protective aspects of the oil, is the theme of the holy war of Deuteronomy 20, which Aphrahat puts in a baptismal context in his seventh *Demonstration*.

The *rushma* of oil on the forehead thus introduces two quite different sets of reference, both biblical; on the one hand it reflects, as we have seen in the previous chapter, the anointing of kings, priests and prophets, who, according to the Talmud,[131] were marked with a *chi* (in other words, the cross-shaped *tau* of the Palaeo-Hebrew script); on the other hand it is linked to the Passover narrative of Exodus 12, and the marking of the door posts

---

[128] D § 11, The theme of the former 'wolves' (i. e. gentiles) who become 'sheep' or 'lambs' is to be found in *H. Epiph.* 3.7; *Liber Graduum* V. 1 (*PS* 3, col. 100); Jacob of Serugh *On the apostle Thomas* (ed. Strothmann) III lines 781, 907, and elsewhere.

[129] Cp Ignatius, *Letter to Polycarp* 6.2 'let your baptism remain as your shields.'

[130] Athletes, but without reference to oil and wrestling (for the latter, note *Testament of Job* § 27).

[131] BT *Kerithoth 5b, Horayoth* 12a.

with blood, together with the marking of the foreheads of the faithful Isra-
elites with the letter *tau* in Ezekiel 9; both of these are passages where the
mark is at the same time protective and a mark of identification or ownership.

This background in Exodus 12 and Ezekiel 9 is never brought out explicitly in any of the baptismal services, but the passages are clearly in the
minds of several of the commentators.[132] Narsai, in particular, dwells on the
protective aspect of the *rushma*:[133]

> The priest traces the three names (of the Trinity) on his face as on a
>   shield
> so that the tyrant may see the image of the divinity on his head.
> The reason for the marking on the forehead is to cause confusion for
>   the devils:
> when they see it on his head they will be overcome...
> On their forehead they receive the spiritual stamp so that it may be
>   bright before angels and men...
> The devils see the sign of God's name upon a man and recoil from him;
> the name of the divinity looks out from the mark on the forehead,
> and the eyes of the crafty one are ashamed to look upon it.

Explicit reference to Exodus 12 is regularly brought out in the later Syrian
Orthodox commentators; thus George, bishop of the Arabs, says:[134]

> The fact that he is signed on his forehead indicates that he will become
> fearsome in appearance to the demons at all times, just as was the case
> in Egypt, where the destroyer feared to come near the doors on which
> the type of the cross was marked.

Rather remarkably, several of these later commentators also say that one of
the reasons for the postbaptismal anointing with myron was 'so that he may
be fearsome to the demons, and not dependent on their help'[135]—another
good example of how the postbaptismal anointing attracts to itself attributes which originally belonged to the prebaptismal *rushma*.

Much more prominence is given in the baptismal services themselves
to the oil as 'armour' in the battle against Satan. The formula at the two
prebaptismal anointings in *Severus*[136] opens 'N is signed/anointed with the

---

[132] Eg. John Chrysostom (ed. Wenger), pp. 92, 146.
[133] Ed. Mingana I, p. 366 (ET p. 43).
[134] Ed. Connolly-Codrington, p. 13 (= 5*).
[135] E.g. Moshe bar Kepha § 18.
[136] For the complex textual tradition here, see 'Studies,' pp. 29–33.

oil of gladness so that he may be armed with it against every working of the adversary.' In the Maronite *Jacob*, before the anointing in position III, we have a prayer:[137]

> Strengthen our weakness, O Lord, in the battle against Satan, and give us victory at all times in the face of his temptations. Clothe us in the armour which repels all falsehood; put Satan to shame before us.[138]

And at the anointing/laying on of hands in position IV in the East Syriac service the priest says:[139]

> May the pledge of the Holy Spirit which you have received, the mysteries of Christ of which you have partaken, and the living sign (*rushma*) which you have received, the new life you have acquired and the armour of righteousness which you have put on—may all this preserve you from the evil one and his forces.

Finally from the baptismal services themselves, we may quote the prayer from the Melkite *Basil*, said over the oil:

> ...may the oil become armour that terrifies away every working of the accuser; for the expulsion of all hostile powers, and for the punishment, burning and destruction of all evil spirits...

(For the full text of the prayer, see above (2) (a)).

It is at first surprising that Aphrahat states that the 'armour' is put on from the water, rather than the oil:[140] 'he who has put on the armour of the water, let him not take this armour off, lest he be worsted in battle. 'The reason for this transfer would seem to lie in the popularity of the imagery of the font as a furnace: 'I did not go down to the fountain of the Jordan to take a shield for myself, but in order to forge mighty armour for warriors,' is what Jacob makes Christ say.[141]

It is Narsai who dwells at greatest length on the connection between oil and armour:[142]

> The oil is an armour with which the earth-born are anointed, so that they may not be captured by the evil spirits in the hidden warfare.

---

[137] The opening is found in D, before position II.
[138] This probably has in mind the oil as an apotropaic mark.
[139] U, p. 79.
[140] *Dem.* 6.1 (*PS* 1, col. 252).
[141] Ed. Bedjan I, p. 180.
[142] Ed. Mingana I, p. 366 (ET p. 43).

As we have already seen, for Narsai the oil also provides the identification mark of the soldiers in the army of the King of kings.

Narsai also speaks of the baptized as athletes who go down to the arena,[143] but he does not develop the games imagery. This is brought out very clearly by Moshe bar Kepha, who gives as the first reason for the anointing:[144]

> to show that he is entering on a contest and a wrestling match with Sa-
> tan. Because he who enters on a wrestling contest is anointed with oil,
> so that the hands of him with whom he is striving may slip from him.
> So too the baptized is anointed that he may not be held fast by the de-
> mons.

Such associations, which essentially belong to the Greco-Roman cultural world, were alien to the unhellenized milieu of the early Syriac church, but they did have a counterpart in the imagery of the pearl diver smearing his body with oil, much better suited to the mercantile background of at least some strands of early Syriac Christianity. For Ephrem the baptized are pearl divers who oil their bodies before plunging into the depths to search for Christ the Pearl:

> In symbol and in truth is Leviathan trodden down by mortals:
> the divers strip and put on oil; as a symbol of Christ they snatched you
>   and came up;
> stripped, they seized the soul from his embittered mouth.

> (*H. Fid.* 82.10)

The double entendre of *'amode*, 'divers,' but also 'baptismal candidates' here is again to be found in one of the Epiphany hymns:

> The diver too raises up
> from the sea the pearl;
> dive down (in baptism) and take up from the water
> the purity that is hidden there -
> the pearl that is entwined in the crown of divinity. (*H. Epiph.* 7.18)

In another hymn of Ephrem's, where pearl diving is once more in the background, he elucidates the parallel roles of the oil (*meshha*) and Christ (*mshiha*):

---

[143] Ed. Mingana I, p. 368 (ET p. 45); cp John Chrysostom (ed. Wenger), p. 147.
[144] § 10.

Oil in its love accompanies the baptized in his need,
when, despising his life, he descends and buries himself in the water:
oil by its nature cannot die, yet He clothed himself in a mortal body,
he was baptized, and so raised up from the water
a treasure of life for the race of Adam. (*H. Virg.* 7.10)

(iii) *Healing and cleansing*

These related concepts are also closely associated with the oil of the prebaptismal anointing; in both cases the object healed or cleansed away is sin.

In the *Acts of Thomas* (§ 121), as Judas casts the oil on Mygdonia's head he prays:

Heal her of her old wounds, and wash away from her her sores, and strengthen her weakness,

In popular tradition, however, the healing may sometimes be physical as well as spiritual. In his famous homily on the baptism of Constantine, Jacob of Serugh relates how Constantine was born with leprous marks on his face, which no doctor could heal. The priest who prepares him for baptism tells him:[145]

'Before you are baptized I will cleanse you with oil.'
And so the priest gave orders for the oil of anointing to be brought;
he opened his mouth and spoke to him saying,
'By means of this oil, with which I shall anoint you, you shall be cleansed,
for you should not take down this foul leprosy into the font.'
The priest began to anoint the king, full of uncleanness,
and his leprosy dropped off, a great wonder for him to see.

In Syriac tradition where one of the most popular Christological titles was 'Good Doctor,'[146] it is not surprising to find sin frequently described in terms of disease; Aphrahat's Demonstration 7 and Ephrem's hymn 34 in the Nisibene collection are notable examples of the way in which this imagery can be developed. For Narsai it is the priest who acts as 'doctor' at

---

[145] Ed. Frothingham, p. 234.

[146] In the *Teaching of Addai* King Abgar addresses Jesus as 'good doctor' (the corresponding Greek text of Eusebius *Eccl. Hist.* 1.13 has 'good saviour'); the title is very common in Ephrem. Cp also Murray, *Symbols*, pp. 199–202. For the importance of healing imagery in early Syriac writers, see especially A. Shemunkasho, *Healing in the Theology of St Ephrem* (Piscataway NJ, 2002).

baptism, as he anoints the candidates. This delightful passage merits quotation in full:[147]

> The office of a physician too does the priest exercise toward the limbs,
> touching the exterior and causing sensation to reach into the hidden
>   parts.[148]
> To body and soul he applies the remedies of his art;
> both open and hidden disease does he heal by the divine power.
> In divine way he mixes the medicine[149] that is given into his hands,
> and by its power he heals all diseases without fail.
> Like a chemist shop, he has opened up the door of the holy church;
> he tends the sicknesses and binds up the diseases of his fellow servants.
> With the external sign (rushma) he touches the hidden diseases that are
>   within,
> and then he lays on the medicament of the Spirit[150] with the symbol of
>   the water.

In the East Syriac service Jesus is called the 'healer of our souls,
through the medicament of whose words he binds up our wounds and heals
our sicknesses.'[151] Likewise in the West Syriac services there is also some
medical imagery present, sometimes in direct connection with the oil. In the
Maronite litany for the oil we find:[152]

> May God cause his glorious, splendid and hidden light to dwell in the oil
> and may it drive out from them sicknesses and diseases, both hidden
> and visible...

In the Syrian Orthodox *Timothy* the priest addresses God as follows:[153]

> our Father, and the Father of Abraham, Isaac and Jacob, the God of our
> fathers, glorify your Son Jesus Christ with miracles and mighty deeds

---

[147] Ed. Mingana I, p. 366 (ET pp. 42–3.)

[148] The oil is seen here, not as soothing, but as cutting (see above).

[149] Similarly p. 358 (ET p. 35) 'in heavenly fashion did he mix the medicine for
the disease of our iniquity.'

[150] The same phrase is used in connection with the consecration of the water
(p. 343 = ET p. 48).

[151] U, p. 60.

[152] JS II, p. 331. Compare *Testament of our Lord* (ed. Rahmani) pp. 122–4 : '*drive
out* from the souls of these your servants all sickness and disease.'

[153] T § 34. Compare also § 33: 'our iniquity...could not be *healed*.' The biblical
source for much of this imagery will be Isaiah 53:5, as well as Psalms such as 41:4.
T § 34 comes shortly before the pouring of the 'oil of the horn' on to the water.

and manifold acts of power, and with healings of all kinds of sicknesses, both hidden and manifest, of the soul and of the body, by the coming of your living and holy Spirit into this water…

Related to the healing qualities of the oil is its ability to lubricate and cleanse:[154]

Oil, the beneficial fountain, accompanies the body, that fount of ills;
for oil wipes out sins, just as the flood wiped out the unclean;
for the flood, acting in justice, wiped out the wicked:
those who had not subdued their lusts drowned,
having brought on the flood through these lusts;
but oil, acting in goodness, wipes out sins in baptism,
for sin is drowned in the water and cannot live with all its desires.

At the end of a prayer in the East Syriac rite, already quoted, the healing and cleansing qualities of oil are linked:[155]

Praise to you who healed the sickness of our body by means of the oil and water that you applied to our wounds; you wiped away the pus of sin from our soul by the Holy Spirit, as with a sponge.

The passage is clearly directly related to one in Narsai, although which is the derivative text is not clear:[156]

He wished to wipe the pus of wickedness from mortal men, and his providence applied the sponge of the Spirit to the hand of our body.

In another passage Narsai again speaks of pus (or rust), but this time he introduces the idea of paint as well:[157]

The rust of the passions has defaced our excellent beauty;
he came again and painted us in spiritual colours which cannot be effaced.
Skillfully he mixed the colours for the renewal of our race,
with oil and water and the invincible power of the Spirit.

---

[154] Ephrem, *H. Virg.* 7.9.

[155] U, pp. 60–1. The word translated 'pus' can also mean 'rust,' but this seems less likely in the the context. It is very probable that an allusion to the parable of the Good Samaritan is intended (this is given a specifically baptismal reference by Jacob of Serugh, ed. Bedjan II, p. 327, and others).

[156] Ed. Mingana I, p. 357 (ET pp. 33–4).

[157] Ed. Mingana I, p. 341 (ET p. 46).

In his fine baptismal hymn, no. 7 (stanza 5) in the collection on Virginity, Ephrem too describes the prebaptismal *rushma* in terms of painting with oils: the oil depicts the image of Christ, thus restoring the 'image of God' that Adam had spoiled:

> A royal portrait is painted with visible colours,
> and with oil that all can see is the hidden portrait of our hidden King
> portrayed on those who have been signed:
> on them baptism, that is in travail with them in its womb, depicts the
>   new portrait,
> to replace the image of the former Adam which was corrupted;
> it gives birth to them with triple pangs,
> accompanied by the three glorious names, of Father Son and Holy
>   Spirit.

The cooperation between oil and water in this process of repainting the 'image' is seen as very close by Ephrem. Narsai employs the same motif on another occasion, but without reference to oil, treating the surface of the water as the canvas:[158]

> God taught the priests a spiritual artistry, so that they became depicters
> of the image of life on the tablet of the water.

Although this imagery is not employed in the liturgical texts themselves, it is picked up again by some of the commentators, referring to the consignation in position I, without oil; here they give rather a different slant:[159]

> He seals him first of all without oil for this reason. It is as when a
> painter comes to an image which is already old and has the paint rubbed
> off. First he scours it and cleans from it the marks of its age, and after
> that he puts paint on it and adorns it. Because if he put paint on it be-
> fore he had cleaned and scoured it, he would ruin the paints. Likewise,
> when the priest comes to the baptized, who is old and sullied with sin,
> he first seals him with the cross without oil, thus cleaning off his marks
> of age, and afterwards he signs him with oil, restoring him to his pristine
> beauty.

---

[158] Ed. Mingana I, p. 357 (ET p. 34); cp p. 356.
[159] Moshe bar Kepha § 7.

(c) Myron

As we saw in chapter III originally the term myron could even be used for the oil at the prebaptismal anointing, but by the fifth century it came to be reserved for the unguent employed at the post-baptismal anointing (and of course various other occasions) and for pouring on the water at the consecration of the baptismal water. As such, its use was confined to West Syriac tradition.

The occurrence of the term myron in the Song of Songs (1:3, Septuagint, but not Peshitta) gives this anointing the overtones of baptism as a betrothal in the eyes of some writers,[160] but more frequently it is the anointing of Christ's feet with myron (John 12:3) which is uppermost in the consciousness of writers and commentators; indeed, according to a baptismal address attributed to Athanasius,[161] the myron makes the baptized a 'sharer' in the anointing Christ himself received on his body, and as a result he becomes a 'sharer in Christ's body' (cp Eph. 3:6) and a 'sharer in his blood.'[162] Jacob of Serugh, in his homily on the anointing of Christ's feet,[163] speaks of the episode as a type of Christian baptism, and he describes how Christ himself provides the oil (sic) with the sweet scent.

The composite nature of the myron, olive oil and scented balsamon, plays an important part in the earliest commentators, such as Jacob of Edessa and George bishop of the Arabs,[164] who stress that its 'composition' from olive oil and balsamon symbolically represented the incarnate Christ, himself a union 'composed' of humanity and divinity (following the Syrian Orthodox terminology developed by Severus, on the basis of Cyril of Alexandria). This interpretation continues to be given by commentators up to the late thirteenth century, when the Coptic practice of employing a large number of ingredients was taken over.[165]

---

[160] E.g. John of the Sedre, British Library Add. 12165, f. 260b; George of the Arabs, *ibid.* f. 263a (= ed. Ryssel, p. 50.)

[161] Ed. Brock, § 11.

[162] This is based on Cyril, *Cat. Myst.* III. 1–2 (*PG* 33, col 1089).

[163] Ed. Bedjan, II, p. 424.

[164] Add. 12165, f. 250b (Jacob), f. 264b (George, = ed. Ryssel, p. 61); Moshe bar Kepha, *On the Myron* (ed. Strothmann) § 7. George is the first of the commentators to trace the myron back via Seth to Paradise; the idea goes back to the Greek *Apocalypse of Moses* (for the medieval western tradition see E. C. Quinn, *The Quest of Seth for the Oil of Life* (Chicago, 1962)).

[165] Siman, *L'Expérience*, p. 96.

According to Severus in his letter to John the Soldier,[166] the myron is the 'perfecter of the gifts of the Holy Spirit,' and this basic understanding is reflected both in the words of the actual formula for the post-baptismal anointing ('with the holy myron, the sweet scent of Christ, the imprint[167] of true faith and perfecting of the gifts of the Holy Spirit, is N imprinted...'), and in the later commentaries. In this letter Severus actually speaks of the myron as a symbol of the Spirit, but most writers regard it rather as symbolizing Christ.[168]

In both liturgical texts and in the commentaries the myron is described as conferring an 'imprint' (tab'a) or 'seal' (hatma); in the earliest treatises on the myron, however, by John of the Sedre, Jacob of Edessa and George bishop of the Arabs, the 'imprint' of the myron is surprisingly also referred to as the rushma as well, and they see it as conferring many of the things that the old Antiochene pre-baptismal anointing conferred—sonship, mark of ownership in the flock of Christ, protection etc. Thus the Patriarch John writes:[169]

> By the imprint of this holy oil we are inscribed as sons of the heavenly Father; by means of this mark (rushma) or imprint (tab'a) of this heavenly oil we become the sheep of Christ, a priestly kingdom (I Pet. 2:9)...we are strengthened against the accuser, the enemy...and are freed from the slavery of sin.

Likewise Jacob of Edessa comments:[170]

> This holy oil is the beginning of the heavenly path and the ladder which takes us up to heaven, the armour against the hostile powers, the indissoluble imprint (tab'a) of the King, the sign (ata) which delivers from fire, the guardian of the faithful, the cause of flight to the demons, the cause of joy to the angels. We should supplicate Christ to appoint it as mighty armour, invincible against every working of demons and evil men; and that all who are imprinted with it may be freed from sin and be numbered in the divine flock.

This makes it quite clear that the post-baptismal anointing was seen as having very much the same significance as the old pre-baptismal rushma, which

---

[166] Ed. Brock § 6.

[167] 'Seal' is found in several texts; see *Le Muséon* 83 (1970), p. 427.

[168] Severus, *Letter to John the Soldier* § 10, quoted by Moshe bar Kepha, *On the Myron* § 5 (Moshe prefers to see the myron as symbolizing Christ).

[169] Add. 12165, f. 261b.

[170] Add. 12165, ff. 250–1.

it both duplicated and replaced; this is further born out by the prayers associated with the myron in the three West Syriac services, where we find present such themes as priesthood and protection[171] which originally belonged to the *rushma*. Only a few new elements, such as the ideas of perfecting, of fragrance, and of union[172] (Eph 4:3), appear to be added.

(3) THE INVOCATION OVER THE BAPTISMAL CANDIDATES

An epiclesis specifically asking for the sending of the Spirit on the candidates is found in all the West Syriac services, but is absent from the East Syriac. Normally these epicleses occur in close conjunction with the anointing in position II. Thus the Maronite *Jacob* provides an epiclesis over the candidates immediately after the *rushma*;

> May your living and holy Spirit come, Lord, and reside and rest upon the head of this your servant, and may he be marked with your name, O living Father, and the name of your only-begotten Son, and of your Spirit, the Paraclete who brings remission of sins.

The epiclesis over the candidates in *Timothy* comes in the prayer immediately before the *rushma*, which reads:[173]

> Almighty God, King of powers, who alone over all ages is good, and Saviour of the whole race of mankind, we pray you, Lord, send the Spirit of your mercifulness upon these your servants who have been prepared for holy baptism, and give them strength and wisdom, knowledge and understanding, against all the wiles of the evil one, so that they may be completely delivered from the whole tyranny of the adversary. Confirm them in your faith, keep them in your hope, seal them in your love, put upon them your imprint, form them with your Spirit in the likeness of your Christ, making them worthy of the new incorruptible birth; to whom, along with you and your living and holy Spirit, let us offer up praise, now and always and for eternal ages.

It will be noticed that, whereas *Jacob* employs the archaic type of wording for the epiclesis ('may your Spirit come'), *Timothy* uses the later one ('send'), as does *Severus*, where rather surprisingly we find three epicleses over the candidates; the first of these comes in the prayer of thanksgiving that follows the *syntaxis* or 'greeting' of Christ:

---

[171] Priesthood: T, B (see my commentary to T § 45); protection: S.
[172] See chapter IV (2) (a) (i).
[173] T § 15.

> We thank you, Lord, that you have made this your servant worthy to come to holy baptism and to renounce the evil one, consorting not with flesh and blood, but with your grace and the loving kindness of your only begotten Son, our Lord and our God, Jesus Christ. Be pleased, Lord, to send your Holy Spirit upon him; overshadow him and search out all his limbs, cleanse first of all and sanctify him so that he may be made worthy of the holy anointing and the perfect faith in our Lord Jesus Christ, with whom, together with your all-holy and good Spirit, you are blessed now and for ever.

The phrase 'cleanse first of all and sanctify him' is intriguing since it appears to tie up with the characteristic Syrian Orthodox interpretation of Gabriel's message to Mary in Luke 1:35, touched on above in chapter I; as Jacob of Serugh put it:[174]

> The Holy Spirit sanctified her and then the Son of God overshadowed her.

The present prayer seems to ask for this initial sanctification so that Christ can then 'overshadow' the baptismal candidate at the anointing, just as he 'overshadowed' Mary at her conception.

The second epiclesis over the candidates in *Severus* is to be found in the prayer that now introduces the *rushma*, although originally it belonged, (as was pointed out in chapter IV (1)) to an imposition of the hands:

> Holy Father, who gave your Holy Spirit to those who were baptized by the hands of your holy apostles, do you now too, using the shadow of my hands, send your Holy Spirit upon those who are about to be baptized, so that being filled with Him and his divine gifts, they may produce fruit thirtyfold and sixtyfold and a hundredfold.

The single epiclesis over the candidates in the Melkite *Basil* employs the same prayer as *Severus* (also prefacing the *rushma*), although this service preserves the imposition of hands at this point as well.

The third epiclesis of this kind in *Severus* is to be found right at the end of the long consecration prayer of the water at a point where the corresponding section of the prayer in the Melkite *Basil* has an epiclesis over the water, rather than the candidates. In *Severus* the prayer reads:

> You effected the economy of baptism on earth, and you sent your Holy Spirit in the form of a dove upon your only-begotten Son, God the Word, you sanctified the streams of Jordan; now too, Lord, be pleased

---

[174] Ed. Bedjan, S. p. 632.

to cause your Holy Spirit to overshadow these your servants who are being baptized, and perfect them, and appoint them associates of your Christ, cleansing them by your washing that gives salvation, so that, being gloriously renewed and filled with your grace and strength, they may preserve the deposit of your salvation and be prepared for the incorruptible and blessed life, and may they become participants in the good things of heaven, which you promised to those who please you, in the grace and loving kindness of your Christ, along with whom to you is fitting glory, together with your Holy Spirit, excellent and life-giving, consubstantial with you, now and for eternal ages.

It will be noticed that again the verb 'overshadow' is employed, thus providing a hinted parallel with the Annunciation (see chapter VII, below).

Whereas the eucharistic epicleses normally ask for the coming or sending of the Holy Spirit 'upon us' as well as upon the Bread and the Wine, in the baptismal services such an addition is not to be found in the various epicleses at the consecration of the baptismal water. There is, however, one apparent exception, in prayer to be found in some texts of *Severus:*

Have mercy on us, O God the Father almighty, and send *upon us* and upon this water that is being consecrated, from your dwelling which is prepared, from your infinite womb, the Paraclete, your Holy Spirit, the Establisher, Lord, Life giver, who spoke in the Law and in the prophets and in the apostles, who everywhere is close at hand, who fills all things; with authority does he act authoritatively, and not like a minister, with those whom he wishes, through your good will; who is simple in nature, and many-sided in action; the source of divine gifts, who is consubstantial with you, who proceeds from you, who is equal on the throne of the kingdom that belongs to you and your only-begotten Son, our Lord and our God and our Saviour, Jesus Christ.

An examination of the manuscript traditon revealed that this prayer does not belong to the long consecration prayer at all, but has been interpolated into it as part of the process of the multiplication of epicleses that we considered above.[175] As a matter of fact the prayer comes from the Anaphora of St Mark, and thus its eucharistic origin explains the otherwise surprising presence of the words 'upon us.'

Finally in this section mention should be made of one more epiclesis to be found in *Severus*, in which the priest asks for the sending of the Spirit

---

[175] See chapter V (1) (a).

upon himself. This occurs in a prayer for the priest himself, which comes shortly before the consignation in position I:[176]

> O Lord God almighty, who knows the minds of men and who searches out the heart and reins, although I am miserable and unworthy, yet, through your mercy you have called me to this ministry; do not there-fore, Lord, abhor me or turn away your countenance from me; blot out my offenses, wash the defilement of my body, cleanse the impurities of my soul, and make me entirely holy; may I not be found a slave to sin as I pray on behalf of the faithful flock and ask forgiveness for their sins; may your poor servant not turn back ashamed, Lord, but rather send upon me your Holy Spirit and strengthen me so that I may administer this great and heavenly sacrament.

---

[176] SH, p. 23.

6 THE HOLY SPIRIT AND THE EUCHARIST

As we have seen in chapter IV the fathers regularly interpreted the wedding garment of Matt. 22:12 as a reference to the 'robe of glory' put on at baptism; the wedding feast itself, which immediately ensues, is the Eucharist, for which the wedding garment must be kept unsoiled:[1]

> The Firstborn wrapped himself in a body, as a veil to hide his glory;
> the immortal bride shines out in that robe.
> Let the guests in their robes resemble him in his;
> let your bodies, which are your clothing, shine out,
> for they bound in fetters the man whose body was stained.
> O whiten my stains at your banquet with your radiance!

From a modern western point of view, used not only to infant baptism but also to a considerable lapse in time between baptism proper and confirmation and first communion, it might appear strange to include a chapter on the Eucharist in a work primarily concerned with the role of the Holy Spirit in the baptismal mystery. From an oriental point of view, however, the procedure is an entirely logical one, since the communion of the newly baptized is the culminating point in the Syrian (and other oriental) baptismal services, and time and time again we find writers stressing the very close links between baptism and communion.[2]

Syriac liturgical tradition is uniquely rich in its anaphoras: as is well known, three are preserved in the East Syriac rite, but originally several more must have been in use. Fragments of one of these survive in a sixth-century manuscript, and a description of two others is to be found in Narsai's homilies 21 and 32.[3] But it is in the West Syriac tradition where we find

---

[1] Ephrem, *H. Nisib.* 43.21.

[2] Witness, for example, the commentaries on the baptismal service, which always include the communion of the newly baptized.

[3] See R. H. Connolly, 'Sixth-century fragments of an East Syrian Anaphora,' *OC* ns 12/14 (1923/4), pp. 99–128, and E. C Ratcliff, 'A note on the anaphoras described in the liturgical homilies of Narsai,' in ed. J. N. Birdsall and R. W. Thomson, *Biblical and Patristic Studies in Memory of R. P. Casey* (Freiburg, 1963), pp. 235–49 (reprinted in E. C. Ratcliff, *Liturgical Studies*, London 1976).

the real profusion, for there over seventy anaphoras survive, of which a little over a dozen are (or have been) used by the Maronites as well as by the Syrian Orthodox.

The focal point of the role of the Holy Spirit in the eucharistic liturgy is of course the consecration of the bread and the wine at the epiclesis. Before looking at the texts of some of these, it will be helpful to consider briefly the wider implications of the Spirit's action, as understood in Syriac tradition.

At the epiclesis the Holy Spirit brings about the proper relationship of the created world to the Creator: the bread and wine, 'fruit of the earth and work of human hands,' is transformed into the saving Body and Blood of Christ. What we have here is a paradigm of the transforming power of the Holy Spirit, hinting how, on the one hand, the material world can become a sacrament, and on the other, the Christian too can become transformed by his cooperation with the Holy Spirit. In the Eucharist Christians have the assurance that the Holy Spirit effects this altered set of relationships in the eucharisic elements, but if this process of sanctification is to be allowed to extend into the rest of the world, and into human life in general, this requires the cooperation of man, just as the Incarnation itself required the cooperation of Mary with the Holy Spirit. Furthermore, whether the Body and Blood turn out to be for sanctification or for judgement depends on the attitude of each individual who receives them (I Cor. 11:27–29).[4] 'In awe and in love let us approach the Medicine of Life, showing discernment,' says Ephrem,[5] echoing St Paul; and in the tenth hymn of the collection on Faith he goes on to illustrate the dual role of the Bread and Wine, destroying sin, but sanctifying the penitent who has dissociated himself from his sin:[6]

Your Bread slays the greedy one who had made us his food,

---

[4] Specifically referred to in several of the epicleses quoted below.

[5] Armenian hymns no. 49, line 11.

[6] H. Fid. 10. 18; see also the stanzas quoted above in chapter II (a). Compare also Armenian hymns, no. 47, lines 5–6 and 13–14;

'For everyone who does not receive it worthily is like him who has not received.'

And

'He who receives it unworthily, takes on his own judgement.'

The same idea of judgement and condemnation as self-imposed is again brought out by Ephrem in his Letter to Publius (ed. Brock, Le Muséon 89 (1976)) §§ 9, 22–3.

your Cup destroys death who had swallowed us up;
we have eaten you, O Lord, we have drunken you—
not that we will consume you up, but through you we shall be saved.

The nature of this judgement implicit within the Eucharist is entirely analogous to that described in John 3:16–21, where it is not Christ himself who
judges; rather, people provide their own condemnation by refusing to be-
lieve in him, seeing that the whole purpose of his presence in the world—
continued *par excellence* in the Eucharist—is that the world should be saved.
As we shall see, the destruction of sin, in the form of its forgiveness, is one
of the recurrent themes of the eucharistic epicleses themselves.

What is required on the part of the individual is essentially the eye of
faith, which discerns the hidden realities behind the sanctified oil and water
at Baptism and behind the sanctified Bread and Wine at the Eucharist. As
Moshe bar Kepha puts it, speaking of both the Eucharist and the Myron:[7]

> The Eucharistic Offering and the Myron bring profit to those who no
> longer look with the physical eye at what can be seen, that is to say the
> bread and the wine, but who, using the eyes of the soul, apprehend and
> perceive God the Word united to the bread and wine and to the oil of
> the myron.

By faith the individual can allow the process of sanctification to overflow
and spill out, as it were, beyond the Sacraments so that the world itself becomes to him a sacrament. As Philoxenus put it:[8] 'without faith everything
is ordinary; when faith has come, even mean things appear glorious.' We
can get a glimpse of how the Eucharist can transform the whole of human
life from a beautiful passage in Isaac of Nineveh:[9]

> When we have found love, we eat the heavenly bread and we are sus-
> tained without labour and without weariness. Heavenly bread is that
> which has descended from heaven and which gives the world life; this is
> the food of angels. He who has found love eats Christ at all times and
> becomes immortal from thence onwards; for whoever eats of this bread
> shall not taste death in eternity. Blessed is he who has eaten from the
> bread of love which is Jesus! Whoever is fed with love is fed with Christ,
> who is the all-governing God. Witness is John, who says 'God is Love'

---

[7] Ed. Strothmann § 47. Philoxenus makes the same point in his *Three Tractates
on The Trinity and the Incarnation* (ed. Vaschalde), p. 118.

[8] Ed. Budge, *Hom.* 3, p. 53. For the world transformed into a sacrament, see
Abdisho, quoted in chapter VIII.

[9] Ed. Bedjan, pp. 316–7=ET (Wensinck), pp. 211–2.

(1 John 4:16). He who lives in love in this world breathes in life from God; he breathes here the air of the resurrection, in which the righteous will delight at the resurrection. Love is the kingdom of which our Lord spoke when he symbolically promised the disciples that they would eat in his kingdom: 'You shall eat and drink at the table of my kingdom' (Luke 22:30.) What should they eat, if not love? Love is sufficient to feed man instead of food and drink. This is the wine that gladdens the heart of man (Ps. 104:15.) Blessed is he who has drunk from this wine. This is the wine from which the lascivious have drunk and they became chaste, the sinners drunk and they forgot the ways of offence, the drunkards drunk and they became abstinent, the rich and they became desirous of poverty, the poor and they became rich in hope, the infirm and they became strong, fools and they became wise.

With this by way of introduction we can now turn to the actual form of the eucharistic epicleses in some of the different anaphoras. We have already had occasion in an earlier chapter to study the epiclesis from a purely formal point of view, and there we saw that epicleses can be classified into two main types, those introduced by 'come,' and those introduced by 'send.' In the former category the Holy Spirit is always the subject of the verb (or verbs) of consecration, while in the latter the subject may be either the Father or the Holy Spirit, depending on the construction used.

What is the situation in the eucharistic liturgies? An examination of the various forms of their epicleses will also provide the opportunity to see exactly what the Spirit is asked to effect, and to what end.[10]

The East Syriac anaphoras introduce the epiclesis by the words 'may the Holy Spirit come':

> *Addai and Mari:* May your Holy Spirit come and rest on this offering of your servants, and bless and sanctify it, so that it may be for us, Lord, for the forgiveness of wrongdoings and remission of sins, for the great hope of the resurrection from the dead and for new life in the kingdom of heaven with all those who have pleased you.

> *Theodore:* May the Grace of the Holy Spirit come upon us and on this offering and reside in and overshadow this bread and this cup, and bless,

---

[10] For the East Syriac anaphoras I use the Urmia edition, for the West Syriac the editions in *Anaphorae Syriacae* (Rome 1939–), where available, supplemented by Cambridge Add. 2887. For the various epicleses in the Anaphoras, see further my 'Towards a typology of the epicleses in the West Syrian Anaphoras,' in H.-J. Feulner, E. Velkovska and R. Taft (eds), *Crossroad of Cultures. Studies in Liturgy in Honor of Gabriele Winkler* (OCA 260; 2000), pp. 173-92.

sanctify and seal them in the name of the Father, Son and Holy Spirit; and may this bread become, through the power of your name, the holy body of our Lord Jesus Christ, and this cup the precious blood of our Lord Jesus Christ; and to all who eat of this bread and drink of this cup in true faith, Lord, may they be for forgiveness of wrongdoings and remission of sins, for the great hope of the resurrection from the dead, for salvation of body and soul, and for life and eternal glory; and make us all worthy, through the grace of our Lord Jesus Christ, to enjoy the kingdom of heaven and the good things to come that do not pass away, together with all those who have done your good pleasure and lived according to your commandments.

Nestorius: May the Grace of the Holy Spirit come, Lord, and reside and rest upon this offering which we have offered before you, and may he bless and sanctify it, making this bread and this cup the body and blood of our Lord Jesus Christ, changing and sanctifying them by the working of the Holy Spirit, so that the receiving of these glorious and holy mysteries may be to all those who participate of them for life and resurrection from the dead, and for the forgiveness of body and soul, for illumination of the mind, for confidence before you, and for that eternal salvation which you promised us through our Lord Jesus Christ, so that we may be joined to one another in one company, in one bond of love and peace, and may we be one body and one spirit, just as we have been called in the one hope of our calling; may no one eat and drink to the condemnation of his body and soul, may it not result in sickness or illness because of his sins, seeing that he is eating of this bread and drinking of this cup in an unworthy way; rather, may we be strengthened and fortified in all things that please you, seeing that we have been held worthy to partake of the body and blood of your Christ with a pure conscience.

Two points may be noticed in passing. As in the East Syriac baptismal service, great emphasis is placed on the resurrection; secondly, two of these epicleses lack the words (may the Holy Spirit come) *upon us* (as well as upon the bread and wine) in contrast to the norm of the West Syriac eucharistic epicleses.

The same pattern using the verb 'come' (in the Greek anaphoras found only in that of Basil) occurs in a certain number of West Syriac anaphoras, notably the Maronite 'Sharrar' (which has many affinities with the East Syriac anaphoras), and the Syrian Orthodox anaphoras attributed to Jacob of Serugh (1), Basil, Gregory Iohannan, Eustathius, Dioscorus of Gazarta, and some others: Thus for example:

Sharrar: Hear me, Lord, and answer me, Lord, answer me, Lord; may your living and holy Spirit come, Lord, and reside and rest on this offering of your servants; may it be to those who partake of it for forgiveness of wrongdoings and remission of sins, for a blessed resurrection from the dead, and for a new life in the kingdom of heaven.

Jacob of Serugh I: Yea, we beseech you, Lord God Almighty, have mercy on us and may the gates on high be opened and may your Holy Spirit come, he who is consubstantial with you and your only-begotten Son, and may he overshadow and hover above and rest on us and on these offerings laid out, and change them, appointing the bread as the precious body of our Lord Jesus Christ, and this cup as the living blood of our Lord Jesus Christ, amen; and may he make them a single body and blood, a single holy thing, worthy, belonging to our Lord, so that, when it is mingled in our souls and bodies, it may be for us and for those who receive it, for growth of faith in you, for the washing away of all stains; may sinners be forgiven by it, may the penitent be sanctified, may wrongdoers be put right, may those who stray be turned back by it, may those who are full of anger with others be reconciled by it, may those full of resentment be calmed by it, may those who are violent become peaceful by it, may those who are in grief receive joy by it, may those who mourn find comfort by it, may those who are oppressed find alleviation in it, may those who are sick find healing in it; so that from all, in all and for all, we may offer up to you praise and thanksgiving and to your only-begotten Son, and to your Spirit, holy and good.

The wording 'come' is even found in some of the late anaphoras, such as that by Dioscorus of Gazarta (end of 13th century,) whose long epiclesis opens:

May the Holy Spirit come, he who proceeds in a hidden way from you, Father, who spoke by the prophets, telling us of your Child, who came down upon the Jordan and appeared to us in the form of a dove together with the unembodied voice, who shone out for us with your beloved Son, who proceeds from you and participates in your radiance, who gave wisdom to the apostles and who crowned the martyrs, giving them a crown of glory; who is timeless, who proceeds uninterruptedly, who perfects, unhampered by time, who brings to completion in a divine fashion; may he come at your compassionate will and overshadow these mysteries and perfect them, expelling, by their holy nature, all unclean thoughts of my soul, making me pure and spotless before you, O God the Father; and may he cleanse and purify me and this congregation present, making us worthy of these mysteries of Christ our God; may we appear without spot of sin. In you grace and great mercies hear me, may he come overshadow and hover over these mysteries, changing this bread...

A notable feature in some of the West Syriac anaphoras is the fusion of the two types of wording, producing 'send your Spirit…and may he come' (or the reverse order); this is found for example in the anaphoras of Dioscorus (I), John Saba, Jacob of Edessa, Ignatius bar Wahib, and others. As a sample I give that attributed to the patriarch Dioscorus:

> Yea, Lord, may your Holy Spirit come and overshadow with his grace, sanctify and perfect, this sacrifice set before us; and may he effect for us a cleansing. Do not deprive your faithful people of your heavenly gift, but in the abundance of your grace send your Spirit to us, and may he fill us with his divine gifts; and as he rested upon your only-begotten Son in the Jordan in the form of a dove, and upon the holy apostles with tongues of fire, so may he reside and rest on us and on these offerings, so that, hovering in his grace, he may make this bread into the body of Christ our God, and the mixture in this cup into the blood of Christ our God; so that, as we enjoy these life-giving mysteries, our souls and bodies may be sanctified; may they not lead to our confusion at that last day, but be for salvation and defence, so that we may come prepared before you and be held worthy of the blessings, along with the glorious saints in your spiritual light, in the grace, mercy and loving kindness of your only-begotten Son, through whom glory honour and power are due, along with your Spirit, holy and good.[11]

Whereas in the West Syriac baptismal epicleses introduced by the verb 'send,' the first imperative was regularly followed by a second, making the Father the subject of the verb of consecration, this is rather rare in the Syriac anaphoras, and is found notably in those attributed to Timothy of Alexandria and Severus (among the Greek anaphoras it is the pattern of the epiclesis in John Chrysostom):

> *Timothy:* Turn and send to us, Lord, from the holy heavens, from the seat of the kingdom of your glory, from your impenetrable bosom, your Holy Spirit, unchangeable and unchanging, consubstantial with you, who proceeds from you, not alien to your Godhead or to that of your only-begotten Son, our Lord God and Saviour Jesus Christ; (send him) upon us and upon these offerings set out, sanctify them, so that this bread may become the life-giving body, the heavenly body, the body that saves our bodies and souls, the body of our Lord God and Saviour Jesus Christ, for forgiveness of sins and for eternal life; likewise with the

---

[11] For all the changes to be effected, compare Philoxenus, *Three Tractates on the Trinity and the Incarnation* (ed. Vaschalde), p. 119 (where the context is baptism rather than the Eucharist).

mixture in this cup, (that it may become) the blood of the new covenant, the life-giving blood, the heavenly blood that brings deliverance to
our souls and bodies, the blood of our Lord God and Saviour Jesus
Christ, for forgiveness of sins and for eternal life. Effect that they are
not to us for judgement or condemnation, but for the justification of
our lives after numerous failings, for the increase of faith, for the repel-
ling of every evil action, for the receiving of incorruptibility, and for
participation in your Holy Spirit, now and always.

The normal pattern in the West Syriac anaphoras follows up the initial
imperative with a final clause, making the Spirit the subject of the verb of
consecration. The popularity of this pattern is not surprising, for it is the
one found in the Greek and Syriac anaphora of St James, which exerted an
enormous influence on the authors of the later Syriac anaphoras:

Have mercy on us, God the Father Almighty, and send upon us and
upon these offerings set out your Holy Spirit, Lord and Giver of life,
who shares your throne, O God the Father, and who shares the kingdom with your Son, who is consubstantial and coeternal with you, who
spoke in the law and in the prophets and in your New Testament, who
descended in the likeness of a dove upon our Lord Jesus Christ in the
river Jordan, who descended upon the holy apostles in the likeness of
tongues of fire; hear me, O Lord; hear me, O Lord; hear me, O Lord,
and have mercy upon us; so that, descending, he may make this bread
the lifegiving body, the redeeming body, the heavenly body, the body
which liberates our souls and bodies, the body of our Lord God and
Saviour Jesus Christ, for the remission of sins and for eternal life to
those who receive; (and may he make) the mixture that is in this cup the
blood of the New Covenant, the redeeming blood, the lifegiving blood,
the heavenly blood which liberates our souls and bodies, the blood of
our Lord God and Saviour Jesus Christ, for the remission of sins and
for eternal life to those who receive it; so that they may be, for all those
who partake of them, for the sanctification of souls and bodies, for
fruitfulness in good works, for the strengthening of your holy Church
which you founded on the rock of the faith, against which the gates of
Sheol will not prevail, delivering it from all heresy and from the stum-
bling-block of those who do wrong, up to the end of the world.

This is not the place to dwell on details in these epicleses, beyond
drawing attention to the specific allusion in some of them to Christ's baptism and to Pentecost. Instead we shall consider certain facets of the Holy
Spirit's role in the Eucharist which are brought out by the earlier Syriac fathers and which are characteristic of Syriac liturgical tradition.

The wording of the archaic epicleses, 'may your Spirit come and rest and reside upon...' helps to bring out an important aspect of the understanding of the Eucharist in this tradition: the Holy Spirit not only effects the transformation of the bread and wine into the Body and Blood of Christ, but the Spirit is also himself present in them. As Ephrem puts it in a hymn we have already had occasion to quote:[12]

> In your bread there is hidden the Spirit who is not consumed,
> in your wine there dwells the Fire that is not drunk:
> the Spirit is in your bread, the Fire in your wine,
> a manifold wonder, that our lips have received.

> When the Lord came down to earth to mortal men
> he created them again in a new creation, like angels,
> mingling fire and spirit within them,
> that in a hidden manner they might be of fire and spirit.

By virtue of the Holy Spirit 'mixing'[13] in the baptismal water and in the eucharistic bread and wine, these representatives of the material world not only take on a new mode of existence, but are rendered capable of conveying this new mode of existence to those who participate in the sacraments of baptism and the Eucharist: the fire of the Holy Spirit becomes mingled in the baptized, transforming them into angelic beings, denizens of Paradise.

We have already seen how Baptism is frequently described as the re-entry into Paradise; so too the Eucharist helps to make the Christian aware that, through the working of the Holy Spirit, he has already potentially entered Paradise, in sacred time. Thus Ephrem describes the Eucharist as 'the spiritual bread which becomes for everyone an eagle that conveys to Paradise' (*H. Azym.* 17.12). Ephrem is also conscious of the tensions between liturgical and ordinary time, between what is already achieved in sacred time, and the realization of this achievement in historical time:

> We have eaten Christ's body in place of the fruit on the Tree of Paradise, and his altar has taken the place of the garden of Eden for us; the curse has been washed away by his innocent blood, and in the hope of the resurrection we already walk in this new life, in that we already have the pledge of it. (*Comm. Diat.* 21.25)

---

[12] *H. Fid.* 10.8–9; compare *H. Fid.* 6.4.

[13] As we have already noticed above, in chapter I and elsewhere, this phraseology is characteristic of Syriac tradition.

The aim of the liturgical poets is to stimulate awareness on the part of the baptized that the Eucharist provides a continuous means of effecting the coming together of the two times, an awareness that life in the Spirit is the recovery of Paradise, that the Eucharist is participation in the messianic marriage feast. Thus a *qolo* from vespers on the 12th Sunday after Pentecost introduces the same bridal imagery that we met in connection with Baptism:[14]

> Happy are you, holy and faithful Church, for in his love your Lord has set before you fair and heavenly pasturage, and at your wedding feast he has mixed a draught from which those who drink shall never thirst again. Arise and consume Fire in the Bread, drink the Spirit in the Wine, so that you may be adorned with the Fire and Spirit and enter with your Lord into the bridal chamber.

Ephrem compares this wedding feast with that at Cana, and here the soul is itself the bride, rather than just a guest at the banquet:

> I have invited you, Lord, to a wedding feast of song,
> but the wine, the utterance of praise, at our feast has failed.
> You are the guest who filled the jars with good wine,
> fill my mouth with your praise.
>
> The wine that was in the jars was akin and related to
> this eloquent wine that gives birth to praise,
> seeing that that new wine gave birth to praise
> from those who drank it and beheld the wonder.
>
> You, who are so just, if at a wedding feast not your own
> you filled six jars with good wine,
> do you, at this wedding feast, fill, not the jars
> but the ten thousand ears with its sweetness,
>
> Jesus, you were invited to the wedding feast of others,
> here is your own pure and fair wedding feast:
> gladden your rejuvenated people,
> for your guests too, Lord, need your songs; let your harp utter.
>
> The soul is your bride, the body your bridal chamber,
> your guests are the senses and the thoughts.
> And if a single body is a wedding feast for you,
> how great is your banquet for the whole Church ! (*H. Fid.* 14.1–5)

---

[14] *Fenqitho* VII. p. 154a.

At the Fraction in the Anaphora of St James the priest specifically refers in his prayer to John 19:34, and Jacob of Serugh uses this passage as a
starting point to bring out the paradox of the wedding feast where the
Bridegroom is slain: [15]

> From the baptismal water comes the chaste and holy union
> of Bride and Bridegroom, united in spirit in baptism.
> Women are not joined to their husbands
> in the same way as the Church is joined with the Son of God.
> What bridegroom dies for his bride, apart from our Lord?
> What bride sought out a slain man to be her husband?
> Who, from the beginning of the world, ever gave his blood as the wed-
>   ding gift,
> apart from the Crucified one, who sealed the marriage with his wounds?
> Who has ever seen a corpse placed in the middle of a wedding feast,
> with the bride embracing it, waiting to be comforted by it?
> At what wedding feast apart from this did they break
> the body of the bridegroom for the guests in place of other food?
> Wives are separated from their husbands by death,
> but this Bride is joined to her Beloved by death!
> He died on the cross and gave his body to the glorious bride,
> who plucks and eats it every day at his table;
> he opened up his side and mixed his cup with holy blood,
> giving it her to drink so that she might forget her many idols.
> She anointed him with oil, she put him on in the water,
> she consumed him in the Bread, she drank him in the Wine,
> so that the world might know that the two of them were one.
> He died on the cross, but she did not exchange him for another:
> she is full of love for his death, knowing that from it she has life.

In a stanza we have already quoted Ephrem says:

> See, Fire and Spirit are in the womb of her who bore you...
> In the Bread and Cup are Fire and Holy Spirit. (*H. Fid.* 10.17)

Although Christ's Baptism and Pentecost are specifically referred to in
some of the eucharistic epicleses quoted above, the Annuciation and Nativity are not; yet Syriac writers are very conscious of the links between the
coming of the Holy Spirit upon Mary and the coming of the Holy Spirit

---

[15] Ed. Bedjan III, pp. 290–1. This is attributed to Ephrem in *Fenqitho* VI, pp.
334–5.

upon the bread and wine. As Dionysius bar Salibi puts it in his *Commentary on the Liturgy:*[16]

> The Body and Blood are called 'mysteries' because they are not what they appear to the physical eye to be; for to look at, they are just bread and wine, but properly understood, they are the Body and Blood of God. Just as Jesus appeared to the physical eye to be man, yet he is God, similarly they appear outwardly to be bread and wine, but they are in fact the Body and Blood. Even though it is the Spirit who effects the mysteries, making from them the Blood, nevertheless they are the Body and Blood of the Son, just as happened in the case of the Virgin: even though it was the Spirit who provided the Son with a body, it was still the Son who was embodied. Likewise when the angel said 'that which is born in you is holy and comes from the Holy Spirit,' even though the Holy Spirit was the cause because he formed the body, nevertheless the person conceived and born was the Son. It is the same with the altar, which is the type both of Mary's womb and of the grave; the Holy Spirit overshadows it and changes the bread and the wine, making them the Body and Blood of the Word who once became flesh in the womb. Although the body is that of the Son, it is given us by the Holy Spirit from the Father.

A little later on he says[17] 'The priest's invocation of the Holy Spirit symbolizes Gabriel's annunciation to the Virgin of her conception.'

Now the descent of the Holy Spirit as Fire into the 'watery womb' of Mary gives conception to Christ the Pearl:

> Hail to you, Mary, from whom the resplendent Pearl appeared.[18]

'Pearl' *marganita,* is also a technical term for the consecrated Bread (or Bread and Wine together); as Ephrem says:[19]

> Christ gave us pearls—his holy body and blood.

As we have seen the origin of this usage lies in the mythology that had grown up in antiquity around the genesis of the pearl: the pearl's 'birth' takes place when lightning strikes the mussel of the pearl-oyster in the sea; from this conjunction of disparate elements, fire and water, the mussel opens and the pearl is born—'a precious stone born from flesh' (i.e. of the

[16] Ed. Labourt, pp. 61–2 (cp also pp. 67–8).
[17] Ed. Labourt, p. 68.
[18] *Brev. Chald,* II, p. 543 (Annunciation).
[19] *Sermones* II iv. lines 9–10 (homily on the sinful woman).

mussel), as a Greek text attributed to Ephrem puts it.[20] The pearl is thus an eminently suitable symbol for Christ; its miraculous birth from two disparate elements corresponds to Christ's birth from Mary and the Holy Spirit; its being raised up from the depths of the sea to take its place of honour on the royal crown finds a double parallel in the ascent from the Jordan and the ascent from Sheol. Using language deliberately reminiscent of the Annunciation Jacob of Serugh speaks of the analogous genesis of the Eucharistic 'pearls':[21]

> The Holy Spirit proceeds from the Father,
> descends, overshadows and resides upon the bread,
> making it the Body, making of the bread priceless pearls.

We have already seen how the imagery of pearl-diving was used in connection with baptism, with the baptized diving for Christ the pearl. Yet further aspects of the pearl are to be found in Ephrem's famous group of five hymns 'on the Pearl' at the end of the collection 'on Faith': besides being a symbol of Christ, the pearl is also one of faith[22] and of virginity,[23] while in later writers, in particular Jacob of Serugh, the pearl may be Adam in Sheol, and Christ himself the pearl-diver:[24]

> Christ was baptized in the pit (of the dead); groping in Sheol, he drew
>   out Adam,
> feeling around in the mud of the dead he sought out the pearl.

Or:[25]

> He went down to the lake of the dead, diving in like a bather,
> from it he brought up the pearl on which was depicted his own image.

In some passages in the *Fenqitho* the pearl actually *is* Adam's lost image:[26]

> Having borne all that belongs to mortals.

---

[20] Ed. Assemani II, p. 263. Compare *H. Fid.* 83.11 and 84.14.

[21] Ed. Bedjan IV, p. 597.

[22] Cp also *H. Fid.* 16.7; similarly (at some length) in Jacob of Serugh's *Letter* 16 (ed. Olinder), pp. 74–6.

[23] Cp *H. Epiph.* 6.17.3; in Sahdona (ed. de Halleux II, p. 71) the pearl is spiritual virginity.

[24] Ed. Bedjan II, p. 599 (*Fenqitho* V, p. 317).

[25] Ed. Bedjan III, p. 423 (very similarly in III, p. 642); compare also *Fenqitho* V, p. 442a.

[26] *Fenqitho* V, p. 384b.

you were exalted with all that belongs to divinity,
you rose from the grave without corruption,
victoriously extracting the plunder stored up there over the ages,
bringing back with you to the region of Life those exiles whom
Death had confined in darkness, raising up the precious pearl, Adam's
     image, from the womb of Death.

Jacob, in the second passage quoted, goes on to state that the pearl had
been stolen by the serpent, and it is possible that Jacob here has in mind the
famous 'hymn of the Pearl' in the *Acts of Thomas*,[27] where the King's Son
goes down to Egypt to bring back a pearl, guarded by the dragon.

Thanks to Ephrem's fertile poetic mind, the pearl is also able to bring
us back to that focal point of Syriac typology, Christ's pierced side whence
flowed the twin mysteries of Baptism and the Eucharist, thus providing us
with a suitable place to close this chapter: (Ephrem addresses the pearl)

Your nature resembles the silent Lamb
with his gentleness: even though a man pierce it,
takes it and hangs it on his ear,
as it were on Golgotha, all the more does it throw out
its bright rays on those who behold it!
In your beauty is the Son's beauty depicted:
—the Son who clothed himself in suffering; nails went through him,
through you the awl passed, you too did they pierce
as they did his hands. But because he suffered he reigns,
just as your beauty is enhanced through your suffering.

                                        (H. Fid. 82.11–12)

---

[27] *Acts of Thomas* §§ 108–113. Since the hymn is poorly attested in the manuscript tradition, Jacob's awareness of it is of some interest.

7 THE HOLY SPIRIT AND MARY

Just as the Eucharist provides the model for the proper relationship between the material world and the heavenly, so too Mary provides the model for cooperation between man and the Holy Spirit. This is very much brought out in Syriac tradition where the descent of the Holy Spirit on Mary at the Annunciation is seen in very similar terms to the Spirit's descent on the baptismal water and on the Bread and Wine.[1] In the course of the previous chapters many examples of the way in which phraseology and imagery properly belonging to Mary has been transferred to a baptismal or a eucharistic context, and the reverse, have been given; here we shall simply try to draw together the main points.

THE HOLY SPIRIT 'OVERSHADOWS'

We have already seen in chapter I how 'overshadow' (*aggen*) soon became a technical term for the Holy Spirit's activity, and so found its way into the phraseology of several Syriac baptismal and eucharistic epicleses. The origin of this terminology can safely be identified in the angel Gabriel's greeting to Mary, 'The Holy Spirit shall come upon you and the Power of the Most High shall overshadow you' (Luke 1:35).[2]

The term 'overshadow' never occurs in the New Testament accounts of baptism or the eucharist, but is frequently found in these contexts in Syriac writers and liturgical texts. In the Maronite baptismal service the deacon proclaims:[3]

> The baptismal water has been sanctified by the Holy Spirit, and has been perfected by the overshadowing of the Holy Spirit.

---

[1] For the latter, see the passages quoted in the previous chapter.

[2] The usage must have originated in a milieu which identified the 'Power' with the Holy Spirit, rather than with the Word (as often understood by Syrian Orthodox writers; cp chapter I).

[3] JS II, p. 344.

Similarly the East Syriac Anaphora of Theodore has for its epiclesis:

> May the Grace of the Holy Spirit come upon us and upon this offering,
> may it rest upon and overshadow this bread...

Indeed, 'overshadow' in the wording of the eucharistic epiciesis occurs in roughly half of the very numerous West Syriac anaphoras that survive. It is interesting that in two out of the three epicleses said over the baptismal candidates in the Syrian Orthodox *Severus*, quoted in chapter V, the same verb is used. Mary's receptivity at the Annunciation thus very clearly serves as a model for all Christians to imitate.

THE THREE 'WOMBS'

Jacob of Serugh saw the Nativity, Baptism and Descent as a series of three 'staging posts' in the course of the Incarnation, and elsewhere, along with other Syriac writers, he describes these as 'wombs,' the first real, the second and third metaphorical.[4] The relationship between these three wombs is well brought out in a beautiful prayer common to the Maronite service and the old Syrian Orthodox one in Add. 14518:[5]

> Your greatness, Lord, was pleased to save us by your unsparing love,
> and you sent, for our salvation, your only-begotten Son and everlasting
> Child, who was born of you without a beginning, who left his hidden
> abode, descended and dwelt in the Virgin's womb so as to appear visibly
> in bodily birth; remaining entirely with you, he came entirely to us, and
> though he was not wanting or lacking in anything he was baptized in the
> river Jordan and sanctified for us the womb of water, to be a womb full
> of health and power. He, Lord, by his own will and by your will dwelt in
> the world for our sake in three different abodes, in the womb made of
> flesh, in the womb of baptism, and in the gloomy abode of Sheol.

The parallelism between Mary's womb and the Jordan's womb led Ephrem to see Christ's presence in Mary's womb as her own baptism, thus anticipating his sanctification of baptismal water at his baptism:[6]

> The Light settled on Mary as on an eye,
> it purified her mind, it cleansed her understanding,

---

[4] See 'Baptismal themes.'

[5] § 31.

[6] Likewise the presence of Christ in Mary's womb effects the baptism of John the Baptist in Elizabeth's womb (based on Luke 2:41, 'the child stirred in her womb'): Jacob of Serugh (ed. Bedjan) I, pp. 156, 183; S, pp. 646–7.

it washed her thought, it made her virginity shine.

The river in which Christ was baptized conceived him again symbolically,
the damp womb of the water conceived him in purity
and bore him in holiness, made him rise up in glory.

In the pure womb of the river you should recognize the daughter of
man
who conceived without the aid of man, and gave birth as a virgin, and
who brought up, through a gift, the Lord of that gift.

(*H. Eccl.* 36.2–4)[7]

and more explicitly:

O Christ, you have given birth to your own mother in the second birth
that comes from water.

(*H. Nativ.* 16.9)

Although the three 'staging posts' or 'wombs' are separate in ordinary time,
they nevertheless come together in sacred time, forming a single unit, seeing
that their salvific content is essentially single. Thanks to this insight,
Ephrem can boldly reverse the apparent sequence of events in ordinary
time.

The relationship between Mary's womb and the womb of baptism is
again brought out in a striking prayer, attributed to Philoxenus, who puts
the following words into the mouth of Jesus at his own baptism:[8]

Do you, Father, open the heavens at my prayer and send your Holy
Spirit upon this baptismal womb, and as the Spirit descended upon the
womb of the Virgin and formed me from her, so may he likewise descend into the womb of the baptismal water to sanctify it, to fashion
men and to give birth from it to new children, making them your sons
and my brothers and fellow heirs of the kingdom…Every time the
priests of the new covenant baptize and call upon you, do you send the
Holy Spirit upon the baptismal water with which they are baptizing
men. May the fact that the Spirit has appeared visibly at the present
moment be an indication that he will descend invisibly whenever they
baptize…

---

[7] For the whole poem, with commentary, see *Eastern Churches Review* 7 (1976),
pp. 137–44,

[8] Quoted by Dionysius bar Salibi, *Comm. Gospels*, ed. Vaschalde (II (2)), p. 304.

Rather a different slant is given to the parallelism between Mary the mother of Christ and Baptism, the 'mother' of Christians, in a passage by Jacob of Serugh:[9]

> Mary gave a body for the Word to become incarnate,
> while Baptism gives the Spirit for men to be renewed.

Stated in formulaic terms we have here the contrasted pattern:

> Through Mary the Divine becomes human
> Through Baptism the human becomes divine.

THE NEW EVE

The typological contrast between Eve and Mary provides yet more ties between Mary and Baptism. The Syriac poets develop the intricacies and nuances of the Eve-Mary typology with consummate skill, and it is important to recognize the different emphases that lie uppermost at any given moment. In the following passage, by Jacob of Serugh, the interest centres on the theme of miraculous birth-giving:[10]

> As our father Adam begot our mother without intercourse,
> so did Mary give birth, just as Adam did before he had sinned.
> The Holy Spirit blew on Adam's face, and he gave birth to Eve:
> this Spirit did Mary too receive,
> and she gave birth to a son...
> Adam gave birth to the 'mother of all living things' without intercourse,
> thus depicting the birth of our Lord, who is the fountain of all life.

This gives the pattern

> Adam: Eve: : Mary: Christ.

Not far below the surface, however, lie the contrasted relationships between the First Adam and the Second Adam, and between the Old Eve and the New Eve, with the pattern

> Adam: Christ: : Eve: Mary.

---

[9] Ed. Bedjan I, p. 204.

[10] Ed. Bedjan, S, p. 634 On Eve-Mary typology in Syriac writers, see also R, Murray, 'Mary the Second Eve in the early Syriac Fathers,' *Eastern Churches Review* 3 (1971), pp. 372–84, my *Mary in Syriac Tradition* (Ecumenical Society of the Blessed Virgin Mary, 1977), and 'The Mysteries hidden in the side of Christ,' *Sobornost* VII. 6 (1978), pp. 462–72; cp also chapter V (1) (b) (vi) and (viii) above.

Thanks to that focal point of Syriac typological thinking, John 19.34, Baptism is just as much at home in this context, in the same role as Mary:[11]

> The virgin earth gave birth to Adam in holy fashion,
> so as to indicate clearly Mary's giving birth.
> Adam in turn slept, and his side was pierced:
> from it came forth Eve to be mother for the whole world,
> serving as an image of that sleep of death upon the cross
> and that side which gave birth to baptism.
> Adam slept, and gave the whole world a mother;
> the Saviour died, and there flows from him baptismal water.
> If the side gave birth to Eve, as is written,
> then a virgin too gave birth to the Son, as is indicated.

This passage now gives a double set of miraculous birthgivings

Earth : Adam: : Mary: Christ

Adam : Eve: : Christ : Baptism

Both Mary and Baptism thus fill the role of the New Eve; Mary gives birth to Christ, Baptism to Christians. In the consecration prayer common to the Maronite and the older Syrian orthodox services,[12] the priest prays that 'instead of the womb of Eve, which produced children who were mortal and corruptible, may this womb of water produce children who are heavenly, spiritual and immortal.'

As a result of this parallelism, Mary shares many titles with the baptismal font. But at the same time she is an ordinary mortal, and shares equally with other mortals. She is in fact the exemplar of what the Christian should become as a result of the gift of the Spirit at baptism, the model of the person who cooperates fully and completely with the Holy Spirit. Viewed from this angle, we can see something of the profundity of Ephrem's insight that Mary's conception at the Annunciation was also her baptism.

The sanctification that Mary receives through the presence of Christ in her womb is thus closely analogous to the presence of the 'fire' of the Holy Spirit in both the baptismal water and in the eucharistic elements. This comes out very clearly in Ephrem's stanza:

> See, Fire and Spirit are in the womb of her who bore you,
> Fire and Spirit are in the river in which you were baptized;
> Fire and Spirit are in our baptism,

---

[11] Jacob of Serugh, ed. Bedjan III, p. 320.
[12] T § 35 = D § 36 = JS II, pp. 339–40.

and in the Bread and Cup are Fire and Holy Spirit.

(*H. Fid.* 10.17)

In the case of the baptismal water and the eucharistic bread and wine, we have the assurance that the Holy Spirit will come and make effective the sanctification or consecration. In the baptism of a Christian likewise we have the assurance that the Holy Spirit will come and reside in the newly baptized, but at this point there is difference, for the cooperation of the individual is required if the Holy Spirit is to effect the process of sanctification: the Christian receives the potential for sanctification—it is up to him whether he responds and allows this sanctification to take place, as Mary preeminently did.

8 BAPTISM AS PENTECOST

John the Baptist told his hearers that He who was to come 'will baptize you with the Holy Spirit and with fire' (Matt. 3:11), and shortly before his Ascension Jesus himself promised his disciples 'before many days you shall be baptized with the Holy Spirit' (Acts 1:5). Addressing the Upper Room where the disciples were gathered at Pentecost, Jacob of Serugh says:[1]

> In you was accomplished that promise of baptism
> for in you were all the disciples baptized with Holy Spirit and fire.

Given their predilection for fire imagery in connection with the Holy Spirit, the Syriac fathers found no difficulty in identifying Christian baptism with 'baptism in the Holy Spirit and in fire,' and the awe they felt at the presence of the Holy Spirit and fire there is well brought out in the following words uttered by the deacon in the Maronite *Jacob*:[2]

> How fearful and full of awe is this moment when the supernal beings stand in silence above this baptismal water—thousand upon thousands of angels, ten thousands of Seraphim hover over this new mother, holy baptism, the spiritual mother who gives birth to spiritual children who enter into the bridal chamber of life that is full of joys. The angels in their ranks, the cherubim with their wings, the fiery beings with their holy nature, the watchers in their pure splendour: all these are born of fire and reside in fire, they now mix fire into this water so that the children of earth-born Adam may find forgiveness there; they carry veils of fire and stand by the river Jordan to receive the Son of God who has come to perfect baptism. The Holy Spirit descends upon him from the uppermost heights, not to sanctify him, but to bear witness to him; for John the true herald has cried out and said 'This is the Lamb of God

---

[1] Ed. Bedjan II, p. 679 (cp 680, 683), Philoxenus, in his *Homily on the Indwelling of the Holy Spirit* (ed Tanghe, p. 46) says: 'this descent of the Holy Spirit (at Pentecost) he calls baptism, because the apostles' baptism there was by the Holy Spirit alone, for they had already been baptized in water by John.' (It is interesting that Philoxenus, unlike his contemporary Jacob, recognizes a post-baptismal anointing; see the passage quoted in chapter III (2) (b) (iii)).

[2] JS II, pp. 332–4; cp SA I in Assemani pp. 291–2.

who takes away the sin of the world.' Come let us fall down and worship him, all peoples nations and tongues, him at whose word the heavens, the earth, the seas, the rivers, and all that is in them, were created.

Thus baptism is also a Pentecost, a charismatic event. This is an insight
that the liturgical poets explore at some length. It is the Upper Room, identified as the locale of the Spirit's outpouring,[3] that provides a starting point
for the parallelism that was seen between Pentecost and Baptism. We have
already had occasion to see that the baptismal water as a furnace was a
popular image; in the West Syriac Office for Pentecost the Upper Room is
likewise described as a furnace:[4]

> On this day the disciples were poured out like gold in the furnace of the
> Spirit, and their splendour shone out to the four quarters of the world,
> and they preached the name of Jesus throughout the world.

And a little further on:[5]

> The Holy Spirit poured them out like gold in the furnace of tongues.

This is very like Narsai's simile:[6]

> As in a furnace He poured forth our image in baptism, in the place of
> our dross, making us spiritual gold.

The image of the furnace leads on to another one that is already familiar from the baptismal texts, the forging by the Spirit of armour.[7] Thus, in a
passage that is incorporated into the *Fenqitho*, Jacob of Serugh speaks of the
Spirit and fire as[8]

> forging armour for the disciples, and clothing them in it.

Both the East and West Syriac breviaries frequently make use of this
imagery; thus:[9]

> Christ clothed his apostles with the armour of the Holy Spirit, and the
> disciples[10] are armed with the armour of the Spirit.

---

[3] Interpreting Acts 2:1 in the light of 1:12–14.
[4] *Fenqitho* VI, p. 211a.
[5] *Fenqitho* VI, p. 217b.
[6] Ed. Mingana I, p. 356.
[7] See above, chapter V.
[8] Ed. Bedjan II, p. 677 (= *Fenqitho* VI, p. 203).
[9] *Brev. Chald.* III, p. 73.

And Christ is made to say[11]

> Behold, I clothe my workers with armour and divine power.

It is interesting in this connection to compare Jacob of Serugh's homilies on Christ's baptism with those on Pentecost, for he uses very similar phraseology in connection with both events. Thus in a passage from the homily on Pentecost already quoted, the Spirit and fire 'forge armour for the disciples,' while in that on the baptism of Christ, Christ states that his purpose in going down to 'the fountain' was not

> to take a shield for myself
> but to forge mighty armour for warriors;[12]

and a few lines further on in the same homily Christ says

> I am making baptism into an armoury,

while in the homily on Pentecost the Upper Room is addressed:[13]

> You have become like an armoury for the apostles,
> and from you they have put on the might of the Spirit to subdue the
> wild.

We have already seen the role that the imagery of armour plays in the baptismal texts themselves.

Baptism culminates in the Eucharist, and the liturgical texts for Pentecost in both the East and West Syriac traditions associate the outpouring of the Holy Spirit at Pentecost with wine. The source of this wine is specified as Christ's pierced side (John 19:34), which, as we have seen, is also the source of baptismal water according to many baptismal texts.

Whereas in Acts Peter pours scorn on the charge that the disciples were drunk, the liturgical texts for Pentecost give a different slant to the accusation: they are indeed drunk—but not with ordinary wine. Thus in the *Fenqitho*:[14]

> The living Cross, with its wine, inebriated them so that they spoke;
> from it they received, in amazement, a new scripture that required no
> learning:

---

[10] *Brev. Chald.* III, p. 58; cp *Fenqitho* VI, p. 220b.
[11] *Fenqitho* VI, p. 217a.
[12] Ed. Bedjan I, p. 180.
[13] Ed. Bedjan II, p. 679.
[14] *Fenqitho* VI, pp. 215–6.

the strong drink that the lance had trodden out taught them every-
tongue.

The East Syriac Breviary uses very similar terms:[15]

> They were drunk with wine that had been trodden out by the lance,
> which is none other than the precious blood.

The phraseology here is traditional, and we find it turning up in the
early poets and homilists; thus Jacob of Serugh, in his homily on Pentecost,
writes:[16]

> What wine can teach letters in this way? It is the Cross, with its wine,
>   that inflamed them to speak...
> the strong wine that the Nation trod out on Golgotha,
> the new wine that the side of the Son of God made to flow.

An anonymous writer, probably slightly earlier than Jacob, puts it in this
way:[17]

> The Jews, always resistant to the Holy Spirit, said; 'They have drunk
> wine and become inebriated.' You have spoken the truth—but it is not
> quite as you think. They have not drunk the wine of the vine; rather, a
> new drink has flowed down from heaven for them, it is the wine re-
> cently pressed out on Golgotha. The apostles have drunk of it, and in
> turn they have inebriated creation with this draught.

Elsewhere in the liturgical texts for Pentecost, in both East and West
Syriac tradition, similar language is common; the Chaldean Breviary speaks
of 'the drink of the Spirit'[18] while the *Fenqitho* says 'make us drunk with the
drink of your grace,' and talks of 'the divine wine from the gift of the
Spirit.'[19]

Related to this imagery is that of the Upper Room as a fountain:

> The Upper Room became a fountain gushing forth rivers,

---

[15] *Brev. Chald.* III, pp. 55–6.

[16] Ed. Bedjan II, pp. 680–1.

[17] In Overbeck, *Ephraemi Syri aliorumque opera selecta*, p. 97 (French translation
by T. Jansma in *L'Orient Syrien* 6 (1961).

[18] *Brev. Chald.* III, p. 61.

[19] *Fenqitho* VI, pp. 237a, 200a respectively. This corresponds to the well-known
motif of *sobria ebrietas* in Greek and Latin writers. For this theme in Syriac literature,
see further my '*Sobria ebrietas* according to some Syriac texts,' *Aram* 17 (2005), pp.
185–91.

says Jacob,[20] and 'fountain' of course is frequently used to describe the baptismal water, and from it the baptized 'drink ,' as well as wash in it:[21]

> The King's bride has made a wedding feast for all the world;
> O nations and worlds, come to the banquet of the glorious maiden,
> she has opened up for the world living water from the Father,
> all who are thirsty, drink the draught of hope from her fountain.

The Syriac fathers are well aware that the pentecostal effects of baptism do not necessarily manifest themselves at baptism itself, but may be delayed until later: the 'pledge of the Spirit,' the potential, however, is already present as a result of baptism. One of the great East Syriac mystics, Abdisho, describes these subsequent 'workings of the Spirit which you received at baptism':[22]

> The first sign of the effective working of the Spirit is when the love of God burns in the heart of a man like fire. From this are born in his heart the hatred and the complete renunciation of the world, and the love of solitude and asceticism, which is the mother and educator of all virtues.
>
> The second sign through which you will feel, my brother, that the Spirit which you received from baptism is working in you, consists in true humility being born in your soul. I am not alluding to the humility of the body, but to the true humility of the soul, which induces a man to consider himself dust and ashes, a worm and no man (Ps. 22:6), notwithstanding the great and wonderful things done to him by the Spirit who dwells in him. All men are also in his eyes great and holy, and there is no one who in his mind is good or bad, just or unjust. It is from humility that peace, meekness and endurance of tribulations are born in the soul.
>
> The third sign of the working of the Spirit in you consists in the kindness which represents within you the image of God, through which, when your thoughts extend to all men, tears flow from your eyes like fountains of water, as if all men were dwelling in your heart, and you affectionately embrace them and kiss them, while you pour your kindness on all. When you remember them your heart is kindled with the power

---

[20] Ed. Bedjan II, p. 688; the rivers divide up into twelve streams, an idea also found in *Fenqitho* VI, p. 218a.

[21] Ed. Bedjan I, pp. 194–5. Note the use of the episode of the Samaritan woman at the well in the Chaldean Breviary at Pentecost (III, p. 79, 81); she features in connection with Christ's baptism in both *Brev. Chald.* I, p. 421 and *Fenqitho* III, p. 288a.

[22] Ed. Mingana (Woodbrooke Studies 7), pp. 165–7.

of the working of the Spirit in you as with fire, and from this, goodness and kindness are born in your heart, so that you do not utter an unkind thing to any man, nor does your thought think evil of anyone, but you do good to all men, both in your thought and in your deed.

The fourth sign from which you will know that the Spirit is working within you consists in true love, which does not leave in your thought any remembrance but remembrance of God alone, which is the spiritual key through which the inner door of the heart is opened, in which is hidden Christ our Lord, whose dwelling place is spiritual and broad, and whose vision is a light that is ineffable. It is from this love that is engendered the faith which sees the hidden things which the mind is not allowed to confide to paper, and which the Apostle called 'the sustenance of things hoped for' (Heb. 11:1), which are not known to the eyes of flesh but are known clearly to the eyes of the mind, in the inward abode of the heart.

The fifth sign of the working in you of the Spirit which you received in baptism consists in the illuminated vision of your mind, which is seen in the firmament of your heart like the sapphire sky (Ex. 24:10), It is this vision that receives the light of the Holy Trinity, and it is this sign that leads you to the vision of the material natures from which you rise again to the knowledge of the intelligible natures. From the latter you will then ascend to the revelations and the mysteries of the divine judgement and providence. It is this gradual ascent that raises you up and makes you participate in the holy light of the vision of Christ our Lord. From this glorious and holy vision you will fall into ecstasy over that broad world, the benefits of which are ineffable. From this ecstasy you will derive a flow of spiritual speech and the knowledge of both worlds: of the one that has passed and the one that shall pass, and also a consciousness of the mysteries of future things, together with a holy scent and taste; the fine sounds of the spiritual intelligences; joy, jubilation, exultation, praise, glorification, songs, hymns and odes of magnification; communion with the spiritual hierarchies; vision of the souls of the saints; sight of Paradise: eating from its tree of life, and intercourse with the saints who dwell in it, together with other ineffable things.

The above are the signs, by which if you find in yourself, you will know that the Holy Spirit, which you received from holy baptism, is working within you.

What Abdisho is describing clearly corresponds to what the liturgical poets, quoted above, have been portraying as the inebriating effects of baptism itself.

There has been a constant temptation among Christians to focus on these subsequent manifest workings of the Holy Spirit at the expense of the hidden workings at baptism. Among some Messalians in antiquity, and some pentecostal groups in the present century, this has led to the abandonment of the sacrament of baptism altogether, while in more orthodox circles there has sometimes been a tendency to regard entry into the monastic life as the true realization of baptism, with the rite of profession being closely modelled on the baptismal service.

Philoxenus describes the tension between the hidden and manifest workings of the Spirit in the following way:[23]

> You have two baptisms, one of grace, which takes place in the baptismal water, the other, of your own will, when you are baptized out of the 'world' in love for God.

And again, later in the homily:[24]

> It appears that the man of God experiences three births: the first, from the womb into creation; the second, from slavery into freedom, from being a man to becoming a son to God—something that takes place by grace at baptism; while the third birth is when a person is reborn of his own will from a corporeal way of life to a spiritual one, and he himself becomes a womb which gives birth to complete self-emptying.

What Philoxenus is saying here is something of great value. He is looking at the relationship between the personal experience of Pentecost, of the coming of the Holy Spirit on to the individual and the actual rite of baptism, in a context where, because of the practice of infant baptism, the two events may be separated by many years in time. Philoxenus' point is that the rite itself confers the gift of the Spirit, but that, since giving also involves receiving, a conscious act of the will, accepting the gift, is required on the part of the recipient, if he is to experience properly the benefits that result from the gift. This acceptance involves the self emptying that Christ himself underwent (Phil 2:7): only once the ego has been stripped away can the gift of the Spirit be fully experienced. The 'two baptisms' are thus but two aspects of the one sacrament, the first seen from the point of view of the Giver, second, from that of the receiver.

---

[23] *Homily* 9 (ed. Budge, p. 276).
[24] *Homily* 9 (ed. Budge, p. 342).

APPENDIX 1

THE TRANSITION TO A POST-BAPTISMAL ANOINTING IN THE ANTIOCHENE RITE

It is well known that the early Syrian baptismal rite had no post-baptismal anointing with myron, only a pre-baptismal one (with olive oil). The post-baptismal anointing is still unknown to John Chrysostom in the 380s, but before the end of the century it is specified in the Apostolic Constitutions.[1] In the course of the fifth century it gained widespread use in the Antiochene area, although in a few localities the old pattern continued to be operative: thus neither Narsai (who died in 502) nor Jacob of Serugh (who died in 523) mention any post-baptismal anointing, and it is still absent from a manuscript of the eleventh or twelfth century containing a short Melkite baptismal service; likewise, the two earliest Syriac commentaries on the baptismal rite pass over it in silence, and presumably know of none.[2]

My aim here is to examine the relationship between the pre-baptismal and post-baptismal anointings in the Antiochene rite, and to consider some of the reasons that led to the re-interpretation of the old pre-baptismal anointing.

---

[1] For a claim that a post-baptismal anointing was present in Syria at an earlier date, see A. H. B. Logan, 'Post-baptismal chrismation in Syria: the evidence of Ignatius, the Didache and the Apostolic Constitutions,' *Journal of Theological Studies* 49 (1998), pp. 92–108, but on this see J. G. Mueller, 'Post-baptismal chrismation in second-century Syria: a reconsideration of the evidence,' *Journal of Theological Studies* 57 (2006), pp. 76–93.

[2] For Jacob, see my 'Baptismal themes in the writings of Jacob of Serugh,' *Symposium Syriacum* II (OCA 205; 1978), pp. 325–47; the Melkite short service is published in *Parole de l'Orient* 3 (1972), pp. 119–30; the commentaries are edited in my 'Some early Syriac baptismal commentaries,' *Orientalia Christiana Periodica* 46 (1980), pp. 20–61 (reprinted in *Fire from Heaven. Studies in Syriac Theology and Liturgy* (Variorum Reprints, 2006). ch. XV).

By the end of the fourth century there were actually two pre-baptismal anointings present in the Antiochene rite,[3] a signing, or marking (*rushma*) of the forehead with olive oil (*meshha*), and an anointing of the whole body (*mshihuta*), also with olive oil. If they are separated in time (which is not necessarily the case), the *rushma* comes immediately before, and the *mshihuta* immediately after, the sanctification of the water. These two pre-baptismal anointings, with the addition of a post-baptismal one with myron, constitute the norm in the later formularies of all the West Syriac Churches.[4]

The two pre-baptismal anointings definitely represent a duplication, and at an earlier stage it is certain that there was just a single anointing, the *rushma*, involving the forehead only; such a pattern actually survives in some of the later Syrian Orthodox formularies[5] (probably representing the more conservative Tagrit, as opposed to the Antioch, rite), and is presupposed in the outline of the baptismal rite in the second chapter of Ps. Dionysius the Areopagite's Ecclesiastical Hierarchy—in both cases, of course, with the addition of the post-baptismal anointing.

There has been considerable discussion over the meaning of the pre-baptismal anointing(s),[6] but unfortunately much of this has been vitiated by the use of loose and misleading terminology, and by the (often unconscious) attempt to fit the evidence into the straight-jacket of purely western

---

[3] This is clear from John Chrysostom's Catechetical Homilies, amongst others.

[4] In the East Syriac tradition myron is not employed; there the post-baptismal anointing is in some texts replaced by an imposition of hands.

[5] See my 'Studies in the early history of the Syrian Orthodox baptismal liturgy,' *Journal of Theological Studies* ns 23 (1972), pp. 16–64, esp. pp. 31–2.

[6] In particular it has been argued that the pre-baptismal anointing was essentially exorcistic and cathartic, and that consequently it has a completely different meaning from the later post-baptismal one and the latter's western equivalent of Confirmation. For this view see H. B. Green, 'The significance of the pre-baptismal seal in St John Chrysostom' *Studia Patristica* 6 (1962), pp. 84–90, and especially E. C. Whitaker, 'Unction in the Syrian baptismal rite,' *Churches Quarterly Review* 162 (1961), pp. 176–87, Sacramental Initiation Complete in Baptism (Bramcote, 1975), and 'The prayer *Pater Sancte* in the Syrian Orthodox baptismal liturgy,' *Journal of Theological Studies* ns 28 (1977), pp. 525–8. Whitaker based his case on late fourth- and fifth-century writers; as will be seen below, a shift in conceptual models and imagery at about this time led to a re-interpretation of the *rushma*, and so it is important to get behind these writers in order to discover the full significance of the *rushma*. For a balanced survery, see E. J. Lengeling, 'Vom Sinn der präbaptismalen Salbung,' in *Mélanges liturgiques offerts à Dom B. Botte* (Louvain, 1972), pp. 327–57. There is also a good discussion in L. Ligier, *La Confirmation* (Paris, 1973), pp. 182–7.

developments, without allowing the texts to speak for themselves as a whole. I shall attempt here to avoid these pitfalls by simply abstracting the dominant themes that are associated with the pre-baptismal anointings (above all with the *rushma*) in the earlier literature, paying particular attention to the imagery used. As it happens, many of these themes are preserved in their original context in the later formularies.[7]

(1) The *rushma* is the mark of ownership

This idea is recurrent in texts of all periods; its equivalent under the Old Covenant was circumcision, a fact of which all early writers are very much aware: the East Syriac *ordo* indeed speaks of the baptized being 'circumcised by it (sc. the oil) with a circumcision without hands, stripping off the flesh of sins with Christ's circumcision,'[8] and Narsai describes the priest as holding 'the iron of the oil on the tip of his finger' and sharpening the oil (i.e. at the epiclesis) like iron to cut away iniquity.'[9]

Very frequently the mark of ownership is viewed as a brand mark, identifying the baptized as sheep in Christ's flock. This particular pastoral imagery, found already in the Acts of Thomas (sections 25, 131 etc.), is extremely common in all the formularies.[10]

(2) The anointing is also protective

Here again there is an Old Testament basis in Exodus 12:23 and Ezekiel 9:4. The second passage (where the Peshitta actually uses the term *rushma*) indicates that originally this concept belonged to the *rushma* on the forehead, rather than the *mshihuta*. It is found already int he Acts of Thomas (section 157) but does not play an important part in the earlier Syriac texts on baptism; in John Chrysostom, Theodore and Narsai, however, it takes on a very prominent role.

---

[7] For details, see chapter V (2) above.

[8] Urmiah edition, p. 68.

[9] R. H. Connolly, *The Liturgical Homilies of Narsai* (Texts and Studies VIII; Cambridge, 1909), pp. 41–2.

[10] In John Chrysostom, Theodore and Narsai the idea of ownership is extended to that of enrolment as a soldier of Christ.

The imagery employed varies: the *rushma* on the forehead may serve to 'dazzle' Satan;[11] or the oil may be described as providing spiritual armour, an idea which obviously best suits an anointing of the whole body (even though in some texts it is applied to the *rushma*). Again, in areas where Greek culture was predominant, the anointing of the whole body may represent that of athletes in preparation for the arena;[12] in less hellenized regions the *mshihuta* was compared to the oiling of pearl divers.[13]

Only very rarely, as far as the Antiochene area is concerned, is the oil regarded as exorcistic as well as protective. On the other hand, it is frequently seen in positive terms as providing healing and cleansing; the latter may be associated with the idea of the *rushma* as a mark of ownership, as in Ephrem's important Hymn 7 in the collection On Virginity, where the oil cleanses and refurbishes the divine image in each human person (Gen. 1:26).[14]

(3) The anointing confers the royal priesthood on the baptized

This is a prominent them in the earlier texts, but one which tended to be pushed into the background later on. The biblical basis is provided by Exodus 19:6 and I Peter 2:9 (in the Peshitta, 'You shall be a chosen race, serving as priests for the Kingdom'). When the baptized receive this dignity, they are understood as sharing in the kingship and priesthood of Christ himself, in that they too are no 'anointed ones.'

As will be seen, originally this theme must have been tied to the *rushma*, even though some of the *ordines* associate it with the *mshihuta*. The reason for this shift may be because the idea was sometimes expressed in terms of investiture with the 'robe of glory' (on which, see below), where the imagery was thought better to suit an anointing of the whole body (in later writers it gets transferred to the water).

---

[11] See John Chrysostom, *Catechesis* II.23 (ed. Wenger).

[12] John Chrysostom, *Catechesis* II.23, incongruously links this with the anointing of the forehead.

[13] E.g. Ephrem, *Hymns on Faith* 82:10 (English translation in my *The Harp of the Spirit: 18 Poems of St Ephrem* (Studies Supplementary to Sobornost 4, 1983), no. 4).

[14] English translation if *The Harp of the Spirit*, no. 8; stanza 6 of this poem contains one of the very rare early Syriac mentions of 'the seal of the Spirit' (here in the sense of a signet, leaving an impression to denote ownership).

(4) The *rushma* conveys sonship

In Syriac writers this features as one of the most important gifts of the
Spirit conferred in the baptismal rite; as they point out, it is the indwelling
of the Holy Spirit which now allows the newly baptized to address God as
Father (Romans 8:15), and so use the 'Our Father.' The conferring of sonship is still associated with the *rushma* in many of the early texts of the formularies, and the presence, in some manuscripts, of the Our Father before,
and not after, the baptism in water simply emphasizes this.[15]

The gift of sonship is closely linked to the public proclamation of
Christ's sonship at his baptism.

*

Looking back at this summary outline, it is possible to see that the early
Syrian baptismal rite has a strongly Jewish background. The rite as a whole
was essentially modelled on the Jewish rite for admitting proselytes, circumcision followed by baptism, with the circumcision replaced by an anointing,
the *rushma*, and the baptism having as its model Christ's own baptism in the
Jordan. The choice of anointing of the forehead to represent and replace
circumcision as the new mark of identity was very probably governed by the
Old Testament practice of anointing kings, priests and prophets, since, according to the Talmud, priests were anointing with a *chi* on their forehead.[16]
Finally, the *rushma* was also connected with the protective mark of Exodus
and Ezekiel, where the latter again points to the forehead as the part of the
body anointed. Emphasis on the protective aspect may represent a subsequent development.[17]

*

In practically all writers of the late fourth and early fifth century there is a
strong tendency to transfer all the positive gifts of the Spirit to the baptism
in water, leaving the pre-baptismal anointing as essentially cathartic or protective in character. This is very noticeable in John Chrysostom and Theo-

---

[15] See 'Studies in the early history,' p. 61.

[16] BT *Kerithoth* 5b, *Horayoth* 12a. Oil was also poured over their hands—
whether before or after was disputed—and this may provide one of the reasons for
the duplication of the pre-baptismal anointing (note that in early descriptions of
baptism the priest sometimes is described as 'casting' the oil on the head of the
candidate).

[17] So G. Winkler in her important study, *Das armenische Initiationsrituale* (OCA
217, 1982). I am most grateful to her for many new insights in the course of discussion.

dore, and John Chrysostom even associates the conveying of priesthood with the imposition of the priest's hand in the act of baptism.[18] Among Syriac writers we can observe the same tendency in Narsai (although he is still much concerned with the oil) and Jacob of Serugh.

There seem to be a number of different factors at work which led to this change of understanding of the role of the pre-baptismal anointings. Fundamentally the shift came about as a result of altering conceptual models and imagery, and the following considerations would seem to be of prime importance here:

(1) With the rapid Christianisation of the Roman Empire in the fourth century consequent upon Constantine's conversion, there was a tendency to push the Jewish origins of Christianity into the background as Christian culture took on a more hellenized character. As far as Baptism was concerned, this meant that the original conceptual basis for the Syrian rite (circumcision—baptism) lost its former significance and faded into the background, while oil imagery which belonged primarily to the Greco-Roman world gradually predominated at the expense of the older more biblical symbolism; this new imagery encouraged a protective interpretation of the anointing (and may well have been a contributing factor in the duplication of the pre-baptismal anointing so as to include the whole body). Needless to say, it is chiefly Greek, rather than Syriac, writers who most reflect this new emphasis. The other Old Testament basis for the pre-baptismal anointing, the anointing of priests, kings and prophets, being essentially charismatic in character, also tended to be pushed into the background as Christianity became more institutionalized; where the concept is preserved, it is transferred from the *rushma* to the baptism proper, or (as will be seen) to the post-baptismal anointing once that had been introduced.

With the loss of awareness of the old Jewish conceptual model for the Syrian baptismal rite, a new one is sought out in the New Testament: Christ's own baptism. As a matter of fact the model itself was not new, only the understanding of it, for Christ's own baptism, seen as sanctifying all baptismal water,[19] had always been seen as the model for the baptism in water. At the end of the fourth century, however, Christ's baptism becomes

---

[18] PG 61, col. 417, 'thus you become a king, a priest and a prophet in the (baptismal) bathing.'

[19] See my 'The Epiklesis in the Antiochene Baptismal *Ordines*,' in I. Ortiz de Urbina (ed.), *Symposium Syriacum* (Orientalia Christiana Analecta 197; 1974), pp. 183–218, esp. 204–6 (reprinted in *Fire from Heaven* (Variorum Reprints, 2006), chapter VII).

the conceptual model for the baptismal rite *as a whole,* and attention is now paid to the fact that the Holy Spirit only appeared after Christ had gone up from the water.[20] With such an overall model, there is obviously no room for a pre-baptismal anointing which has important associations with the Holy Spirit. In John Chrysostom, who still knows no post-baptismal anointing, this dominance of Christ's baptism as a conceptual model has simply meant that he has to transfer all the positive elements originally connected with the *rushma* to the baptism.

(2) The great rarity of references in early Syriac literature to Paul's understanding of baptism in Romans 6 is very noticeable. Rather, baptism is primarily seen as a rebirth to a new mode of existence, with little attention paid to the idea of dying to the old. Thus the baptismal water as a grave plays no part at all in Syriac writers prior to Narsai and Jacob of Serugh. One element of the Pauline phraseology in Romans 6 does, however, feature prominently in early Syriac tradition, namely 'the old man'; but instead of 'being crucified with Christ' (Romans 6:6), he is 'stripped off' (Col. 3:9).

One of the recurrent themes of Syriac baptismal tradition is the putting on, at baptism, of the 'robe of glory,' lost by Adam and Eve at the Fall but recovered for humankind by the Second Adam at his baptism.[21] Earlier writers also associate the 'robe of glory' with the *rushma,* whereas later ones characteristically transfer it to the water. Also, following Jewish tradition, this robe is at the same time a priestly and royal one. But even here, the emphasis of the Syriac writers is significant, for they are primarily interested in what is put on (i.e. the 'robe of glory'), and show little concern with what is put off, the 'old man' and the 'garment of skin' (Gen. 3:21) upon which Greek writers loved to speculate.

In the Syrian area it is Theodore of Mopsuestia who is the first to lay great stress on the Pauline view of baptism as a death and resurrection. The consequent introduction of the imagery of the font as a grave obviously clashes badly with the earlier understanding of the *rushma* as conveying anything positive, such as sonship; thus it is no surprise to find Theodore giving the *rushma* a low-keyed interpretation as a protective marl of owner-

---

[20] E.g. Theodore, *Cat. Hom.* XIV, 23–27; Jacob of Serugh (for whom, see note 1). Underlying this emphasis there is also anti-adoptionist polemic.

[21] See my 'Some aspects of Greek words in Syriac,' in A. Dietrich (ed.), *Synkretismus im syrisch-persischen Kulturgebiet* (Abhandlungen der Akademie der Wissenschaften in Göttingen III.96; 1975), pp. 80–108, esp. 98–104 (reprinted in *Syriac Perspectives on Late Antiquity* (Variorum Reprints, 1984), chapter IV).

ship.[22] There is, however, a tell-tale relic of the older, positive, meaning attached to this anointing: Theodore's emphasis on *parrhesia* in connection with the *rushma* indicates clearly that he is working within a catechetical tradition that once associated the gift of sonship (the source of *parrhesia*) with the pre-baptismal anointing.[23]

We can thus see that in the late fourth and early fifth century a combination of several different factors led to the emergence of a new understanding of the *rushma* as primarily cathartic and protective: the positive elements formerly associated with it, notably sonship (implying the indwelling of the Holy Spirit) and royal priesthood, have to be pushed to some point later in the service; the way is thus open for the introduction of a post-baptismal anointing to take over these positive elements that formerly belonged to the *rushma*.

A further contributing factor that favoured the emasculation of the meaning given to the *rushma* lay in an over-literalist interpretation of some of the imagery employed in connection with baptism. Thus, even after the late fourth century, Syriac writers—and the *ordines* themselves—prefer to call the font a womb (based on John 3:4–8), rather than a grave. The font, instead of the anointing thus comes to be seen as a more logical source for the gift of sonship. Further examples of this nature could be adduced.

It is not the object here to discuss the immediate provenance whence the Antiochene rite borrowed the post-baptismal anointing; there is certainly much to be said for Ratcliff's view that it comes from Jerusalem.[24] Rather, the aim has been to indicate how the tensions brought about by developments in the late fourth century created an inner dynamic within the rite itself which cried out for the introduction of a new post-baptismal

---

[22] The anointing of the whole body is for him just 'a sign that you will receive the garment of immortality' (i.e. from the water), *Cat. Hom.* XVI.8.

[23] On *parrhesia* in baptism, see R. Coquin, 'Le thème de la *parrhesia* et ses expressions symboliques dans les rites d'initiation à Antioche,' *Proche Orient Chrétien* 20 (1970), pp. 1–17.

[24] E. C. Ratcliff, 'The old Syrian baptismal tradition and its resettlement under the influence of Jerusalem in the fourth century,' in his *Liturgical Studies* (ed. A. H. Couratin and D. H. Tripp; London, 1976), pp. 135–55; cf. also *Journal of Theological Studies* ns 23 (1972), pp. 38–9 (the imagery of olive grafting, from Rom. 11). B. Botte adduces another factor, the need to receive back heretics, using an anointing ('L'onction post-baptismale dans l'ancien Patriarcat d'Antioche,' in *Miscellanea G. Lercaro* (Rome, 1967), pp. 795–808; English translation in *Studies on Syrian Liturgical Rites*, ed. J. Vellian (Syrian Churches Series 6; Kottayma, 1973), pp. 63–71).

anointing to take over those characteristics which it was no longer thought possible to associate with the *rushma*.

It remains now to show how, in the understanding of Syriac writers, the new anointing has simply taken over (or duplicated)[25] attributes formerly belonging to the *rushma*. Needless to say, there are some new elements, culturally of Greek origin, such as the term 'seal' (very rare in early Syriac writers) alongside 'imprint' (*tab'a*), the idea of 'union' (Eph. 4:3), and that of the Holy Spirit 'perfecting' the rite, as well as the imagery specifically associated with myron as opposed to live oil; but these represent supplements to, rather than a totally altered understanding of, the *rushma*.

The clearest evidence of all in support of this contention is to be found in the seventh-century Syriac treatises on the myron; not only do they retain the use of the term *rushma* for the post-baptismal anointing, but they list as the effects of this anointing precisely those things that had originally belonged to the pre-baptismal *rushma*—even including the apotropaic elements! Thus the Patriarch John I (died 648) writes of the myron used in the post-baptismal anointing:[26]

> With the imprint of this holy oil we are inscribed as sons of the heavenly Father; by means of the *rushma* or imprint (*tab'a*) of this holy oil we become the sheep of Christ, a priestly kingdom (I Peter 2:9, not Peshitta), a holy people.

And he goes on to say

> We are strengthened against the accuser, the enemy and the might of all evil spirits.

The protective and apotropaic element is brought out even more clearly by Jacob of Edessa (died 708) in his treatise on the myron:[27]

> This holy oil is the beginning of the heavenly path and the ladder which takes us up to heaven, the armour against the hostile powers, the indissoluble imprint (*tab'a*) of the king, the sight (*ata*) which delivers from fire, the guardian of the faithful, the cause of flight to demons, the cause of joy to angels. ... It is named myron by the all-wise teachers.

---

[25] This has happened in many of the *ordines*.
[26] British Library, Add. 12165, f.261b; ed. J. Martikainen, *Johannes I Sedra* (GOFS 34; 1991), p. 198.
[27] British Library, Add. 12165, f.250a-b = sections 10–11 of my edition in *Oriens Christianus* 63 (1979), pp. 20–36.

The same thing can be seen in the Syriac *ordines* themselves: here there is a great deal both of duplication in the understanding of the pre- and post-baptismal anointings, and of the transference to the post-baptismal anointing of themes that originally belonged to the *rushma*. Here a single example must suffice. In the old Syrian Orthodox *ordo* attributed to Timothy of Alexandria the prayer introducing the post-baptismal anointing read as follows:[28]

> O God, whose gifts are very great, Father of our Lord and our God and our Saviour Jesus Christ, you raise up to adoption by yourself these persons who are being filled with the scent of your Christ, the promise of whom you have given in this myron which through invisible power you are wont to sanctify; grant through his imprint (*tab'a*) the union of your living and holy Spirit, the honour of priesthood and the heavenly kingdom to those who are sanctified; and grant, in the coming of your Christ, glorious honour and priestly produce, since to you all things are simple and easy; and may they be made worthy to offer up, together and in company and companionship with us, praise for your mercies towards us, Father, Son and Holy Spirit, now and always.

Here, very obviously, we have the fusion of new (scent, union) with old (sonship, royal priesthood).

The situation may be summed up as follows: the originally single pre-baptismal anointing, the *rushma*, besides being the new Christian equivalent of circumcision, also took over from Judaism the anointing of the baptized into the royal priesthood. At the *rushma* the baptised 'put on the robe of the Spirit' and thus became children to the Father; the *rushma* was also the protective mark of ownership. The altered situation of Christianity in the later fourth century, which brought with it a change of conceptual models and imagery, necessitated a radical re-interpretation of the *rushma*, leaving it with only a protective and cathartic meaning, and transferring its positive elements from the oil either to the water or, in due course, to the newly introduced post-baptismal anointing with myron. The post-baptismal anointing now takes on the positive roles formerly played by the *rushma*, at the same time introducing some new themes, although many vestiges of the older understanding of the *rushma* are also preserved in the new position, owing to the conflation of elements of varying antiquity, both in the formularies themselves and in the later commentators.

---

[28] Section 45 of my edition in *Le Muséon* 83 (1970), pp. 367–431; for parallel texts in other *ordines*, see the commentary there.

APPENDIX 2

THE HOLY SPIRIT AS FEMININE IN EARLY SYRIAC LITERATURE

In his commentary on Isaiah[1] Jerome quotes from a passage in the Gospel according to the Hebrews where Jesus proclaims that 'my mother the Holy Spirit has taken me ... (and conveyed me to Mount Tabor).' No one should be scandalized on the matter, comments Jerome, in the 'Spirit' is feminine in Hebrew, but masculine in 'our language' (Latin) and neuter in Greek, 'for in the Deity there is no gender' (*in divinitate enim nulla est sexus*). Here some of the repercussions of this grammatical feature of the Semitic languages are explored in the history of the only early Christian literature to have been written in one of these languages, namely Syriac.

Although the New Testament was written in Greek, Christianity was born in a Semitic milieu and Jesus himself will have spoken Aramaic (of which Syriac is a dialect). Likewise, in those parts of the eastern Roman Empire where Aramaic, rather than Greek, was both spoken and written (such as much of Syria and Palestine), Aramaic became the language of many early Christian communities; accordingly, when these communities spoke of the Holy Spirit they naturally used the standard Aramaic word for spirit, *ruha* (which can also mean 'wind,' as *pneuma*), which, like Hebrew *ruah*, is grammatically feminine. Thus, when referring to the Holy Spirit, they used the feminine forms of adjectives, verbs etc. What effect does this purely grammatical feature have on their understanding of the role of the Holy Spirit? In what way does it affect the images and metaphors they use of the Spirit? In particular, is the image of the Holy Spirit as 'mother' found elsewhere, as well as in the Gospel according to the Hebrews?[2]

---

[1] On Isaiah 40:9 (Corpus Christianorum, Series Latina 73, p. 459).

[2] For these questions see also S. A. Harvey, 'Feminine imagery for the Divine: the Holy Spirit, the Odes of Solomon, and early Syriac tradition,' *St Vladimir's Theological Quarterly* 37:2–3 (1993), pp. 11–39; also my '"Come, compassionate Mother, ... come, Holy Spirit:" a forgotten aspect of early Eastern Christian imagery,' *Aram* 3 (1991), pp. 241–57, repr. in *Fire from Heaven* (Aldershot, 2006), ch. VI.

Before turning to the evidence of Syriac literature, it is helpful to look briefly at the role of grammatical gender in different languages, for it is important to realize that differences in this role will give rise to different sensitivities. For the present purpose it will suffice to notice five different possibilities:

(1) In English there are separate pronouns, 'he,' 'she,' 'it,' but no special feminine forms for the article, for adjectives or for verbal forms. Gender is thus mostly confined to persons.

(2) French has only the masculine and feminine pronouns, but it also has separate feminine forms for the article and adjectives. Thus, for example, l'Esprit is grammatically masculine. Gender affects things as well as persons.

(3) The situation in Greek is similar to that in French, except that there are three separate pronouns. Thus *to pneuma to hagion* is neuter.

(4) In Hebrew, Aramaic and Syriac, while there are only two pronouns, masculine and feminine, separate feminine forms exist for verbs as well as for adjectives (but not for the article).

(5) In certain languages, such as Armenian, no grammatical gender exists, and a single pronoun covers both 'he' and 'she.' Revisers of modern liturgies and biblical translations will lament that the English language does not have this simple solution to the problem of 'sexist language.'

This difference in the role played by grammatical gender in different languages means that we should not necessarily think that the surprise which we may feel if we hear the Holy Spirit described as 'she' would also have been felt in a language where the word for spirit is feminine anyway.

With these preliminaries we can turn to see what happens in the literature of the Syriac-speaking Church. First of all, it is important to look at these texts in historical perspective, for over the course of time practice can be observed to change. Three stages can be identified:

(1) In the earliest literature up to about AD 400 the Holy Spirit is always treated grammatically as feminine. This is the norm in the three main monuments of early Syriac literature, the Acts of Thomas, and the writings of Aphrahat and Ephrem.

(2) From the early fifth century onwards it is evident that some people began to disapprove of treating the Holy Spirit as grammatically feminine; accordingly, in defiance of the grammatical rules of the language, they treated the word *ruha* as masculine wherever it referred to the Holy Spirit. Perhaps this shift in practice was in part due to the ever-

increasing prestige of the Greek language, though of course *pneuma* is neuter, rather than masculine.

(3) From the sixth century onwards what had been only sporadic practice in the fifth century now becomes the norm: *ruha*, referring to the Holy Spirit, is regularly treated as masculine. Even so, the original feminine is not completely ousted, for it can still sometimes be found, especially in liturgical texts and in poetry (where some poets use either the masculine or the feminine, depending on which best fits their immediate metrical requirements).

This three-stage development happens to be neatly reflected in the history of the biblical translations into Syriac. Thus in the Old Syriac translation of the Gospels, dating from the late second or early third century, the Holy Spirit regularly features grammatically as feminine. In the revised translation of the Syriac New Testament, the Peshitta, produced in the early fifth century, we find that, although the feminine has been preserved in many places, there are also some where the grammatical gender has been altered to masculine. Finally, in the early seventh-century version of the Harklean *ruha* is regularly treated as masculine wherever it refers to the Holy Spirit. It is likely that this practice was also adopted in the Philoxenian revision of 507/8, now lost apart from quotations.

These developments may be illustrated by means of some examples, beginning with the Syriac Bible.

Rather surprisingly there are only two places in the Gospels where the revisers who produced the Peshitta chose to alter the feminine of the Old Syriac to masculine; it so happens that both are passages where the Holy Spirit 'teaches' (Luke 12:12 and John 14:26). Much more frequently in the Gospels the Peshitta simply retains the feminine of the Old Syriac; this includes two contexts of central importance, the Annunciation (Luke 1:35) and the Baptism of Christ.[3] It is, curiously, in Acts that the Peshitta provides the highest number of cases where a masculine form is used in connection with the Holy Spirit (nine instances),[4] but even in that book the

---

[3] Matt. 3:16, Luke 3:22, John 1:32 (at Mark 1:10 'dove' rather than 'Spirit' could be subject of the feminine verb). Other passages where the feminine is kept are Matt. 10:20 'speaks,' Mark 1:12 'took him out,' Luke 2:25 'was,' 4:1 'led him,' John 6:63 'who gives life,' and 7:39 'was given.'

[4] Acts 1:16 'foretold,' 2:4 'gave,' 10:19 and 11:12 'said,' 19:6 'came,' 20:23 'testifies and says,' 20:28 'set up,' 21:11 'said,' 28:25 'spoke.'

feminine survives in a further seven passages.[5] There appears to be no clear rationale behind this variation in usage. In the Peshitta of the Epistles, on the other hand, the archaic usage with the feminine is kept throughout.[6]

The only consistent alteration made by the Peshitta revisers (and this is confined to the Gospels) concerns the precise Syriac terminology for the Holy Spirit. Although the Old Syriac normally employs the phrase 'Spirit of holiness,' *ruha d-qudsha*, of Jewish origin,[7] in five passages[8] it uses instead the feminine adjective, *ruha qaddishta*, 'Holy Spirit'; all five of these are altered in the Peshitta to *ruha d-qudsha*, though the feminine form of the accompanying verb is retained in one case (Luke 2:25), thus indicating clearly that it is the feminine adjective to which objection was taken. The situation here is quite different from that in the Peshitta Epistles, where *ruha qaddishta* is to be found at Eph. 4:30 and I Thess. 4:8. It comes as no surprise to find that the form of the masculine adjective, *ruha qaddisha*, occurs only in the post-Peshitta version of the minor Catholic Epistles (early sixth century?), and in the Harklean New Testament.[9]

The alteration to masculine of biblical passages which originally had feminine forms can also take place at a subsequent stage, either in the manuscript tradition of the Syriac Bible, or in quotations by later writers. Two examples will suffice. In the much used Psalm 51 the original Peshitta text has the feminine adjective in verse 13, 'Take not your Holy Spirit, *ruhak qaddishta*, from me'; this is preserved only in a few of the oldest manuscripts,[10] and the alteration to the masculine *qaddisha* is already found in the

---

[5] Acts 1:8 'shall come,' 8:18 'is given,' 8:29 'said,' 8:39 'snatched,' 10:44 'overshadowed,' 13:2 'said,' 16:7 'permitted.'

[6] Rom. 5:5 'was given,' 8:9, 11 'dwells,' 8:16 'testifies,' 8:26 'assists, prays,' 1 Cor. 2:10 'searches out,' 3:16 and 6:19 'dwells,' 12:11 'performs, distributes,' Eph. 1:13 'is promised,' 2 Tim. 1:14 'dwelt,' Heb. 3:7 'said,' 9:8 'indicated,' 10:15 'testifies,' 1 John 5:7 'testifies.'

[7] Cf. H. Parzen, 'The *Ruach hakodesh* in Tannaitic literature,' *Jewish Quarterly Review* 20 (1929/30), pp. 51–76.

[8] Mark 13:11, Luke 2:25, 26, 11:13, John 20:22.

[9] Several editions of the Syriac NT based on late manuscripts have altered Eph. 4:30 to masculine, *qaddisha*. In early Syriac literature *ruha d-qudsha* is the norm, but *ruha qaddishta* is also sometimes found, e.g. *Acts of Thomas* (ed. Wright), p. 323 line 10; Aphrahat, *Demonstration* VI.14, XXIII.61; Ephrem, *Hymns against Heresies* 55:5; *Liber Graduum* IX.1. For the masculine *qaddisha* in the Odes of Solomon, see below.

[10] 6t1, 8a1*, 8t1, 10t4.5 in the notation of the critical edition, *Vetus Testamentum Syriace* II.3 (the first numeral denotes the century to which the manuscript is dated).

earliest complete Syriac Bible, the Codex Ambrosianus, of the sixth/seventh century. Another important verse is I Cor. 3:16, where the Peshitta uses the feminine: 'the Spirit of God dwells ('*amra*, feminine) in you.' The great Syrian Orthodox theologian Philoxenus (died 523) alters the verb to the masculine ('*amar*) when he quotes the passage;[11] the same phenomenon can be observed when he quotes other key New Testament passages referring to the activity of the Spirit, such as Luke 1:35.[12] It is thus likely that the (lost) Philoxenian revision of the Syriac New Testament regularly removed usage with the feminine, anticipating the Harklean's practice. The same phenomenon can be observed in the transmission of the Christian Palestinian Aramaic biblical texts. In this version (of uncertain date, possibly fifth century), the feminine is the norm, but at Luke 3:22, for example, some manuscripts have altered the verb to the masculine form.

Before turning to non-biblical literature one further analogous feature of the Syriac Gospels should be mentioned. In Syriac, the Greek Logos 'Word' is translated by another feminine noun, *mellta*. Accordingly in the Prologue of the Gospel of John the Old Syriac treats *Melltha*, the World, as feminine, and this usage is reflected, not only in the fourth-century writer Ephrem (which is to be expected),[13] but also very occasionally in texts of the fifth, or even later centuries,[14] even though in the Peshitta revision, the grammatical gender had already been altered to masculine.

In the non-biblical literature of the earliest of the three periods outlined above it is very exceptional to find cases where the Holy Spirit is treated grammatically as masculine. Curiously enough, the one text where

---

At another important verse, Isaiah 11:2, Codex Ambrosianus (7a1) is the only manuscript to alter the accompanying verbs to masculine forms.

[11] E.g. *Tractatus tres de trinitate et incarnatione* (ed. Vaschalde, CSCO Scr. Syri 9), p. 168, line 31. An earlier writer who sometimes makes such alterations of gender in his biblical quotations is the monastic author John the Solitary (or John of Apamea; first half of the fifth century), e.g. Letters (ed. Rignell), p. 113, line 9, quoting John 7:39.

[12] Substituting a masculine for the feminine form of the verb 'shall come,' e.g. *Comm. on the Prologue of John* (ed. de Halleux, CSCO Scr Syri 165), p. 41, line 2. The same change is often made in liturgical texts, e.g. *Fenqitho* (Mosul edition), II, p. 83b, 87a, 88b, 95b etc.

[13] Excerpt on the Prologue of John, *apud* T. Lamy, *S. Ephraimi Hymni et Sermones*, II, col. 511; *Hymns on the Resurrection* 1:7 (quoted below).

[14] *Fenqitho* II, p. 65a (in a prayer which on other grounds must belong at least to c.7th century), p. 272b; VI, p. 107b, etc.

the masculine adjective (*ruha*) *qaddisha* does occur several times is the archaic Odes of Solomon,[15] though it may well be that in the rather late manuscripts which preserve this work an original *qaddishta* has been consciously or unconsciously altered to the masculine form. Apart from the Odes, the only other occurrences of usage with the masculine are a few passages in the hymns of Ephrem[16] (who otherwise regularly employs the feminine). It should be noted that usage with the feminine is also the norm in early translations from Greek into Syriac (e.g. Eusebius, *Theophania*, *Ecclesiastical History*, *Palestine Martyrs*).

The fifth century is clearly the period of transition, and it would be of interest to trace in detail the development of usage over the course of the century in different texts. This task remains to be done, but a general impression suggests that it is those writers who are more theologically aware (aware, that is, of contemporary controversies) who are more likely to employ masculine forms. Thus, towards the end of the century, both Narsai (in the Antiochene christological tradition) and Philoxenus (in the Alexandrine) use the masculine, while the author of the Life of Simeon the Stylite still employs the feminine.[17] The great poet Jacob of Serugh (died 521) is happy to use both feminine and masculine, indifferently.[18]

From the sixth century onwards usage with the masculine (and normally with *ruha qaddisha*, rather than *ruha d-qudsha*) appears to be invariable in theological writing, and it is only sporadically in poetry that the feminine is still to be found. Many examples—still in liturgical use today—can be gathered from the pages of the *Fenqitho* and *Hudra*, the Sunday and Festal Hymnaries of the Syrian Orthodox Church and the Church of the East.

Thus far we have solely been concerned with surface phenomena connected with the grammatical structure of the language. Does this fact that the Holy Spirit is grammatically feminine in the earliest Syriac literature have any effect on the way people envisaged the role of the Spirit? That it did is suggested by a passage in the Gospel according to Philip, a work preserved

---

[15] *Odes of Solomon* 6:7, 11:2, 14:8, 23:22 (in the older manuscript). Usage with a feminine verb (but not adjective) also occurs (including 19:2, quoted below).

[16] Hymns on Faith 12:6, on the Church 45:15.

[17] For Narsai, e.g. *Homily on the Nativity*, line 151; *on Epiphany*, line 298 (both in Patrologia Orientalis 40). For Philoxenus, see above. Life of Simeon the Stylite: ed. Bedjan, *Acta Martyrum et Sanctorum* IV, p. 617, "The Holy Spirit caused to be written down (*aktbat*, fem.) the resplendent deeds of the faithful ..."

[18] Metrical considerations are evidently uppermost in his choice of masc. or fem. (an example is cited below).

only in Coptic (among the Nag Hammadi finds) but probably having a Syrian background. Here, in §17 we find: "Some have said. 'Mary conceived of the Holy Spirit.' They are wrong…when did a woman ever conceive of a woman?" Passages implying that the Spirit acts in a male role as the source of Mary's conception can be found in some later liturgical texts, such as the following, where Gabriel addresses Mary: "You shall discover a wonderful conception: without (human) seed or intercourse, your conception shall be from the Holy Spirit, O Virgin."[19] It was perhaps in order to obviate such a literalist reading of Luke 1:35 that many later Syriac writers deliberately distinguish between the 'Holy Spirit' and the 'Power of the Most High' in that verse, identifying the Power (*hayla*, masculine in Syriac) as the Logos.[20]

The author of the Gospel according to Philip clearly sees the Spirit as female, and it is this, evidently Semitic, tradition that is represented in a number of early Syriac works where we encounter the Spirit as 'Mother.'[21] The Acts of Thomas, perhaps of the third century, is the earliest of these. This work, whose original language was Syriac, survives in a re-worked Syriac form and in a Greek translation which was made from a more primitive form of the Syriac original. Thus, in the course of several prayers uttered by Judas Thomas, the Greek text includes several invocations to the Holy Spirit as 'Mother.' In the surviving Syriac text, however, this term is always absent, presumably having been removed on the grounds that it was

---

[19] *Fenqitho* II, p. 108b. Compare the polemic in Ephrem, *Hymns against Heresies* 55:3. Cf. also A. Orbe, *La teologia del Espiritu Santo* (Rome, 1966), pp. 69–116, 687–706.

[20] See my remarks in *Novum Testamentum* 24 (1982), p. 227, and further in *Mélanges A. Guillaumont* (Geneva, 1988), pp. 121ff. Jacob of Serugh explains the different roles of the Spirit and the Power as follows: "The Spirit of Holiness first sanctified (fem. form of verb) her, and then (the Son of God) tabernacled in her. The Spirit freed (masc. form of verb) her from that debt, so that she might be above any wrongdoing when (the Son of God) resided in her in holy fashion" (Homily on the Virgin, *apud* P. Bedjan, *S. Martyrii qui et Sahdona quae supersunt omnia* (Paris/Leipzig, 1902) = Bedjan (repr., ed. Brock), *Homiliae Selecta Mar-Jacobi Sarugensis* VI (Piscataway NJ, 2006), p. 632.

[21] On this see especially R. Murray, *Symbols of Church and Kingdom* (Cambridge, 1975; 2nd edn Piscataway NJ, 2004), pp. 312–20, and W. Cramer, *Der Geist Gottes und des Menschen in frühsyrischer Theologie* (Münster, 1979), pp. 36–8, 68–9.

no longer considered appropriate. The relevant passages in the Greek text are as follows:[22]

> §27 (In a baptismal context; the invocation is addressed to both the Son and the Spirit). Come, O holy name of Christ, which is above every name; come, Power of the Most High, and perfect mercy; come, exalted gift (i.e. the Holy Spirit); come, compassionate Mother,…(for 'compassionate Mother' the Syriac has nothing corresponding).

> §50 (An invocation to the Spirit in the context of the Eucharist). …Come, hidden Mother,…come, and make us share in this Eucharist which we perform in your name, and (make us share) in the love to which we are joined by invoking you. (The Syriac again removes the reference to the Spirit as 'Mother').

> §133 (In the course of a trinitarian invocation in the context of the Eucharist). We name over you (= the newly baptized) the name of the Mother. (Syriac: the name of the Spirit).

In one further passage, a prayer in §39, the Greek text has an intrusive 'and,' wrongly separating the epithet 'Mother' from the Holy Spirit: "We hymn you (Christ) and your unseen Father and your Holy Spirit *and* the Mother of all created things."[23]

In these passages we have clear evidence of a Trinity envisaged as consisting of Father, Mother and Son. Traces of this are also to be found in the archaic poem known as the Hymn of the Pearl (or, of the Soul), incorporated into the Acts of Thomas. The poem described how a royal son was sent by his father and mother, the king and the queen, from the highlands of the East (i.e. the heavenly realm) to go to Egypt (i.e. the fallen world) in order to collect a pearl from the mouth of a dragon. Although the interpretation of the poem has been much disputed,[24] a reasonable case can be made out for seeing the son as representing in some sense both First Adam/humanity and Second Adam, Christ the Word who rescues him. In Egypt the son receives a letter from his parents which begins: "From your father, the King of kings, and your mother, the Mistress of the East," and

---

[22] For §27 and §50 there is a detailed study by H. Kruse, 'Zwei Geist-Epiklesen der syrischen Thomasakten,' *Oriens Christianus* 69 (1985), pp. 33–55; also now S. E. Myers, *Spirit Epicleses in the Acts of Thomas* (Tübingen, 2007).

[23] For 'Mother,' the Syriac has 'hovering over' (based on Gen. 1:2, on which see below).

[24] A helpful survey is provided by P-H. Poirier, *L'Hymne de la Perle dans les Actes de Thomas* (Louvain-la-Neuve, 1981).

later he uses the names of his father and mother in an invocation to charm the dragon so that he can extract the pearl. In some sense or other it seems likely that the king and the queen are to be identified as the Father and the Holy Spirit. In any case, this was the Christian reading of the poem in antiquity.

The Acts of Thomas might be considered as belonging at best only to the fringes of orthodoxy. It is not, however, the only place in early Syriac literature where we encounter the Spirit as Mother. A thoroughly orthodox witness to this tradition is Aphrahat, writing towards the middle of the fourth century. Aphrahat, or the Persian Sage as he was called, lived within the Sasanian Empire, and so it is no great surprise that his theological language seem archaic when compared with that of his contemporaries writing within the Roman Empire. In a work dealing mainly with virginity, he has the following interpretation of Genesis 2:24 ("a man shall leave his father and mother"):[25]

> Who is it who leaves father and mother to take a wife? The meaning is as follows: as long as a man has not taken a wife, he loves and reveres God his Father and the Holy Spirit his Mother, and he has no other love. But when a man takes a wife, then he leaves his (true) Father and his Mother.

The seeds for such an interpretation had already been sown by Philo (not that Aphrahat would have read him) in his *Allegorical Interpretation* (of Gen. 2–3). At II.49, after quoting Gen. 2:24, he says:[26]

> For the sake of sense-perception the Mind, when it has become her slave, abandons both God the Father of the universe, and God's excellence and wisdom, the Mother of all things, and cleaves to and becomes one with sense perception, and is resolved into sense-perception so that the two become one flesh and one experience.

Closer to Aphrahat in time, space and spirit, however, are the Macarian Homilies, whose Syrian/Mesopotamian origin in the fourth/fifth century is now generally admitted. Here we encounter the following passage, which again reflects Genesis 2:24:[27]

---

[25] Demonstration 18:10.
[26] Translation by G. H. Whitaker (Loeb edition, p. 255).
[27] Homily LIV.4.5 in H. Berthold, *Makarios/Symeon. Reden und Briefe*, II (Berlin, 1973), pp. 156–7.

It is right and fitting, children, for you to have left all that is temporal
and to have gone off to God: instead of an earthly father, you are seek-
ing the heavenly Father, and instead of a mother who is subject to corruption, you have as a Mother the excellent Spirit of God, and the heavenly Jerusalem. Instead of the brothers you have left you now have the
Lord who has allowed himself to be called a brother of the faithful.

It is important to realise that the image of the Holy Spirit as Mother is
by no means confined to Syriac writers or those working in a Semitic milieu.
Thus, Hippolytus, writing in Greek c.200, describes Isaac as an image of
God the Father, his wife Rebecca as an image of the Holy Spirit, and their
son Jacob as an image of Christ—or, of the Church.[28] Most striking in this
respect, however, is the second Hymn of the highly cultured Synesios,
Bishop of Cyrene from 410–413. After addressing the Father and the Son
he turns to the Spirit: [29]

I sing of the (Father's) travail, the fecund will, the intermediary principle,
the Holy Breath/Inspiration, the centre point of the Parent, the centre
point of the Child: she is mother, she is sister, she is daughter; she has
delivered the Hidden Root.

Examples of the same kind of imagery used of the Spirit can also be found
in a few Latin writers, most notably Marius Victorinus (mid fourth century).

Thus among early Christian writers, Greek and Latin as well as Syriac,
one can find scattered pieces of evidence which may suggest that there was
once a fairly widespread tradition which associated the Holy Spirit with the
image of mother.[30] The roots of such a tradition are to be found, not only
in the grammatical feature of the Semitic languages where 'Spirit' is feminine, but also in the links which the concept of Holy Spirit will have had

---

[28] In H. Achelis, *Hippolytus Werke* (Leipzig, 1897), I.2, p. 54, line 5. For Greek
writers, see S. Hirsch, *Die Vorstellung von einem weiblichen pneuma hagion* (Diss. Berlin,
1926).

[29] On this passage, see S. Vollenweider's excursus 'Mutter Heilige Geist' in his
Neuplatonische und christliche Theologie bei Synesios von Kyrene (Göttingen, 1985), pp. 78–9
(with further bibliography on the subject).

[30] A different model is provided in chapter 9 of the *Didascalia* (a Syrian product
of the third century): there the bishop corresponds to God the Father, 'the deacon
stands in the position of Christ ... and the deaconess in the position of the Holy
Spirit.'

with the personalised figure of Wisdom[31] and with the Jewish concept of the Divine Presence or Shekhina.[32] As is well known, both these features are often connected with mother imagery. As far as extant early Syriac literature is concerned, however, neither Wisdom not the Shekhina is at all prominent, although both feature here and there.

As we have seen, from the fifth century onwards a reaction against the idea of the Holy Spirit as mother must have set in. This may partly have been due to the misuse of the imagery by some groups regarded as heretical, though another factor should also be kept in mind: in the Syriac-speaking areas of the eastern Roman Empire the large-scale influx of new converts to Christianity will have included many people whose background lay in pagan cults in which a divine triad of Father, Mother and Son was prominent.[33]

The archaic tradition of the Holy Spirit as Mother did not, however, entirely disappear, for one can find occasional relics of it, albeit reduced to a simile, in much later Syriac writers. Thus the monastic author Martyrius, writing in the first half of the seventh century, speaks of the person "who has been held worthy of the hovering of the all-holy Spirit, who, like a mother, hovers over us as she gives sanctification; and through her hovering over us, we are made worthy of sonship."[34] The term 'hovering' here will immediately have provided Syriac readers with three resonances, of which Genesis 1:2 is the primary one; more important, however, in the context within which Martyrius is speaking are the resonances of the baptismal rite, where the Spirit 'hovers over' the font,[35] and the eucharistic epiclesis,

---

[31] In the *Acts of Thomas* §50 the Holy Spirit is described as 'the Wisdom of the Son,' but on the whole the figure of Wisdom is not often found in early Syriac literature.

[32] The Peshitta of Chronicles introduces the term in a number of passages (e.g. 2 Chron. 6:18), and it occurs a few times in Aphrahat (*Dem.* IV.7, XVIII.4, XIX.4) and Ephrem (e.g. *Hymns on Paradise* 2:11; *on Unleavened Bread* 13:21), but it only becomes popular in rather later writers such as Jacob of Serugh, and notably in some 7th/8th-century(?) texts in the East Syriac *Hudra*, on which see my *Syriac Perspectives on Late Antiquity* (London, 1984), ch. IV, pp. 106–7.

[33] Such cults are well documented from Palmyra and Hatra from a slightly earlier period.

[34] *Book of Perfection* I.3.13 (ed. de Halleux, CSCO Scr. Syri 86, p. 32). Martyrius is a writer who frequently retains the archaic usage, treating the Holy Spirit as grammatically feminine.

[35] See my *Fire from Heaven* (Aldershot, 2006), ch. XIV, pp. 346–7. Ancient exegetes, as well as modern Bible translators, disputed the sense of *ruaḥ elohim* 'spirit/wind of God' in Gen. 1:2.

where the Spirit is invited to come and 'hover over' the Bread and the Wine and thus transform them into the Body and Blood of Christ.[36]

Another example of the imagery can be found in the writings of the Syrian Orthodox theologian and scholar, Moses bar Kepha (died 903): "The Holy Spirit hovered over John the Baptist and brought him up like a compassionate mother."[37] For the most part, however, in later Syriac literature it will be found that 'Grace' has taken over the Spirit's place as mother.[38]

Whereas the Holy Spirit as Mother, alongside God the Father, is a feature only encountered rarely in Syriac literature, the use of female imagery is much more common. Such imagery is implied, for example every time the term 'hovers' is used of the Holy Spirit (and it occurs very frequently), for this term, based on Gen. 1:2, originally describes the action of a mother bird. Rather than explore this aspect further here, it must suffice to observe that female imagery is by no means confined to the Holy Spirit: many examples can be found (and this applies to Greek and Latin literature, as well as to Syriac) where female imagery is employed with reference to the Father and the Son as well. What seems to us a bizarre example can be found in the Odes of Solomon (late second century?):[39]

> A cup of milk was offered to me, and I drank it in the sweetness of the Lord's kindness. The Son is the cup, and the Father is he who was milked, and the Holy Spirit is she who milked him. Because his breasts were full, and it was undesirable that his milk should be ineffectually released, the Holy Spirit opened her bosom, and mixed the milk of the two breasts of the Father.

An interesting example is provided by the Syriac translation of John 1:18, "No one has ever seen God: the only Son, who is in the bosom of the Father, he has made him known." In order to render the Greek word *kolpos*,

---

[36] Many of the Syriac anaphoras employ the term 'hover' in the wording of their epicleses (see further, *Fire from Heaven*, ch. VIII). It is already used in a Eucharistic context by Ephrem (*Hymns on Faith* 10:16), even though he elsewhere states that the 'spirit' of Gen. 1:2 is not to be identified as the Holy Spirit.

[37] In a homily edited by F. Nurse in *American Journal of Semitic Languages and Literature* 26 (1909/10), p. 95.

[38] E.g. Jacob of Serugh, *Homiliae Selectae* (ed. Bedjan), IV, p. 313 (though on p. 52 he has 'the Divinity is a compassionate Mother'); similarly *Fenqitho* III, p. 137a.

[39] Odes of Solomon 19:1–4, as translated by R. Murray, *Symbols of Church and Kingdom*, p. 315. Similar imagery can be found especially in Clement of Alexandria; a collection of references is provided by H. J. W. Drijvers, "The 19th Ode of Solomon," *Journal of Theological Studies* 31 (1980), pp. 344–5.

'bosom,' the Syriac translator employed a word which also means 'womb' (*'ubba*); that at least some Syriac readers then understood *'ubba* in the sense of 'womb' at John 1:18 is shown by a number of passages in Ephrem's hymns where he sets the 'womb' of the Father alongside the 'womb of Mary.' Thus in the Hymns on the Resurrection, 1:7,

> The Word (fem.) of the Father came from his womb
> and put on a body in another womb:
> the Word proceeded from one womb to another—
> and chaste wombs are now filled with the Word.
> Blessed is he who has resided in us.

Ephrem happens to be a writer who is particularly fond of female imagery,[40] even though he perhaps deliberately avoids any overt description of the Spirit as mother. Two examples will suffice here. In one of his Nativity Hymns (4:149–50) he describes the infant Christ, who sucks Mary's breast, as himself being 'the living breast':

> He was lying there, sucking Mary's milk,
> yet all created things suck from his goodness.
> He is the living breast; from his life
> the dead have sucked living breath—and come to life.

Elsewhere, in the Hymns on the Church (25:18), Ephrem compares God to a wet-nurse:

> The Divinity is attentive to us, just as a wet-nurse is to a baby,
> keeping back for the right time things that will benefit it,
> for she knows the right time for weaning,
> and when the child should be nourished with milk,
> and when it should be fed with solid bread,
> weighing out and providing what is beneficial to it
> in accordance with the measure of its growing up.

In using female imagery of God Ephrem and other Syriac writers are simply following the lead set in the biblical writings themselves where such imagery applied to God is by no means infrequent—even though traditionally male-oriented eyes have usually been blind to this. In fact, throughout Christian

---

[40] See especially K. McVey, "Ephrem the Syrian's use of female metaphors to describe the deity," *Journal of Ancient Christianity* 5 (2001), pp. 261–88, and "Images of joy in Ephrem's Hymns on Paradise: returning to the womb and the breast," *Journal of the Canadian Society for Syriac Studies* 3 (2003), pp. 59–77; also my *The Luminous Eye. The Spiritual World Vision of St Ephrem* (Kalamazoo, 1992), pp. 168–72.

tradition an undercurrent can be discerned where feminine imagery is used of God, and of the individual persons of the Trinity. Thus in the medieval West, to take by one example, besides the well-known case of Dame Julian of Norwich, many instances can be found in writers like St Anselm and St Bernard.[41]

Clearly it is important to recover an awareness of, and a sensitivity to, this female imagery already present in the tradition, for it is only by regaining this sensitivity that it is possible to attain to a better appreciation of the fullness of the Godhead: by restricting ourselves only to fatherly images (or only to motherly images) we will end up with a very unbalanced view of God.

At the same time it is essential, as Ephrem points out, to move beyond the metaphors with which God has 'allowed himself to be clothed' in the course of what could be described as his incarnation into human language:

If someone concentrates his attention solely
on the metaphors used of God's majesty,
he abuses and misrepresents that majesty
by means of those metaphors with which God has clothed himself
for humanity's own benefit,
and he is ungrateful to that Grace
which has bent down her stature to the level of human childishness.
Although God had nothing in common with it,
he clothed himself in the likeness of humanity
in order to bring humanity to the likeness of himself.

(Hymns on Paradise, 11:6)

---

[41] See especially C. Bynum, *Jesus as Mother. Studies in the Spirituality of the High Middle Ages* (Berkeley, 1982).

INDEX OF BIBLICAL REFERENCES

4:1	9, 177	5:15	8
4:18	21, 51	8:18	178
4:40–1	56	8:29	178
9:34	9	8:39	9, 178
10:34	59	9:31	9
11:13	9	10:19	177
2:12	9, 177	10:38	21, 51
20:35–6	11	10:44	8, 178
22:30	140	10:45	58
Jn		11:12	177
1:14	8	11:15	8
1:16	67	13:2	178
1:18	187	13:22	78
1:32	8, 177	16:7	178
3:3	96	19:6	177
3:4	91, 102	19:16	8
3:4–8	172	20:23	177
3:8	8	20:28	177
3:16–21	139	21:11	177
5	106	28:25	177
5:4	91	Rom.	
5:7	91, 107	5:5	178
6:63	177	6	96–7, 103, 171
7:37–8	108–9	6:3–4	97
7:39	108, 177, 179	6:4	96
12:3	131	6:5	73, 96
12:3–5	19	6:6	96, 171
14:26	9, 177	8:9	8, 178
15:1	74	8:11	8, 58, 178
16:13f	9	8:14	51
19:34	11, 38, 63–4, 81, 85,	8:15	50, 68, 169
	91, 103, 108–9,	8:16	178
	112–14, 147, 155,	8:17	71
	159	8:26	178
20:22	9, 102, 178	11	74, 121, 172
Acts		11:23	74
1:5	157	12:4	71
1:8	8, 178	13:12	123
1:12–14	158	13:14	61
1:16	177	1 Cor.	
2:1	158	2:10	178
2:4	177	3:16	178–9
2:17–18	9	6:14	71
2:26	8	6:19	58, 178

INDEX OF SYRIAC PASSAGES QUOTED IN TRANSLATION

(B) Syriac Commentators and Later Writers

(C) Liturgical Texts

INDEX OF PERSONS, PLACES, SELECT TERMS

INDEX OF MODERN SCHOLARS

CPSIA information can be obtained at www.ICGtesting.com
Printed in the USA
BVOW012052160113

310750BV00003B/296/P

9 781593 338442